The Dolce Vita Diaries

The Dolce Vita Diaries

Words by Cathy Rogers
Recipes and photographs by Jason Gibb

The Friday Project
An imprint of HarperCollinsPublishers
77–85 Fulham Palace Road
Hammersmith, London W6 8JB
www.thefridayproject.co.uk
www.harpercollins.co.uk

First published by The Friday Project in 2009

A catalogue record for this book
is available from the British Library

ISBN 978-1-906321-31-4

Designed and typeset by e-Digital Design

Printed and bound in Great Britain by
Clays Ltd, St Ives plc

Mixed Sources
Product group from well-managed
forests and other controlled sources
www.fsc.org Cert no. SW-COC-1806
© 1996 Forest Stewardship Council
FSC

FSC is a non-profit international organization established to promote the responsible
management of the world's forests. Products carrying the FSC label are independently
certified to assure consumers that they come from forests that are managed to meet the
social, economic and ecological needs of present or future generations.

Find out more about HarperCollins and the environment at
www.harpercollins.co.uk/green

To Grandfather Jack, who sadly
never did see the grove

Acknowledgements

We'd like to thank Andy and Jane for their support,
tolerance of annoying paperwork and frequent words of wisdom,
Frances and Kerry for running the Nudo 'Buddlemead Branch',
and Madeleine and Mibo, without whose brilliant designs
Nudo would be nothing. Thanks also to Deborah Krasner
for allowing us to use some of her olive oil recipes,
and to Tami for helping us wrestle with the Beast.

Contents

1 The seeds are sown

We'd both been working in TV for a long time, ten years for me, seven years for Jason. I think that ten years is long enough to do anything. I've always admired old people who can look back at their lives and divvy it up into the different chapters, much more than those who have just doggedly pursued one thing. We felt we'd done telly for long enough and we'd started making plans, or at least flirting with the possibility of plans, for doing something else, something *completely* different.

We'd been living in LA for three years, having moved there to set up a US office of RDF Media, the company we both worked for, making programmes like *Faking It, Scrapheap Challenge* and *Wifeswap*. We lived in the hills under the Hollywood sign, bought coffee from a drive-through on our way to work, went surfing at the weekend or visiting the silver Airstream trailer I'd impulsively bought one day up in the mountains by the Kern River. We bought fashion-able clothes, hung out in the kind of bars where you could get your nails done while sipping your martini and having your car valet-parked. Generally we led a pretty charmed, if rather shallow, life.

'New life', as we began to refer to it, had a lot to live up to. Lots of people who make big life changes are escaping something – a job they hate, a country they have come to loathe, a future that just seems too banal and laid out. It wasn't at all like that for us. We both had really good jobs in television, we worked with people we really liked, we were stimulated and we were very well rewarded for our efforts. We'd also enjoyed a bit of public acknowledgement of our efforts because we'd both been in front of the camera as well as behind it – me co-presenting *Scrapheap Challenge* with Robert Llewellyn, and Jason being one of the presenters in a series called *Wreck Detectives*, which investigated the stories of shipwrecks. We also had enough creative rein to mean that our ideas stood a chance of 'making it' to the screen.

But TV was becoming less wholesome. I didn't really want to be making shows like *Big Brother* or *X Factor* or *I'm a Celebrity* or a hundred other programmes that take people and then use them, all for our viewing pleasure. I didn't want constantly to be justifying my latest series with an ever smaller fig leaf of excuses for this exploitation that the programme was 'revealing' or 'helped people understand the world'. And neither did I want to stay and get jaded. We wanted to quit while we were ahead.

But what to do instead? Jason had clearer ideas from the start. He wanted to do something that involved some physical work and to make something which at the end he could hold up with pride and say 'This is the product of my labours and it is good.'

That still left the field pretty open.

We both really liked food and, since the start of our relationship, food and cooking and eating together had been a pretty key element. In fact, from when we first met, Jason was always rummaging around for scraps of paper to jot down some recipe he'd just made, or to write down the pearls of wisdom from a restaurant chef who'd just revealed some cooking secret. In fact, it became a joke that my job was to be constantly buying pretty notebooks to paste in all these scraps of paper, saying there was no point having all these ideas if you could never find them again.

We talked about running a restaurant but everyone we know who does it says, 'Don't don't don't.' It's such a commitment of time and single-mindedness – you don't have the flexibility to do a bit of this and a bit of that, you have to stick with it totally without deviation, every day, every hour. It's a life equivalent of an each-mouthful-the-same plate of risotto rather than the mixed meze we were after.

One day we were in the Grove shopping centre in Hollywood. A place that by all accounts should be horrific and terrifying because it is such a model of super-clean, super-straight, super-capitalist, super-nice America, but which for some reason doesn't quite make you choke in the way that it should. Well, at least there was a shop there we really liked, called O&Co. It's part of that French chain L'Occitane which does stinky unguents to slather yourself in – but O&Co is the food bit that does mainly olive oil and also a few other things like vinegars and mustards. In the one in the should-be-scary Grove, they had lots of different olive oils that you could taste. We'd go in there for a free lunch of bits of slightly stale bread dunked in delicious olive oils from around the world.

Our favourite became an olive oil which was made entirely from Leccino olives and came, improbably, from Uruguay. It was quite smooth and fruity but had a definite peppery kick and a freshness that was just mmmm.

One Saturday we went in for our customary cheapskate snack lunch and the lady there, who knew our game but didn't seem to mind as actually, doh, the joke was on us – given how much oil we bought from them – said, 'You're fond of that Uruguayan oil, aren't you?'

'Well, yes, sure.'

'Well, we've had a 25-litre barrel arrive that's badly dented. We can't really use it as we need a perfect one for the display. But we could sell it to you for cheap if you were interested?'

Interesting.

'How much?'

'Well, shall we say $150 – after all, it's a 25-litre barrel.'

What dilemma and confusion it threw us into. We loved it, it was definitely a bargain. But $150? And 25 litres? It seemed a bit decadent. We went away, telling her we'd have a think about it. It sounds ridiculous now but we really did hum and haw for ages thinking about that barrel of oil. Should we shouldn't we, should we shouldn't we? Then on Monday morning in the office, I just had a feeling that it was a good thing to do and phoned her and said, 'If you still have that oil, we want it – we'll come and pick it up this evening.'

When we arrived, she'd laid out not just the barrel but also about 50 empty half-litre cylindrical tins with their little green lids, so that we could decant the oil at home. We packed up our booty in the car and drove home feeling quite pleased with ourselves.

It was there, attaching the little tap to the barrel and pouring out oil tin by tin, that one of us, we can't even remember which, said, 'Why don't we make olive oil? We love it. It would mean good outdoor physical work and we could be really proud if we made oil that was halfway as good as this stuff.'

So that was it. Life decisions needn't be so terribly taxing. We would make olive oil in our new life. That was that.

We went a bit mad with that oil for a few weeks. We were like crazed apothecaries, experimenting with every kind of flavouring we could think of. In the end we had about thirty little bottles in the cupboard: oil infused with basil leaves, oil with pieces of rosemary thrown in, oil with bits of garlic that we'd try to 'home-sterilize', infusions with mint, some with lemon; every herb and leaf that we could lay our hands on was somehow stuck into a bottle of oil and left to mature in its dark home.

In the end most of it wasn't particularly good and a lot of it went mouldy – which gave us a new-found respect for those Christmas trinkety oils you buy containing baubles of chilli pieces and rosemary. However, in a way, that wasn't the point. Those witching hours stirring cauldrons and making pulps of herbs and concentrating on olive oil were really the start of our plan.

One evening, we decided to have an olive oil tasting. If we were really going to make this stuff, we needed to know our onions. We had invited a bunch of friends round. They weren't perfectly qualified for the job in that none were olive oil experts; they were all Hollywood producers more used to viewing rough cuts than reviewing condiments. But they all loved food and had a good spread of knowledge levels and food snobbishness, so we thought it'd be interesting.

Jason had been devouring every book on the olive he could get his hands on, whether it was about olive cultivation, cooking with olive oil or the historical significance of the olive tree. That night would be a prime opportunity for him to show off his burgeoning knowledge.

Our search for fine olive oils to taste took us to Joan's on Third, a small but well-stocked delicatessen in West Hollywood. They have a mouth-watering display of international oils and a great café with yummy food and fine coffee (depending on which member of staff strikes up the machine). It's not cheap though and the four bottles of olive oil we picked up cost around $80. We couldn't help wondering how much of that the olive farmer claps eyes on.

Jason had read that olive oil is the oldest unadulterated food in the world. And when you think about it, even wine has preservatives added nowadays. Olive oil is the crushed fruit, nothing more, nothing less. Pure as can be. Another of his favourite facts at that time concerned the distinction between 'green olives' and 'black olives'. We, like many, had always assumed that there were different species of olive which turned out either green or black. Imagine our delight when we discovered that no, there was no more difference between a green and a black olive than between a green banana and a yellow – it's just a question of ripeness. How we would be able to wow our friends with these great new factoids.

Thankfully, when we wheeled this out later that evening, everyone was impressed. Jason sounded positively erudite. 'Each olive variety has a specific moment when it's in prime condition – that is, when the oil will be at it finest. The Leccino variety, the one from our Uruguayan booty pack, produces its fruitiest, grassiest oil when it's just turned black. The Coratina produces the bitter, spicy oil it's famed for when it is half purple and half green …'

'Does that mean you have to go round picking the ripe olives one at a time?' asked Rex, ever thoughtful of the labour costs of a job, having always been a film's purse-holder.

'Well, no, you pick a whole tree at once when say 50 percent of the olives are the right colour,' Jason said confidently.

'And what about the difference between olives for oil and olives for the table?'

'Of the hundreds of types of olives, there are specialists. Some, like the black, wrinkled ones from Greece called Kalamata, are best for the table, others like the little pert Picual from Spain are revered for their oil. But there's no olive you can't eat, nor one you can't make oil from.'

Only about 10 percent of olive oil produced is in the top quality extra virgin olive oil bracket. The rest of the stuff is chemically extracted, in other words not simply crushed. The top dogs at the International Olive Oil Council (yes, there really is one), divide olive oil up like this:

Extra virgin olive oil

An acidity of less than 0.8 percent, and an extraordinary range of colours, flavours and textures. To qualify, the oil must be cold pressed and only mechanically. Note to selves: we want to be making this stuff.

Virgin olive oil

An acidity level of less than 2 percent with a 'perfect' aroma, flavour and colour. Cold pressed.

Olive oil

A mix of refined oil. Heat and sometimes chemicals are used to get the remaining oil out of the pulp left over from the first pressing and this is combined with some virgin olive oil. The good stuff gives the taste and the less good stuff gives the bulk. It officially has an acidity of less than 1 percent. We'd use this kind for frying, but nothing else.

Olive pomace oil

Refined oil from the olive residue. Good for oiling the door hinges.

But enough of the facts and figures – it was time to get down to serious tasting.

We didn't agree on which oil was the best. There isn't a right answer. But everyone agreed that olive oil production seemed an estimable and wholesome business to be in. And as we sat under the Californian night sky, illuminated by the twinkly lights of the luscious houses of the Hollywood hills, our path to olive oil producers seemed a simple and dignified one. A quick poll of where we should go to pursue this honest labour was pretty decisive and summed up by Rex:

'Dude, it's got to be Italy.'

Here are our tasting notes from that evening:

The Italian oil
It tastes sweet, of apples or sweetpea. Full flavour and aroma of grass, but a bit thin. Made from Frantoio and Leccino olives. Jax's favourite.

The Moroccan oil
Vanilla, avocado, honey, soil, artichoke heart. What an exotic cacophony of flavours. Creamy at front with a kick at the back. Made from Picholine olives. Aloysia's favourite.

The Spanish oil
Deep, rich olive flavour of grass and fresh mown hay. Peppery, too. From a blend of olive types. Jason's favourite.

The Californian oil
Round mellow and delicate flavour maybe more suited to an American palate. Very pale colour. Picholine olives. No one's favourite.

Olive oil tasting

Ingredients for olive oil tasting
Bread – white

Representing

Africa
Mustapha's Moroccan
Extra Virgin Olive Oil

California
B.R. Cohn Sonora
Gold

Italy
Badia a Coltibuono
Extra Virgin Olive Oil
from Chianti

Spain
Núñez de Prado Extra
Virgin Olive Oil from
Andalusia

Pour each oil into a white saucer, so you can get a good look at the colour and viscosity. Cut the bread into small cubes. Dip in oil and eat. Simple.

Word on the street is that the bread can modify the flavour and mask the subtleties of the oil, so for purists dispense with the bread and instead pour some oil on a teaspoon, suck it into the month with a slurp and wait for it to flow down the back of the throat.

Infusing olive oil

Ingredients for cold infusions
Rosemary – a big sprig
Dried chilli – one large one or several small
Black peppercorns – a small handful
Garlic – a whole bulb

We've worked out two ways to infuse the oil. The first is what we call *warm infusion,* where we gently heat the flavourings in a saucepan of oil for maybe an hour. Then there is *cold infusion,* where we leave the flavouring in the olive oil for a couple of weeks – the flavour slowly ebbs out in a more natural way. Things like lemon rind or basil, which contain water, go mouldy if you cold infuse them. But on the other hand, when we heat up the oil the result is a bit bland because the volatile aromatic flavour compounds are destroyed.

Our success stories so far have been cold-infused dried chillies, rosemary and roasted garlic (we nuke the dastardly bacteria with a good roasting).

Get creative and mix up whatever ingredients take your fancy. You will need a variety of glass bottles, corks and funnels. You are best off sterilizing the bottles beforehand – 10 minutes in boiled water will do the job.

Simply put your flavourings into a bottle and then fill with olive oil so that they are covered and there are no air bubbles.

To roast the garlic, preheat the oven to 190⁰ C /gas mark 5, wrap the whole, unpeeled bulb tightly in kitchen foil and roast for about 40 minutes or until the cloves are soft. Once the bulb is cooled down a bit, pull off individual cloves and shove as many of them down the neck of the bottle as you can. Then fill and cover with oil.

Olives stone-ground with lemons

Just when we'd really got the hang of infusing the lemon rind we discovered a lemon olive oil from Olivier's & Co. which is vastly superior and made in a completely different way. In contrast to an infusion, here the lemons and the olives are crushed together in the olive press. The olives and lemons are 'joined at the pip', Cathy likes to say. We've taken to drizzling this oil on fish and chicken or as a lazy salad dressing (just add a pinch of salt). But best of all we use it to make lemon mayonnaise (gives a citrusy lift to potato salad, or try dipping grilled asparagus spears in it) and lemony ravioli.

Lemon ravioli with sage butter

Ravioli al sapore di limone, con burro e salvia

Ingredients for 4 people
Plain flour – 300g
Eggs – 4
Lemon olive oil – 1.5 tablespoons
Ricotta – 300g
Spinach – 120g cooked and finely chopped
Marjoram – a couple of fresh sprigs
Salt and pepper
Butter – 40g
Sage – a big sprig

Find a nice big clean workspace. Pour the flour into a mound and make a well in the middle. Break 2 eggs into the well and whisk in with a fork, gradually bringing in more and more flour. Add the lemon olive oil (or normal olive oil for a general pasta). When there is a lumpy mass sticking to your fork turn the dough onto a floured surface and knead for 5 minutes. I find it hard to believe 5 minutes is so long when I knead the pasta, so I make myself keep going for a couple of songs on the radio.

When the dough is smooth and homogeneous, cover it with a kitchen towel and leave for half an hour. Then get your pasta machine together – we have a hand-cranked Atlas 150, which has been kicking around for ages and remains faithful.

Cut the pasta into 4 manageable pieces. The trick is to roll the pasta through the machine 10 times on the widest setting, folding it back in half each time. The dough should be beautifully smooth.

Now work your way down the thicknesses on the machine from 1 to about 6. You should have beautiful sheets of pasta, which you need to lay out on a floury surface. This pasta recipe is the basis for all shapes. In general if you need a bit of elasticity (like for ravioli) use olive oil, if not (like fettuccine) go easy on the oil.

To prepare the filling mix together 2 egg yolks, the ricotta, spinach (you can use frozen if you don't have fresh, just make sure it's well thawed and drained), marjoram and a couple of pinches of salt and pepper.

Back to the pasta sheets. Put a teaspoon of the filling mixture at regular, well-spaced intervals. Paint around them with the egg whites. Lay another pasta sheet on top and press down over the mounds of filling. Cut into ravioli shapes with a pasta cutter.

Bring a pot of water to boil, with a bit of salt and olive oil. Cook for about 2 minutes. Whilst it's cooking, make the sage butter. Gently heat the butter in a frying pan with the slightly torn-up sage leaves. Spoon out the ravioli into your serving dish, cover with the sage butter and serve.

2 Dipping our toes in the Dolce Vita

It was our first trip to Le Marche. We'd never heard of the place before and still hesitated to say the name aloud. It sounded so foreign in our mouths. It was hard to believe that the 'ch' wasn't pronounced as it is in 'church'. Also, that 'Le' looked a bit more French than Italian to our unseasoned eye. So we felt we were making a mistake if we said it right, or we'd go the whole wrong hog and pronounce the region 'Les Marchais', which made it sound like a French triumphal march.

Most people still haven't heard of Le Marche. If they have, it's probably because they have seen an article in a Sunday paper entitled something like 'Is Le Marche the New Tuscany?' A question which only serves to underline the fact that it isn't.

We were there because, in the course of conversation with old family friends Noddy and Graham, we'd mentioned our 'new life' plans as a sort of distant hypothetical project. But as a first step, we'd said, we were keen to explore a bit of Italy, starting from the imminent bank holiday weekend. Graham mentioned this place called 'Le Marche'. I think he probably pronounced it lemarshay. He'd spent a lot of time in Croatia, which is just a nip across the Adriatic from the Italian swampy marshland, and he'd heard it was fabulous – 'like Tuscany but more of a secret'. He'd even acquired some little booklets about it. The booklets were full of photos of olive groves and vines and overcolourized photos of plates of food, like a 1970s cookbook. The text was really badly translated from the Italian. All of these facts we took as an excellent sign that it was indeed, unlike Tuscany, charmingly un-up-with-the-times.

Le Marche hadn't exactly featured heavily in Jason's olive oil research, but nonetheless the next day we booked some flights with Ryanair to a place called Ancona, which the ever-informative and ever-growing airline flight map assured us was the capital of this Le Marche. I think at the time they had four or five flights a week, all from London's glistening Stansted Airport.

So it was that we came to be in Le Marche. Which for the record is pronounced 'ley' (like the end of ballet) 'markay'.

When you arrive, the airport is just as you'd hope. One small runway and a cramped single-storey building by way of arrivals, departures, customs, airport shopping, all rolled into one. The look of it, in dusty sunshine, brought to mind one of those impermanent outpost airports constructed quickly for an unworthy war. When the flight disembarked, the one building became full to bursting for a few minutes, only to be returned to sleepy silence within an hour. We knew this because the only car rental place, despite being in an airport where the one daily international flight arrived at 1 p.m., was closed for lunch.

The good thing about being on holiday is that it doesn't matter. We sat in the sunshine and had a delicious tiny coffee and a panino and, before we knew it, there was a smiley man with a tiny dog on his lap at the Hertz reservation desk.

Our little car took us north. We'd decided to follow our noses on this trip. Important as it was that Le Marche cut it on the olive-growing front, and that it produced good olive oil, we also wanted to make sure that we actually liked it. Against instinct, we were trying to approach the trip less as TV producers on a rigorous recce and rather as young hopefuls ready for some romance.

We both love the feeling of seaside places out of season and we spent a few hours kicking sand around in a place called Cattolica. We contemplated swimming but it was just a bit too nippy. We did find one *gelateria* unseasonaly open and couldn't let the opportunity go to waste. I had half chocolate and half hazelnut and, upon one lick along the border separating them, was rushed straight to heaven.

Why is ice cream so much nicer in Italy? I mean, isn't it just milk and then stuff that you can get anywhere like nuts and chocolate? Is it, like the coffee, something to do with having fancy machines that just do the job better? Or is there something they're hiding? Because you go into one of those awful British or American places and the ice cream is just horrid by comparison – vulgar, crude, not even tasting of what it's meant to. The Italians aren't averse to the odd horrid flavour – a bright blue one named after the Smurfs that tastes of nothing on earth, at least nothing this side of Belgium – but at least it seems they're choosing to do it, rather than doing it because they don't know better.

Italian ice cream tastes so good it almost manages to convince you that it's good for you. So, healthily nourished, we headed inland to the pretty little town of Urbino. Up winding roads and through unlikely positioned hilltop villages, access hasn't been made easy and that's partly why it still feels secret. But once you're there, you vow to come again. It is like a miniaturized version of the Tuscan big boys – the Sienas and the Florences. Cobbled streets and spectacular cathedrals and art palaces all positioned in a setting that could be taken straight from the backdrop of a Renaissance portrait. Bar a few telephone lines, the landscape looks unchanged for half a millennium.

We struck lucky with a hostel to stay in – on a steep cobbled hill, a couple of doors away from the house where Raphael was born – it was cheap as chips and right in the middle of town. We got rid of our stuff and went wandering around, a cardiac exercise in itself given that no part of the town is on the flat. Everything seemed to be small – there was a tiny carwash for tiny Italian cars, a tiny petrol pump, it was hard to keep the word 'cute' from your mind. Then, within minutes, the whole town was suddenly awash with luminously dressed cyclists careering around every corner and we kept being offered free Red Bull by passing strangers with funny Red Bull hats on. Yes, it was the day of the Red Bull sponsored cycling race around town and we had arrived in time for the start of festivities, which it transpired would go on all night in the form of Euro rock in the main square.

So this was Le Marche, ancient and modern. And we decided we liked it. That night, our fate was sealed when we tried our first Le Marche olive oil, a delicate oil from a place called Pesaro, on a delicious plate of orecchiette which was simplicity itself. A glass of Verdicchio was the final piece in the puzzle. Le Marche it would be.

A few months later, we were en route to Le Marche for the second time, via London. It was one of those traditional Ryanair journeys which begins at an hour of the day that should really be called night. At 4.30-something you ask yourself whether it is really worth it and at 11 a.m. in Italy you answer yourself 'yes'.

This trip had a different feel about it. It was more than just a holiday, filled with pleasant but aimless wanderings. It was greater than a vague sniffing out of an area. Things had moved on and somehow, without either of us really spelling it out, we knew we weren't just dipping our toes any more. This trip was the first real step towards our new life.

Our plan was to find a house in an olive-friendly area, then find a nearby olive grove to buy afterwards. Secretly, I think we both had hopes of stumbling across a beautiful house positioned in the middle of a huge olive grove, but we knew that was a long shot.

We'd lined up an array of estate agents for the trip. Le Marche covers a pretty big area so we planned to hop from one part to another with a different 'tour guide' for each, hoping that way we'd learn more about how house buying works as well as getting to know the region.

Pretty much all of Le Marche is hilly – the views forming that curvaceousness that is the hallmark of the Italian countryside and that spawns fresh lovers every day. All of these deeply tilting hills are divvied up by the lines made by olive trees, often used as a marker of the border of one farm to the next. It all looked just like the romantic vision we all secretly nurture of a new life abroad.

First up on the estate agent front was a duo: Sandro, a suave Italian in an Audi, and his scatty German assistant, Valeria. We'd told them our plan about the olive grove so occasionally Valeria would excitedly say something like 'This house has fifteen olive trees in the garden', which only served to confirm that we'd never find house and grove together. The important thing, instead, was to make sure the area was suitable – which ruled out places too high (olive trees don't like frost), places too near the coast, where the trees don't tend to thrive, or any shady oak-filled valleys (obviously they need loads of sun).

Most of the houses we were shown 'needed work'. That's what the English buyer wants, we were told. But we weren't sure we wanted trees growing through the middle of our living room, and some of the cracks dividing houses pretty much into two were frankly frightening. Prices varied enormously; the range we were shown started at 45,000 euros and went up to about 200,000 euros. Estimates for restoration at least doubled the price.

We saw about 20 houses that first day, fanatically photograph-
ing and documenting each one. Sandro turfed us out about 6 p.m.,
telling us to have a think and that he'd see us in the morning. He
left us at a place called Hotel Ristorante Giardino in San Lorenzo
in Campo, where he said the food was 'rather good'.

Sandro is master of understatement. The food was exceptional.
We ate one of the most fantastic meals we have ever had. When
the waiter brought the menu, outlining delicious morsels of every
kind of flesh, our hearts sank a little. Jason is a vegetarian and
asked his daily question about the possibility of non-carnal options
and the waiter looked slightly surprised. Oh no, we thought; please
have *something* Jason can eat. But no, he was surprised because
we hadn't seen the vegetarian tasting menu at the back! A vegetarian tasting menu – with five courses of it – in the middle of Le
Marche. We had to live here.

Sandro appeared at a leisurely nine-thirtyish the next morning as
we muddled our way into the day through our food-and-wine hang-
overs. There followed many more houses and much more indecision. But today there was one house which lingered with us: Upupa,
owned by a little bent lady called Pepita. It seemed to be the biggest
house in the world, made up of at least four different chunks, each
of which would probably have sufficed alone. It was half 'done up'
in a deplorable style, which would have to be swiftly and expensive-
ly undone. It had a garden full of olive trees, a vegetable plot and
360 degree views, being perched on top of a hillock. The communal olive press was within walking distance and two minutes away
was a sweet little town where we watched buxom Italian grandmothers
cooing over a tiny baby that for some reason was in a box. But
above all this, it felt like it could become our family home.

The sums, of course, didn't quite add up. We spent the evening moving numbers around, increasing the hypothetical amount we'd sell our London flat for and decreasing the estimated restoration costs of our new house until it sort of worked. As to the restoration, we reckoned that in any case we could do it in different chunks as and when we had the money. Gradually, over the years, the house would become one unified whole. As we looked at the numbers and the estate agent handout of the house, our hearts raced with excitement and terror at the realization that *we might really do this*.

Another day brought two new estate agents. The first was a slightly shady seeming Englishman who'd lived in Le Marche for years and had a sort of freelance estate agent business. He had no office and we met him in a bar where he was sitting smoking a cigarette and wearing a cream-coloured linen jacket that made him look like he thought he was in the Raj. We didn't feel enormous confidence but nonetheless our hearts bounced as we drove up to the first house he took us to. It was beautiful, with flowers growing all round it. Built of pale bricks, it looked to be in good condition, it had plenty of the little add-on bits giving interesting angles (J can't stand big blocky square lumps of houses) and it came with a four-hectare chunk of land right by the house that looked perfect for growing olive trees. The house had fifteen bedrooms and two little outhouses. Better still, the price was a suspiciously reasonable 125,000 euros.

The catch, when it came, was an extraordinary one. It wasn't that there was an abattoir next door or that they were about to build a new shoe factory at the bottom of the garden or anything so mundane. No, the catch was that if we bought it, we'd have to share the house with someone else.

Italian property law is, to our eyes at least, rather eccentric. When someone dies, a Napoleonic decree that still stands says that their property be left in proportion to their relatedness to any living relatives – so if you have three sons they get a third each; if you have one daughter she gets the lot. And if you have three sons, two cousins, five nephews, a niece and an ever-increasing count of grandchildren, you get a lawyer.

The effect of this is that there are lots and lots of farmhouses which lie abandoned because each has a family that never agrees what to do with it – one party wanting to sell up, another saying that selling would be a family betrayal, etc. – so the end effect is that nothing happens.

In the case of this lovely house, most of the owners had reached agreement but there was a sticky uncle who owned effectively a single room in the house which he under no circumstances wanted to sell. But he had been persuaded to let the rest of the sale go ahead.

'But what would that mean?' we asked. 'Could he just come round any time and spend the day sitting in his room?'

'He almost certainly won't.'

'Well, does he have his own key? To get to his bit, he'd need to use our front door, isn't that a bit weird?'

'Maybe you just need to adjust your thinking a bit,' said Mr Linen. 'Italy is a very relaxed place.'

It wasn't hard to say goodbye to him.

Next up was the lovely Anna Paola in Serra de Conti, a pretty village slightly further north. Unlike Sandro and Mr Linen, her office was rather immaculate and she had a computer that did modern things like make projections of how houses would look once they were done up. After the essential coffees and perusal through her offerings on paper, we got in her car to start the day's viewings. Her car had little stickers all over it in English saying things like 'glove compartment' and 'vanity mirror', apparently there to teach her as-yet pre-verbal child the importance of knowing English. Given that she didn't speak much herself, this seemed a clear case of transference. She, too, showed us some lovely houses and our uncertainty grew. We saw one called Graziosa, which had such huge rosemary plants growing all around that the whole microclimate had the most delicious smell, evocative of Sunday roast. We tried to convince ourselves that it was big enough but knew in our hearts it wasn't true.

We really wanted to buy a house from her! We trusted her, even if she told us things we didn't want to hear about how restoration can cost twice as much as many people will tell you. It was probably because she told us things we didn't want to hear that we trusted her. She also told us some interesting specific things, which was nice in a world of indecision and generalities; for example: the legal minimum ceiling height is 2 metres 70 centimetres; you can only extend existing windows vertically downwards and you can't put any new windows in rural properties. She told us that the reason you see lots of houses with four odd pillars in a square or a beaten-up old metal framework in the garden is that they are marking the position of a former outhouse. Any outhouse can be automatically rebuilt without additional permission-seeking, to the same volume as the original – but if you take away the pillars you lose this right.

She showed us some lovely places but they were all just not quite right – a bit too small, a bit not in an olive-growing place, a bit too expensive. That evening, we hatched a plan to buy Graziosa, to do up the outbuilding first and then live in that as we set up our olive business and brought up (hopefully) a baby while we did the work to restore the main house. We went to sleep excited with this image – and with having a plan. But by morning the house had shrunk back to its true size, and there was no further mention of it.

One final day of house viewings; this time with Anna Paola's side-kick Peter, a serious Swede with the longest fingers you've ever seen and that irritating Scandinavian habit of speaking five languages fluently. We saw a few more properties with him, had lunch in an honest workmen's café where we were shocked to see that he drank wine at *lunchtime*, and went on to the two final places of the trip. One was just a bit bunkerish on the outside and a no-no, but as we drove to the last one we turned to each other to note a feeling we both had of familiarity. We wondered whether it was just that in seeing so many houses (about 40 by now) dotted all over the region we were actually getting to know the area quite well. But no, there was more to it than that. As we turned off the *strada bianca* and saw a familiar massive crack down the side of a pretty house next to a field of olive trees, we realized we had been shown this house before, by another estate agent! It was a disappointing way to end but also strangely reassuring in that things were coming full circle.

We said goodbye to all and prepared for our trip back to LA.

Back in LA, our thoughts kept returning to Upupa – the unfeasibly huge house we had unfeasibly fallen in love with, in all its madcap glory. At the distance given firstly by e-mail and secondly by being thousands of miles away in a city where the overriding philosophy is 'If you want it, you damn well go out and get it', we found ourselves composing an e-mail.

At first we played it slightly coy. There was some neighbouring land with lots of olive trees on it, which we would be interested in buying, too. If the agents could confirm whether there was a possibility of our buying this in addition to the house and its existing land, it would make our decision a good deal easier.

A few days later, an e-mail came back confirming that the owner was interested in discussing the possibility of our buying up to two hectares of land in addition to the house.

This was more than enough to puncture our coyness. Our next e-mail could only be described as ... an offer! In our excitement we even forgot the usual etiquette of offering below the asking price and instead just girlishly sort of said 'We want it!' The asking price was 155,000 euros.

Our hearts skipped every time there was the ping of a new e-mail popping into the inbox. But strangely there was no word that day, or the next day, or the next. We sent another e-mail checking that our first had been received safely.

The next day came back the following reply. 'The owner of the house is being rather naughtie and has increased the asking price, on the basis that she has someone interested in paying it. She now wants euros 206,500.00. We are a bit vexed that this has happened as you can well imagine, and wait to hear how you feel about it.'

Quite apart from the insult of the spelling of naughty, this was just a joke, especially given how much we would have to spend on doing up the house. And even more especially since in the meantime we'd learned that the house had been on the market for twenty years. May it long remain there.

That evening, over a consoling beer in the sunshine of our porch, we cheered ourselves up by booking tickets for our next trip back to Le Marche to see more houses. Even though Upupa wasn't to be, there was no going back now.

Orecchiette pasta with cauliflower

Orecchiette al cavolfiore

Ingredients for 4 people
Cauliflower – one medium sized
Garlic – 1 clove
Chilli – 1
Extra virgin olive oil – 2 tablespoons
Orecchiette – 500g
Salt
Parmesan – grated to serve

This is a different take on the more common orrechiette with broccoli, which we found at a lovely little trattoria in Urbino.

Cut the cauliflower into little florets, cook in salted boiling water for 5 minutes and then drain. Peel the garlic and seed and chop the chilli. Heat the olive oil (Marchigiani if you can find it) and gently cook the garlic and chilli for a few minutes. Add the cauliflower and cook for a further 5 minutes so there's a bit of colour to the veg.

Cook the orecchiette in salted water according to the instructions on the packet. Once it's *al dente*, drain and toss into the cauliflower. Serve with a generous handful of grated parmesan.

Pan-fried trout with polenta crust and almonds

Trota in padella con impanatura di polenta e mandorle

Ingredients for 4 people
Trout – 2 whole ones gutted,
rinsed and patted dry
Polenta – 1 cup
Olive oil – 2 tablespoons of the peppery kind
Lemon – cut into wedges
Almonds – $2/_3$ of a cup,
slivered and blanched

Always hungry to extend our cooking repertoire, Cathy and I did a course called 'Flavors of Olive Oil'. It was run by Deborah Krasner, an olive oil aficionado who efficiently taught us the multitudinous uses of fine olive oil, from soups to cakes. Cathy's favourite was the pan-fried trout with polenta crust. Even the crunchy skin was delicious. I was turned on by Deborah's orange and caraway seed cake. It uses olive oil instead of butter, so it's guilt free (low in saturated, high in monounsaturated fats) and apparently very forgiving to make for a cake novice like me.

Roll the fish in a plateful of the polenta. Shake off the excess.

Heat a cast-iron frying pan, and when it's hot, add 1 tablespoon of the olive oil. When the oil is hot add the fish. Brown the fish on both sides, about 4 minutes per side depending on the thickness. Once they're cooked put each fish on a plate with a wedge of lemon.

Wipe the pan and heat the remaining olive oil. Brown the almonds over a medium-high flame and stir continuously. As soon as they are golden and aromatic pour the almonds and oil over the fish. Serve with a flavoursome green salad.

Orange, almond and caraway seed cake

Ingredients

Unbleached flour – 300g
Sugar – 250g
Fine sea salt – $\frac{1}{4}$ teaspoon
Baking powder – 1 teaspoon
Bicarbonate of soda – 1 teaspoon
Eggs – 3 large ones
Full fat milk – 300ml
Olive oil – 100ml of the fruity kind
Orange – grated zest of 1
Vanilla extract – 1 teaspoon
Sliced almonds – 80g
Caraway seeds – 1 tablespoon
Icing sugar

Preheat the oven to 180ºC / gas mark 4. Grease a bundt mould tin (one of the ring shaped ones) with a bit of olive oil and don't forget the middle funnel bit. Sift the flour, sugar, salt, baking powder and bicarbonate through a sieve into a big mixing bowl. Make a well in the middle and add the eggs, milk, olive oil, zest and vanilla.

Using a whisk, beat the wet ingredients together in the centre of the bowl, gradually drawing in the dry ingredients as you do so. Continue until all the ingredients are blended. Now add the almonds and caraway seeds and mix lightly with a spatula or wooden spoon.

Pour the smooth batter into the bundt tin and bake for 50–60 minutes, or until the cake is cooked through (if you stick a metal skewer in it will come out clean) and golden brown. Cool it in the pan on a rack then run a knife around the edge and invert it onto a serving plate. When it's completely cool dust with icing sugar, admire it for a minute and then eat a slice with a cup of tea.

Strozzapreti

'Choking priest' pasta

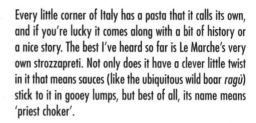

Ingredients for 4 people
plain flour – 250g
Eggs – 2
Olive oil – 1 tablespoon

Every little corner of Italy has a pasta that it calls its own, and if you're lucky it comes along with a bit of history or a nice story. The best I've heard so far is Le Marche's very own strozzapreti. Not only does it have a clever little twist in it that means sauces (like the ubiquitous wild boar *ragù*) stick to it in gooey lumps, but best of all, its name means 'priest choker'.

This, Sandro our estate agent explained, goes back to the time when the church was a big landowner in Le Marche. The farmers' wives would make this pasta to grease the palms, or rather fill the bellies, of the local clergymen. But the farmers would go wild with jealousy (eating your wife's pasta is tantamount to bedding her, Sandro told us) and so wish for the pasta to choke the gluttonous priests to death. Anyway, we've had fun making our own strozzapreti at home. It's just a shame we have no priest friends to invite round for dinner.

Make the pasta according to the instructions for lemon ravioli (page 12). Lay the thin dough on a floury board and cut into long strips about 3cm wide. Take two wooden barbecue skewers and roll a length of dough around first one skewer then the next. You should end up with an 'S' shape, with a skewer in each hole of the 'S'. Give it a further little twist to make sure that the priest really gets it, and place on a well-floured tray.

Once you've made enough for 4 people, throw the pasta shapes into salted, boiling water. When they are cooked they will rise to the surface. Scoop them out and mix them into whatever sauce you have come up with. Our favourite so far has been an asparagus, fresh pea, mint and cream sauce.

Maccheroni di Campofilone

Macaroni with rabbit and olive ragù

Ingredients for 8 people
Parmesan – 50g grated, 400g to make a
wafer to serve each dish on
Olive oil – for frying
Carrot – 1
Onion – $\frac{1}{2}$
Celery – 1 stick
Leek – 1
Vine tomatoes – 300g
Minced pork and veal – 150g
Rabbit – half a boned one
(get your butcher to bone it)
Rosemary – 1 sprig
Salt and pepper
White wine – half a litre
Vegetable or meat stock – if needed
Courgette – 1
Garlic – 1 clove
Black olives – 350g of pitted ones
Macaroni – 1kg of the smallest macaroni
you can find
Butter – a knob

Hotel Ristorante Giardino
After a long day house-hunting, we had been chuffed to find a restaurant with nothing less than a vegetarian tasting menu. It had got even better when we found out that owner and chef Massimo Biagiali prided himself in using only ingredients which grew within throwing distance of his hotel. And then it really got better when Massimo insisted that we drink a different glass of wine with each course. There were a lot of courses. At the end of the evening, rather tired and emotional, we made Massimo promise to give us recipes for our favourite dishes.

We've discovered that in Le Marche rabbit is a standard dish in your everyday trattoria. Usually it's grilled, *alla brace*, over an open flame. In this dish the boned rabbit is cooked in tomatoes, allowing its aromatic flavour to come through in every tender bite.

Method overleaf

Maccheroni continued...

First of all get the parmesan wafers out of the way. Preheat the oven to 200ºC / gas mark 6. Thinly slice the cheese and then arrange it into rough circles with a diameter of about 20cm on a Teflon baking sheet (we also use a non-stick cooking liner called 'Bake-O-Glide'). Make sure that the pieces are overlapping. You may have to make a few batches but they don't take long. Whack it in the oven for 5 minutes or until the cheese has fused, then remove and put each circle on top of an upside-down tumbler so it takes the shape of a basket. When it's rehardened set aside for later. Make a basket per person.

Now for the sauce. First put some olive oil in a deep, heavy-bottomed pan over a low heat and brown the finely chopped carrot, onion, celery and leek. Then add the roughly chopped tomatoes to the pan and cook for another 10 minutes. You can then add the minced meats. While this is cooking cut the boned rabbit into 0.7–0.8cm cubes and then add them to the pan. Also add the chopped rosemary leaves and season with salt and pepper. Cook for a further 10 minutes before you add the white wine and stock, if you need it, to cover. Slowly cook it down.

Cut the skin off the courgette and slice it in batons, julienne style, then sauté them with olive oil and the peeled garlic clove. Once they have a bit of colour, remove and chuck away your garlic clove and add the courgettes to the *ragù*. Also add the black olives. Let this cook while you prepare the macaroni according to the instructions on the packet (Massimo assured us that they make their pasta fresh each day, of course).When it is cooked drain and turn it into a frying pan with the grated parmesan and a knob of butter.

Put a big serving spoonful of the macaroni in each parmesan wafer, then a spoonful of the *ragù* and serve immediately. Eat with a fruity and mature glass of '99 Il Cupo from Le Marche's Ester Hauser.

Aubergine involtini with sapa sauce

Involtini di melanzane con salsa di zabaione di sapa

Ingredients for 4
For the aubergine rolls:
Aubergines – 2 fairly large ones
Salt – 2 tablespoons
Olive oil – 4 teaspoons

For the filling:
Ricotta – 150g
Pecorino – 400g cut into small cubes
Salt and pepper

For the sauce:
Egg yolks – 2
Salt and pepper
Sapa – 100ml
Vegetable stock – 50ml
Balsamic vinegar – 10ml

This recipe uses sapa, which is a popular condiment in Le Marche, but not well known outside of Italy. It's like a sweet, rich, almost toffee-flavoured balsamic vinegar. According to our friend Massimo, sapa was used by the Romans before sugar was introduced to Italy. It's also known as saba and we've found it on the shelves of a couple of delis. If you're not so lucky, use a good balsamic instead. This particular recipe may seem a bit precious, but it's not difficult and is an amazing combination of flavours.

Cut the aubergines lengthways into thin slices of 0.5 to 0.8cm. Cover them with plenty of salt and a bit of water and leave for at least 15 minutes. Rinse them and then pat dry. Lightly brush each side with olive oil and brown them a bit in a non-stick frying pan for about 5 minutes.

In a mixing bowl, combine the ricotta and the pecorino. Add a little salt and pepper. Then take one aubergine slice at a time and put a teaspoonful of the cheese mixture at the thin end. Roll up the aubergine all the way to the other end, like a Swiss roll. Put the roll onto a baking tray lined with baking paper. Do this with all the aubergine slices. You'll want about 4 rolls per person.

For the sauce, beat the egg yolks with salt and pepper, add the sapa, the stock and the balsamic vinegar and mix well. Put the mixture in a Bain Marie (a heatproof mixing bowl on top of a saucepan of boiling water) and carry on stirring at a high heat for a few minutes. Now cook the involtini (rolls) at 220ºC / gas mark 7 for about 5 minutes. Take them out, lay them on plates and pour the sauce over the top. Garnish with a bit of parsley and some chopped tomatoes. According to Chef Biagiali it should be enjoyed with a very cold glass of white wine, such as a Falerio from Vigna Solaria.

3 Somewhere to call home

This time we were taking no chances – we were going to come back with our future home. We had arranged three separate days with three different estate agents and had told them to fit in as many houses as it was feasible to see in a day. By the end of this trip we'd have seen about seventy houses in all.

This time around, we had hooked up, for no particular reason, with property places further south in Le Marche. It's funny how quickly one develops fixed ideas. We had one that leaving Ancona airport, we had to go north. We were smitten with Urbino and San Leo and Serra de Conti and the valleys around Corinaldo – and all of these were to the northwest. But now we found ourselves heading south to poorer (or so we thought, Italy tending to get more so as you go south) and uncharted lands.

First stop was Gualdo, located in a place we have since discovered is nicknamed 'Gualdoshire' for its prevalence of English expats. It certainly seemed tuned in to the desires of the English, with arrangements where agent, lawyer and architect are often thick as thieves and will, if you wish and pay for it, oversee everything from the purchase of your property until moving in, making all decisions about light switches and toilet positioning along the way. The agent drove us first to show us some of the properties his company had already done up – to help us visualize how these dilapidated wrecks could be turned into perfect homes.

Except we weren't sure we liked these perfect homes. They were so of a type, they screamed out 'ENGLISH INHABITANTS' for miles around. For a start, all the pretty brickwork was always sandblasted to within an inch of its life, which meant that the houses looked new. How ridiculous. They were pale and gleaming and, like a Hollywood star with too much botox, unconvincingly hid their life and experience with bland smoothness. Inside, the walls were all plastered, so again the joy of the bricks was lost – except they didn't want to lose it altogether, so at random intervals there would be an amorphous blob of plaster missing so that the bricks could show through. It was like a wedding cake that had rubbed up against the roof of a tin and taken off a big chunk of icing, leaving the cake nakedly showing below. There was always a swimming pool – a boon for the owners but a vile lurid blot in the view for everybody else. And they were always down miles of windy rocky track in the middle of nowhere, as if people moved here not to move to Italy but to move *away* from the rest of the world.

It didn't quite feel like us.

So we schlepped around lots of nonetheless very pretty wrecks with very pretty views and were sort of tempted but not quite enough. We had a feeling that there was something we were missing, but we'd seen so many places and with so many different agents that we couldn't really convince ourselves we weren't being thorough enough.

We sat in the office of the trim and efficient Monica, purveyor of houses to nearly all the English in an area covering a good 100 square miles (well, you would look trim on that wouldn't you?). She thumbed through her files, throwing out the odd place here and there. Then she paused and looked at us sidelong and said, 'You mentioned olive trees, didn't you?'

We replied it was very important we were in an olive-growing region, and ideally we'd get some olive trees with the house, too.

'There is this one house,' she started, without conviction, 'but I don't think it's what you want. It's quite a modern house.'

We gave her a look to say tell us more.

'It does have a lot of olive trees.'

'How many?' we asked.

'Well, the last owner had registered … let me see … about 900.'

'Take us there,' we said.

The journey there was so wiggly and windy that you'd never remember it again even if your life depended upon it. Monica, clearly accustomed enough to Italian entranceways to know not to risk them, parked the car at the top, barely off the road on what seemed a pretty deadly bend. We walked down the short driveway to a big square red-brick modern house.

'Horrible roof,' Jason said.

I could see he was right, though I think I could have gone there a hundred times before I'd have really noticed by myself. I was looking the other way, at the breathtaking view that stretched on and on and on. In Le Marche the views are often quite closed in because the hills have so many little tucks and folds, but here there were two quite separately beautiful views. One which was tucked in: the hill opposite, with a pretty painted campanile tower and a cluster of houses rising out of a picturesquely farmed hillside. The other was one that never appeared to end. It stretched down along the line of a valley seemingly all the way to the sea, which you could imagine there at the end even if you couldn't really quite in all honesty see it. And peeping up every couple of miles along the valley was a little village, always perched on top of a pointy hill and every time with a turret or a tower poking up from the other buildings. It was gorgeous. It was the sort of view you wanted to soak yourself in. I did reverse blinking to try and make it stick.

Estate agents being estate agents, we didn't get too long to stand being whimsical before keys were whisked out for our appointment with the house.

It wasn't the sort of house you would fall in love with. At least, if I imagine the kind of person who might fall in love with this sort of a house it makes me like it less, so I prefer not to. It's not that there was anything wrong with it, but neither was there anything particularly right – it was just sort of a blob of house, just sort of there. Jason likes houses with tacked-on bits and a little ramshackle and he was right and there was none of that. It was quadratic. It was made of functional bricks, not the pretty old Italian ones that the English fall in love with. The roof did not have an aesthetic dimension; its job was to keep out the rain and that was what it did.

Nonetheless, as soon as we saw the house, we knew that it was going to be ours. We even decided that we quite liked that it wasn't the sort of house that English people who move to Italy fall in love with. It made us feel that we were different and that we were coming here for sensible reasons, not for some daft and naïve dream. We liked the fact that it was functional and wouldn't mean sinking all our savings and more into rebuilding magnificent archways or restoring frescos buried under years of plaster and wallpaper. But, of course, in thinking that we were beginning to start our own little dream, to create our own world of expectation and our own sense of place.

I'm omitting, of course, the most crucial element. The house, as Monica had promised, had a very, very large garden – about eight hectares or 20 acres – most of which was planted with olive trees. It had 881 or 977 trees depending on whether you believed the document that went with the house or the form that goes to the local board to claim subsidy on olive trees, which Monica had unearthed and which was, strangely, higher. One day soon, we thought, we'll count those trees ourselves and know for sure. More than that, we will give each one a name or at least a number, and register it on a map with GPS coordinates and write down every detail about it, from how many olives it produces annually, to how much manure we put on it, to the date we prune it each year.

But before that, there was a lot of work to do. When we'd done the tour of the house and were finally allowed a wander round the grove, it was obvious this was not a perfect one, like the covers of pretty Italian photography coffee-table books, with olive trees in neat lines and matching shapes. This grove presented all the ramshackle-ness and chaos that the house didn't. The lines were mostly not even straight. The trees had been pretty much abandoned, with only the ones right at the top of the very steep hill having even been harvested for probably a decade. Worse, the bleak, bleak winter the year before had done some serious damage to the trees. A properly pruned tree can take snowfall because the snow just falls through the branches. But a great big '70s Afro of a tree leaves nowhere for the snow to fall through and it just sits there. Add that to a really cold winter where that snow sits for weeks and even months and the result is broken branches and in some cases even split trunks.

Of course, we didn't know most of that then: we saw lots and lots of olive trees. And we knew we wanted lots and lots of olive trees. The fact that they needed a bit of a love-up was actually almost a plus, in that it would give us something to get stuck into and would immediately help us form a sort of bond with the grove. It would be thanks to us that it would be healthy and productive again. We'd feel that we'd done a bit of good in a little corner of our new world.

We spent about an hour in the grove, frolicking about in the wild flowers and running down the hills and thinking about people thinking how lucky we were. And feeling pretty lucky, even when Jason, who (in contrast to me) is a very unjumpy person, jumped at least two feet in the air with a loud shriek.

'Oh my God, what is it?' I yelled, certain that he must have broken a leg at least.

'A *massive* snake,' he said. 'Like this long' (he held his arms at full stretch) 'and jet black. It just went right across the grass in front of me, almost over my feet!'

Yikes. I'm not sure I like snakes. Though these ones are harmless, according to Monica.

There was another beautiful piece of perilous wildlife. On one of the upstairs windows, attached to the outside of it and protected by the shutter on the other side, was a nest of *calabroni*. They're sort of giant wasps, like hornets but bigger – twice the size of a big bumble bee each, and apparently it only takes a handful to kill a horse. Babies have been killed by a single sting, apparently. I realize that we are going to use the word 'apparently' a lot. It's a slim cover for ignorance. The nest spread over almost the whole window and was an intricate work of practical art – tunnels carved out and passing over each other in all directions to make a crazy and complex lattice of waspy dwellings.

We didn't mind the feeling of sharing our future home with some worthy other dwellers but apparently (you see?) we'd have to call the firemen out for these fellas.

We had planned to make another trip to the house before we committed, but when we tried to return on our own a few days later there was a rainfall so heavy that big chunks of road were gushing away down the hill. I was driving and it was quite nerve-racking, swerving around and skidding all over the place, with flumes of gravel and mud rushing past and round the car. It was almost a relief when the road ahead was closed and meant we couldn't heroically battle on to get there. What this rainfall meant is that we were about to decide to commit our money and our future to a place that we had seen for less time than I would interview someone for a temporary assistant's job. But commit we did.

Back in Los Angeles, the process of idealizing the house began in earnest. Our photos of mouldy cellars and wild flowers running riot evoked in viewers a mixture of cheesy images culled from the vile and legion films romanticizing Italy. In most people's minds, we would have a beautiful room with a view where we would ponder life's mysteries under the Tuscan sun. We half hated their schmaltzy idealization of our future life, but allowed ourselves the odd enigmatic smile, because who is immune to a bit of romance?

A few days after being back, we phoned Monica to tell her that we wanted to buy the house. Slightly chary after our Upupa experience, we made an offer of 215,000 euros, a little less than the asking price of 225,000 euros. Within a few hours, she had phoned back to say that the owners had accepted our offer. And that was that! It seemed too easy. We had a house in Italy. It was in a place called Loro Piceno which we'd learned to pronounce properly. *And* we had enough olive trees – God, I couldn't wait to count them myself – with which to start our new life.

Life continued as normal in LA. We were in the middle of filming the umpteenth series of *Junkyard Wars*, the American version of *Scrapheap Challenge*, and it was boiling. On several days, the temperature in the valley where our salubrious junkyard lay reached 120°F. It was relatively fine for us, the production team, but the poor on-screen teams would be slaving away against the clock to finish their machines with welding torches and grinding discs, lugging cars and machinery all over the place and working their backsides off. We had a few cases of heatstroke, all dealt with calmly by our medic Roy, who had no nose (a result of diving in toxic polluted waters).

A house in Italy with lots of olive trees couldn't have seemed further away.

Then one day I found out I was pregnant. I say it as if it was a shock but it wasn't really. We'd been to see a fertility 'dude' in LA, who was one of those doctors who sees it as his moral duty to bring more children into the world. All around his office – his baby shrine – were pictures of beautiful smiling babies of every colour and shape, offerings to the gods of procreation.

We went to see him because we wanted some more facts about this whole business of ageing and having children. There's so much written about it by a slightly disapproving media, and so many prejudices about older mums, that we just wanted to know the truth. His speech went along these lines. 'Well, you guys seem happy. You've probably been together a while – you've had lots of fun together, right? I mean you've had enough fun, haven't you? You can't play about all your lives. Have kids! Get on with it! I swear to God you'll regret it if you don't.'

Then he drew a chart on a blank piece of paper – I was impressed because it was really good even though he drew it upside down so that it was facing us on the other side of the desk. On the horizontal axis was 'woman: age' and on the vertical 'fertility: odds of getting pregnant'. The line just went down and down till it almost hit the line at the bottom. He then drew a cross where I, at the age of 35, sat on the graph and I felt uncomfortably close to where the line stopped being a graph line and started being an axis. It was one of those pictures that spoke at least a hundred words.

'Do you want more than one child?' he asked.

We'd never really talked about that – it was a big enough thing to think about having one. But, on the spot, we both thought that we probably did.

'Well, then, you really need to get on. This graph doesn't stop just because you have one under your belt. So think about how old you'd be by number two or number three or number—'

'No more than three!' we both yelped.

'Well, whatever, you've still got to think that by then you'll be what 38, 39, maybe even in your forties by number three.'

It was a clear and resounding 'Go forth and multiply', in American.

So we did. And here, astonishingly efficiently and with a distinct V-sign to that maudlin graph, was a tiny growing baby.

I think pregnancies are nine months long not because that wee thing needs that time to get its act together but because the carrier does. Nine months to get your head around the idea, nine months to work out how it might affect your life decisions, nine months to make plans about the future.

In many people's cases, these nine months are a time to nest and to settle and to move house and prepare for a life as more than two. And so it was with us. Before the pregnancy, we hadn't made a definite plan about leaving LA, but as soon as it was there, we did. We both felt we wanted to be at home in London for when the baby was born, near friends and family – so that gave a very clear schedule for our departure. It also gave enough time for our company to make plans for our replacements – another great reason for this nine-month preparation time, clever babies.

As to our bigger future plans, the fact that there would be a baby in among them only made them seem more right. Even from afar, I had always dreaded having that sort of London frenetic motherhood where I was constantly rushing from work to be with baby or rushing from baby to be with work. I am more than prone to feeling guilty about not doing enough, even when I am, and the idea of this constant emotional pull one way or another did my head in, even as a theory.

But equally, the idea of being tied to a house and tied to a routine which everyone tells you a baby needs filled me with terror. The idea of a life with a bit more flexibility, one which included working and finding fulfilment beyond nappies, but without some of the strictures of a more-than-full-time job, had an appeal that felt very tangible.

We didn't really make a definite plan but in our heads we'd be in London for a while, have the baby, hang around for a bit, then head off to Italy a year or so later.

In the meantime, life was busier than ever. So much so that we couldn't make it to Italy to sign the documents on the house purchase as we were in the midst of filming. Instead, my sister Madeleine went over with her boyfriend Dan to do it on our behalf. We had signed power of attorney over to her. It was she who had to rush around finding our lovely lawyer Furio, to get the right documents and open bank accounts on our behalf, and it was she who had to sit through the arcane and archaic process of handing over a house from old owner to new. Compared with the British set-up it's a very formal process, with a notary presiding over the whole thing and making dramatic speeches (all in Italian, of course). But Italy being Italy, there is also the entrenched desire to beat the system, a desire that is not only recognized but facilitated by the authorities.

And so it was that Madeleine came to experience on our behalf our first and rather dramatic example of Italian corruption at first hand. We were anxious to be putting her in such a position though also, if we're honest, a bit jealous. Italian corruption is by now a high art. It has been practised for centuries, its processes refined and perfected, its challengers only serving to propel it onto further cunnings and refinements, its protagonists by now accomplished professionals. It is truly an art. For this, as much as for any other reason, it is almost impossible to stop. As unimaginable as someone in England one day suggesting that the Sunday roast should be stamped out.

In our case, what the corruption meant was that there were two prices that had been agreed for the house. The first amount was the actual sum we would pay to the current owners. The second amount was the one that would be declared on all the official documents – and on which the owners and we would be liable to pay tax.

We'd had huge deliberations beforehand about whether to go along with all this. We are generally very law-abiding and, on a practical note, it seemed rather foolhardy to be letting the best part of 100,000 euros disappear into the Italian ether. But a combination of Furio telling us the owners were insisting on it – and that the sale could therefore be off if we didn't agree to this – and a naïve excitement about learning to play by Italian rules eventually led us to decide that we would.

In practice, what all this meant was some nerve-racking minutes for my poor sister. All of a sudden, the handover proceedings stopped. The notary got up and left the room, 'In order,' he said, 'that the owners, past and present, can talk.' These were the code words to hand over the real money. So Madeleine, nudged on by Furio, had to whip out her sticky bundles of the cash needed to make the sum up to the agreed sale price and pass them under the table to the ex-owners. After a decent interval, the notary re-entered and the rest of the business of signing the official papers was completed without fuss.

And so it was that we were now the official owners of a house on the other side of the world, and Madeleine had had her first lesson in the ducking and diving ways of the Italian 'grey market' as they like to call it. It's not really bad, it's just sensible, common sense, practical. If you had a man like Berlusconi as your leader and paragon, wouldn't you have a sceptical view of national honesty?

By the time it came to have our LA leaving party, I was so pregnant that I needed one of those stretch limos to drive me around all day. Actually, it was stretch Hummers that were the in thing in LA by now. Let's not forget that, despite his latter-day greening, it was Arnie who inspired the purchase of these misanthropic tools of all-American one-upmanship. Our party was all-American glamour. We had been nominated for an Emmy award for *Junkyard Wars* in the first year of a new category called 'Best Reality TV Show'. We despised the label but liked the idea of the invite so swallowed our reservations. It did seem the perfect setting for a Hollywood farewell.

Eloise, our wardrobe genius, made me an amazing dress out of bluey green shimmery silk, festooned with beautiful rusting nuts and

bolts and rivets – it was the attire of a junk mermaid and quite lovely. Everyone else looked fantastic, too, like snakes emerging from
their skins of filthy T-shirts and jeans to squeaky shoes and perfectly
tied bow ties.

Our arrival was a small moment of glory. Everyone else, by tradition, arrives in stretch limos, black and sleek. We've all watched
them on TV, the starlets and the vamps poking a perfectly tanned
leg from a black limo straight onto the red carpet, met by the fire-
work flashes of a thousand paparazzi. We knew we couldn't com-
pete on that level of glamour so decided instead to go our own
way. We'd commandeered the *Junkyard Wars* truck – a massive
whitish transit van with (probably) 'Also available in white' and
'Clean me' daubed in fingertip on the back door. The faces of the
butterfly-tied bouncers lining the entrance route were priceless as two,
five, ten of us emerged in our finery from this scabby half-broken down
van. The creaky door was held open by Dominic, who, wearing
white lab coat, steel toecaps, hard hat and huge red ear defenders,
looked to be lodged in some uncomfortable nether region between
mad scientist and mental health nurse.

I had prepared a speech which was to honour no one in television but instead everyone outside of it who has year-round dirty fingernails and a car chocked up on bricks in the front yard. But, of
course, I never got to say it because *Survivor* won.

Goodbye LA.

Preserving lemons

Ingredients for 1 large jar
Lemons – 10 unwaxed
Salt – 6 teaspoons
Bay leaves – 3
Peppercorns – 21
Coriander seeds – 21
Cloves – 3

Cathy was at the uncomfortable stage of pregnancy, when the soccer-ball-size lump means that you just want the little blighter out. Most mums-to-be would have been putting their energy into nesting, but she couldn't because our nest would be in London and we were in LA. So instead Cathy's suddenly demon-like energies went into preserving. My favourite is her preserved lemons. She uses big, fat juicy ones and they have to be be unwaxed. You can eat the whole preserve, rind and all. The jar is whisked out of the fridge at a moment's notice to brighten up a salad or pasta dish with tiny citrusy nuggets.

Sterilize a three-quarter-litre preserving jar by putting it in a hot oven for 15 minutes. Take 5 lemons and squeeze out as much juice as you can. Keep the juice. Cut the other lemons into wedges and remove the seeds.

Stuff the lemon wedges into the jar to make a layer, then sprinkle 2 tablespoons of salt on top, and a third of the bay leaves, peppercorns, coriander seeds and cloves. Add another layer of lemon wedges and repeat the salting and spicing. Repeat with a third layer. Now pour in the lemon juice, which must completely cover the lemon wedges. Close the jar and store it away. After a month or so the skin will start to go soft.

We usually chop half a wedge up into small bits to sprinkle on salad. The jar will keep for up to a year and it's nice to make an extra one to give away.

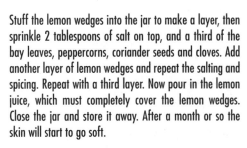

Hollywood pasta

Ingredients for 4 people
Spinach – 400g
Olive oil – 7 tablespoons
Garlic – 3 cloves
Tomatoes – 700g
Tagliatelle – 500g fresh
Salt and pepper
Parmesan – freshly grated

Simple fresh ingredients. The three words that sum up Italian cooking. A wise woman once told me that, faced with a dish that didn't taste quite right, a French chef would think about what ingredient they could *add* while an Italian chef would think about what ingredient they could *take away*, stripping the dish down its absolute essence. This is something that we make along Italian principles. It depends on finding flavoursome, robust spinach where you can almost taste the iron, not the watery, bland supermarket stuff. And, of course, the tomatoes have to be sweet and pert.

Wash the spinach well and place in a colander to drip dry. Heat the olive oil in a saucepan on the lowest heat you can get. Cut the garlic into thin slices and fry in the oil – the test is to cook it as slowly as possible (because there is an element of challenge to this dish blokes seem to like cooking it – that and it's simple as pie).

Chop the tomatoes into decent chunks, cutting out the stringy stalks along the way.

Boil some salty water and cook the tagliatelle with a bit of oil. At the same time put the spinach in on top of the garlic and oil but turn off the heat.

When the pasta is cooked add this on top of the spinach, put the heat back on low, and stir everything together so the spinach is evenly spread. Season with lots of salt and pepper, add the tomatoes and stir once more. The tomatoes should not be cooked too much, just heated through. If it's looking a bit dry add more oil and serve immediately with some parmesan.

Title: Pushing ice
ID: 484000169N

Title: treasure hunt
ID: 530666963T

Title: Three moments of an explosion : stories
ID: 5400363765

Title: great game
ID: 53077884X5

Total items: 4
14/02/2017 09:50

4 Los Angeles ... London ... Loro Piceno

We only just made it back to London before our baby, Rosie, arrived, bang on time, and suddenly we were three. As we left the hospital, our tiny little naked mole rat bundled up and looking teensy in the obligatory car seat, we expected a heavy hand on our shoulder at any moment. It just doesn't seem possible, when you think of all the tiny petty things that the law *doesn't* let you do, that the authorities really think it's OK to hand over the care of a tiny vulnerable little human to terrified amateurs.

We happily lived in the bubble that is early parenthood for a few months, seeing lots of friends and family, being treated like royalty, and sauntering out with Rosie into the charmed London world around us. We did things like take her – at a few weeks of age – to an exhibition of magnified insects at the Natural History Museum, or, stashed under coats, to music recitals. And every Friday night – our sacrosanct 'date night' – we'd walk round and round the block, swinging her in her car seat or singing banal songs until she fell asleep and we'd be able to go out for dinner together, banned from even mentioning the baby word.

Jason did his last stint of work for the *Scrapheap Challenge* juggernaut at the end of 2004 and then said goodbye to TV. We both underestimated the shock of his giving up work. The idea was that he would do part-time Rosie care (my maternity leave having come to an end) and part-time development and research for our life to be. In other words, a rather formless existence, with suddenly no colleagues, no structure, no clocking in and out and, crucially, no pay cheque at the end of the month. Lots of people say money isn't important to them – us included. And what you mean when you say it is that, if you were forced to live on very little money, you feel sure that you could cope. And you're probably right. But the main thing you lose when you give up a pay cheque isn't the money. Instead, you are losing your independence (and I'd say, feminism intact, that for a man this is harder, because the social taboos are so much more potent) and your sense of being valued in the world; you're losing your sense that you are contributing.

Rationally, you know most of this is nonsense – of course Jason was doing valuable work, both with Rosie and for our future. But such is the curse of unpaid work at home – it is unrecognized and unappreciated by society. But people still ask women who stay at home 'But what do you actually *do* all day?'

In terms of the business we were going from a true standing start. And Jason was doing most of it single-handed as I was back at work three or four days a week, the other days looking after Rosie. Our 'To do' list for January read as follows:

TO DO LIST – JANUARY 2005

TO DO FOR BUSINESS	WHEN	BY
Write Business Plan		
Find out about EU grants		
Find out about small business loans		
Investigate starting business in UK v. Italy (consulate)		
Investigate importation rules (licences, food standards)		
Organize pruning lessons		
Capital investment research		
Set up e-mail/website		
Name for company		
UK importer contacts		
US importer contacts		
continued overleaf		

	WHEN	BY
Shop contacts London		
Shop contacts USA		
Talk to Madeleine re design		
Get hold of Italian instructional video tapes on olive trees		
Set up UK company – UK or Italian? Research		
TO DO FOR HOUSE	**WHEN**	**BY**
Work out timetable for building work		
Transfer money/get best rate (check rate daily)		
Kitchen plan – send designs		
Telephone line – talk to Roberto, architect		
Electricity – Francesca says we need 5 or 6 KW		
Franco – other carpentry e.g. bookshelves		
Septic tank – check requirements		
Book tickets for next trip out		
TO DO GENERAL	**WHEN**	**BY**
Italian residency – talk to Furio about deadline		
Find out about language schools in Italy		
Do a proper budget		
Place to get married		
Import car		
Check on stuff shipped from LA		
Buy desktop computer?		
Sell bike		
Write Italian will		
Write English will		
Do at least an hour of Italian every day		

Work was due to start 'pretty soon' on our Italian house. In Italian that seemed to mean anything from 'this afternoon' to 'some time next year'. But we'd found a builder to do the work and an architect / project manager who was going to keep an eye on him as well as coordinate electricians, plumbers, carpenters, septic tank installers, all those folk. It all seemed to be very specialized – with particular experts, 'skilled artisans' we liked to think, to do one specific tiny thing, rather than a single gun-slinging cowboy who often typifies the Brit norm.

As for work, we still had very vague ideas about what we were going to do. We knew we'd make olive oil and we hoped we'd be able to sell it to shops in the UK. But neither of us had any background in marketing or retail or food production or really anything relevant at all. But we somehow hoped that because we were determined and accustomed to learning fast, because we had a hunger for new knowledge and a mortal fear of failure, that we'd somehow manage not only to get by but become successful and rich. Hoping to have our optimism corroborated, we decided to ask some people we knew for advice. An old family friend of Jason, who set up the chocolate company Green & Black's, advised us that the olive oil industry is notorious for its deadly combination of low margins and high levels of competition – basically because any old Tom, Dick or Harry thinks they can chance their arm at it. He suggested we would need something earth-shatteringly unique in order to set ourselves apart from the myriad competition. And with that he wished us the best of luck.

One day I came home from work to discover that Jason had found us an olive tree pruning course. It always amazes me the things that he manages to find out – he would have made an excellent sleuth. On this occasion he'd unearthed a three-day course on 'The Theory and Practice of Pruning Established Olive Trees' in a church hall in a village less than an hour from our Le Marche future home. Hearing this information while drinking a cup of tea in a flat in central London, the murmur of traffic below, felt something like a miracle. We decided to sign up before the mirage vanished.

We didn't yet have the full medical history of the olive grove but we knew that no real work had been done on it for a good decade. There'd been a bit of harvesting here and there – well, who wouldn't take a few olives from orphan trees for a bit of free oil? But it would have taken more of an altruist to get out there with secateurs and saws and actually *prune*. So a pruning course was essential, both for the radical facelift that the grove needed, but also for us – to get our heads out of textbooks and into wellies and practical work. Encouragingly, we'd read that olive trees are generally very resilient and that despite the years of neglect, we should be able to get the grove back on track pretty quickly.

A week later we were in Le Marche. We'd decided to stay in a bed and breakfast near Loro Piceno as our house was still missing a few fundamentals like water and walls. The B&B was basic but functional. The 'breakfast' element consisted of a fruit tart presented on day one, and expected to do for the week. Hooray, we said, this place is definitely not Tuscany.

The drive from Loro Piceno to San Severino Marche where the course was to be held was one of those really sickly ones with too tight curves and pointy tufts of hills that make your stomach roll over, much to giggles from Rosie in the back. We were heading off to sign in, the day before the course proper. Italy still works by nature of this face-to-face exchange. It is normal to sign up for something like this, or even just to book tickets for a show and still have to physically show up. They haven't (yet) developed our fixation for the ease of the telephone and e-mail and I suppose it is simply, admirably (?), because they aren't in such a fret about constantly saving time. This sort of Italian habit is a good example of the sort of thing that is charming when one is on holiday and distinctly less so when one is not. For now we were still on holiday – sort of, a working one – so could swallow it, but rancour mightn't be far off.

The concession they make to the need to communicate remotely is that fantastically archaic device the fax machine, which is still ubiquitous in Italy. I hate them, they are such rubbish and outdated I would rather have a pigeon appear. Even that word 'fax', 'facsimile', conjures images of the '80s and of secretaries with big shiny shoulder pads and electric blue mascara.

For the pruning course, run by a local agricultural association, even the fax wasn't an option, so here we were.

We found the place, at least we thought it was the place, quite easily. It was a completely empty church hall next to a completely empty, in fact locked, church. We were early, that is to say we were on time, so decided to keep the faith and wait a bit. Rosie was in one of those kangaroo pouch things on my front, constantly trying to put my finger in her mouth.

After about quarter of an hour, a very, very old man arrived. He was about 4 feet 10 and his trousers were on a battle against gravity, which might have explained his shuffle. It looked so improbable to us that he was there for the same reason we were, and to him it looked so improbable that we were there for the same reason that he was, that we exchanged nothing more than a sort of cocked neck acknowledgement of each other's existence. A little while later, more tiny old people came in, followed by a few more. And then more still. Then there was a youngish – well, late-middle-aged – man in a suit who breezed in and then breezed as breezily straight back out again. After about another quarter of an hour, there had assembled probably about fifty people, and it dawned on us, belatedly, that some sort of ad-hoc queue had formed. Ad-hoc or not, we were definitely at the back of it. At the front of it, I was not sure how she had snuck in, was a young lady – like properly young, in her thirties, half the age of anyone else in the room.

A baby is like an access-all-areas pass in Italy and I walked boldly to the front, just to check that we weren't in a queue for a wake or something. The young lady was writing things down in what looked like a register and I could see the word 'potatura' which means pruning, written on her sheet, so this really was it. The reason the queue was moving so paralysingly slowly was that these old people were taking an aeon – each – to write their names and phone numbers on it. The weight given to each signature was as slow and deliberate as a judge signing someone's death warrant. Then it occurred to me that for some of these old geezers, their name was probably the only thing they could write, a theory borne out when the breezy man who'd been and gone, came again and, with scolding words, made a spelling correction to one of the old men's scrawlings.

When we got to the front of the queue, we realized we were in more-or-less the same illiterate boat as the rest of them. First of all we got in a muddle trying to explain that we didn't have a phone number – one of those situations where I always say too much. Where 'non telefono' would probably have got the message across, instead I decided to try to explain that we were redoing our house and still waiting for a phone line to be put in; what came out was something like 'The house, yours, is being reseeded and we are late for the string.'

Then we got in a pickle about where to put our first names and where our surnames, and also whether we needed to put Rosie down (London habits making us think that this list might also serve as a checklist should the place be bombed). In the end I put Cathy where I should have put Rogers and Jason where I should have put Gibb – with everything leftover going in the column for first names. The result was that for that evening and for the duration of the course, Jason would be known as 'oceantelfordgibb' and I as 'androsierogers'.

Having signed up, everyone headed into another room where there were several chairs and benches set out in rows. Italians don't like rows and within minutes old men were rearranging them so they could sit next to their buddies in comfy huddles. We managed to squeeze into the end of a Johnny-no-mates row. By this time Rosie was pretty restless, my finger had been chewed to the bone, but Jason managed to unearth some prehistoric biscuit from some nether region of his jacket.

The young lady got up onto the platform/stage area and introduced herself as 'Alfei, Barbara'. She would be taking the pruning course for the next three days. Relief! We were such strangers among these grizzled farmers with filthy fingernails and legs all bent the wrong way that it was great to have someone sort of the same shape as us at the helm. There was nothing more we needed to do today but she'd see us all bright and early in the morning.

The next morning we were all back in the hall again by 8 a.m.

About three-quarters of the people from the night before were there and a few new people, mostly slightly younger ones who must have known to take this whole signing-in business with a pinch of salt.

As Alfei, Barbara set off on her guide to olive-tree pruning, it dawned on us just how far we had to go with our Italian. It didn't help that there was a constant murmur of noise from the assembled farming crowd, who acted as if showing up alone was the point. As fast as our fingers could thumb through our dictionary, we couldn't get a level of detail greater than 'branches, cut, lymph, overall shape', generic things like that. Alfei, Barbara had a charming habit of saying 'OK' which she pronounced 'Ho-kayee' at the end of each sentence, but that wasn't going to get us very far with 1,000 trees to prune. When she came round after the first hour with hand-outs, *with pictures in*, we could have kissed her.

In the break – for coffee, of course – our course-colleagues turned out to be quite friendly. I think that last night they had assumed we were lost tourists looking for a remote Lotto painting, but now that they realized we were there for the same reason they were, things warmed up. Even if our Italian was dire (and it didn't matter because they spoke in that constipated, cauterized language that is the Le Marche dialect), we managed to get by thanks to the ancient art of gesture talk. They would point at Rosie and make snipping movements as if she were pruning an olive tree and we'd laugh, and in return mime her carrying crates of olives up a steep hill, beating her to go faster.

The course carried on in similar vein for the rest of the day. The only difference was that the audience had an ever-growing confidence and would challenge Alfei, Barbara more and more at every stage. We couldn't understand most of the words, but we could understand that there was a clash of cultures of sorts – between ancient farming tradition and modern scientific method. To me it seemed that the fact all these old guys were here at all listening (well, mostly listening) to a whippersnapper of a woman teaching them about ancient country ways was a victory for her in itself. And she clearly earned their respect – not least measured by the fact that they all stayed. She gently took the piss out of them – admonishing the critics of her methodology by insulting their trees as being 'all wood'. This was something we'd read about – that a lot of people who kept olive trees mainly for their own use weren't nearly radical enough in their pruning. They couldn't cut one branch off in preference to another any more than they could choose to feed only one of their children. The result was that trees which should have at the most four main branches ended up with nine or ten – and the resulting tree was 'all wood'. The effort it took the tree to keep all this wood alive meant that there wasn't much left for the productive parts – and the trees would not only look ugly but be woeful olive producers. It's a sort of 'spare the rod and spoil the child' warning shot for olive keepers.

That night, we sat on the cold tile floor of the B&B, our notes all laid in front of us, taking turns to use the Italian–English dictionary. Jason cross-referenced a lot of what Alfei, Barbara had said with a very technical manual published by the University of California, the only technical olive book he'd found that was written in English. It was a close contest whether the unintelligible academic text or the unintelligible Italian was harder to fathom.

By midnight we'd started to make some headway. The good thing about technical jargon is that it's usually derived from Latin and the words are often very nearly the same in English and Italian.

So we found out that the *vaso policonico* that Alfei, Barbara kept referring to was no more mysterious than a 'polyconic vase'. Hang on, that's pretty mysterious. But another pruning book showed us that this meant a tree pruned in such a way that it was like an open bowl in the middle, i.e. empty of growth inside, and that each of the (usually four) main branches was pruned into a sort of cone shape with one main growing tip then giving out to more productive shoots lower down. This was a shape we recognized from trees we'd seen and we liked the sound of it. Trees like that couldn't be accused of being all wood and how clever we'd be to talk about pruning our trees like a polyconic vase. Even in English people would be perplexedly impressed.

The next day was more of the same, except for some reason freezing cold. I think the church heating bill can't have been paid – though they'd really no excuse given the pile the Pope is sitting on. Now whenever Alfei, Barbara mentioned the *vaso policonico* we glanced at each other knowingly. Jason even did a 'casual' sketch of one in a place in his notepad which he knew was visible to the rows behind.

The afternoon brought excitement in the form of some young olive trees offered up to the Alfei altar. There was a gasp from the crowd – well, from my mouth – when she whipped out a pair of secateurs clearly with intent. As she demonstrated how to prune a very small olive tree, that messy bit where theory tries to become practice clouded our vision. And everyone else's. Within seconds, half the audience were up on their feet poking and jabbing at this little tree, pulling a branch here and a twig there – saying cut that bit, leave that bit, everyone sure they knew the answer.

'*Domani*,' said Alfei, Barbara, '*tocca a voi*' ('you will have your turn'). The next day was a Saturday and some of the teensy farmers had brought along their burly wives. It had snowed the night before and everyone was thickly bundled. Rosie was almost rigid in layers, wedged into her papoose like a too fat hotdog in a too small roll. We congregated outside the church, ready to head up the hill to the olive grove which some unwitting volunteer had lent the course for our pruning experiments. Probably saw it as a cheap way of getting the trees pruned. But would you get a bunch of apprentice electricians round to have free run of your home's wiring?

Alfei, Barbara bobbed up and down the ladder like a squirrel, showing why a snip here and a cut there were called for – and how, in some cases, there were branches big enough to justify the saw being brandished. She showed us what to do on perhaps four trees before offering up her secateurs to the first smart Alec who fancied his chances. A sprat of a man bounded up the ladder and was ready to start his 'tac tac tac' when Alfei, Barbara asked the assembled throng to suggest which branches should stay and which should go. A chorus of 'Secondo me ...' ('Well, I think ...') rang out through the valley.

The 'secondo mes' carried on the whole day, with arguments about what and where to cut becoming more impassioned as cold and hunger set in. A nice lady lent me a blanket she'd brought along so that I didn't have to lay Rosie actually on the snow to change her nappy. The lady and her wrinkly husband laughed at us affectionately and called us the 'mad English'.

In terms of learning, the experience was one of feeling like you've got it, then lost it, then regained it, then lost it, then regained it again. There were so many different bits of the theory that, when faced with an actual living tree, one often contradicted another. So the rule that said you should cut off anything blocking light to the centre ran into conflict with the one which said you shouldn't sever a 'principal branch', when the tree you were faced with had one main branch that curled across the middle of the tree and exploded growth out down below. Or how to choose between retaining the end branch that was too vertical and the one which went through an awkward dogleg right at its end? This was life and one had to make compromises. We were sorry when Alfei, Barbara told us it was the end of experiment time and the course.

All that remained was for us all to assemble in a restaurant across the road and eat an enormous feast. I suspect all Italian courses end a similar way. At the end of the meal, a group of dignitaries at the high table got up to speak. The farmer next to me told us that one of them was the local mayor, one the president of the Le Marche olive oil society and various others things I didn't understand. They talked keenly for quite a while and singsongishly enough to send Rosie thankfully to sleep. Then there was a reshuffling of chairs as it became clear that presentations were to be made. Everyone who had completed the course was to be given a certificate! In turn, each grizzled farmer was called up to walk in silence to the high table, shake hands with the mayor and collect his little paper slice of prize.

The mayor said the words 'Oceantelfordgibb and androsierogers' so strangely that it was only when we were jabbed in the back that we realized it was our turn. We felt terrified. Jason said he was more nervous getting this three-day pruning course certificate than he'd been getting his degree after three years of study!

Suddenly, out of the quiet, everyone burst into spontaneous and loud applause, which turned to cheers and whistles and shouts as we walked up, Rosie slumped in her sling. As we shook the mayor's hand and looked out at these lovely grubby rosy smiling faces, it was all I could do to stop myself bursting into tears of gratitude. Gratitude that we had been allowed to fit in.

This was to be our life.

5 Leading
double lives

It *was to be* our life. But we weren't there yet. I was leading a schizophrenic life, half as a TV executive, and half as a budding Italian peasant. Jason, too, was in a strange hybrid life, our Italian plans seeming a chimera juxtaposed against the all too practical everyday duties of nappy changing. Occasionally for him these two worlds collided, as when he made a trip to Italy with Rosie in tow. Being there with her on his own, in the middle of winter (this one just didn't seem to end), staying in the not very nice but very cheap B&B, was no easy feat. Rosie could still barely sit up by herself and the challenge of doing so on freezing cold marble floors was too much – so she'd preferred to be suctioned to Jason most of the day.

Jason had to go for two reasons: first, to check up on the building work on the house and, secondly, to prove that we lived there. Even though we didn't.

Let's take the relative ease of the first. We were having some fairly big work done to the house. It was not on the scale – thank God – of the total restructurings that many embark on and that we had so nearly done. But the house hadn't been lived in for probably a decade and when it had been last inhabited, it was evidently by people who liked cooking in a tiny dark poky corner, hated the view and never had a bath.

The house, like most Italian country houses, was divided into two halves – the half where the animals lived and the half where the humans lived. The animal half was basically a huge lofty room – by lofty I mean you could have fitted in another whole floor just about – with tiny windows. In more recent years, it had been done up as what can only be described as a 1970s pizzeria – with pale pine wood cladding the walls and a disproportionately huge (and that's hard in such a large room) open-plan brick fireplace.

This 'pizzeria' was the site of most of our major work – because this was the room where we thought we'd spend most of our waking hours. So we were changing the tiny windows into big French doors, putting in a big open-plan kitchen, getting rid of the fireplace and clad walls and opening the whole room up with a big archway entrance.

In the rest of the house, we were also changing the garage into our office, stealing one of the bedrooms to make a bathroom and opening up the erstwhile living room with another big archway, instead of its current plywood door. We were retiling all the floors, rewiring all the electricity, putting in a gas hob (which meant a big buried gas container in the garden), installing a septic tank, waterproofing the cellar, redoing the roof and the stairs and repainting and plastering pretty much everywhere.

This work was being done by a chain-smoking man called Rosario, who Jason had nicknamed Fivebellies. From what we could see, Fivebellies himself didn't do very much work, but he did do effective bossing of the rest of his team: the unfeasibly wiry and strong Laddi, the unfeasibly long-suffering Moroccan Marti and his unfeasible offspring Fabio, who was thin and handsome. Even though Fivebellies wasn't one to lift many fingers, he was still the one who needed constant praise and affirmation of the work 'he had done'. If you didn't tell him that the new fireplace he'd put in was one of the most beautiful things you'd ever seen in your life, he would sulk. He smoked constantly and left a trail of ash and butts wherever he went, a fact that drove Jason mad, even though the place was still a building site.

Basically, though, they were a good gang and the work they were doing seemed to be good in that archways appeared to have been knocked through the correct walls and kitchens were landing up where they were planned to touch down. So that it was all encouraging.

The second reason for Jason's trip – the proving that we lived there bit – was a little trickier. The point was this: when we bought the house, we said it was to be our primary residence, which is true. This means that you pay a stamp duty equivalent of 3 percent instead of the 17 percent that you pay if you are buying as a holiday home. All seems quite fair and reasonable; charge those holiday homers we say. To fulfil the obligations of this lower tax, you have a certain period of time in which to take up residency in said house. And that certain period was about to run out. Rules being rules (at least until you've learned how to break them), there is no scope for appeal, for saying 'but the building work is running late because of the hard winter' or 'our plans changed a bit so we're going to be six months later' – you live there within that period or you cough up the extra cash.

So live there we had to. Even though anyone seeing the house for a millisecond could see it was impossible to live in, especially with a baby. Jason would have to become instantly proficient in the ancient Italian art of craftiness, an art he'd be instructed on by, among other people, our lawyer.

Craftiness in this case meant Jason 'hanging out' around Loro Piceno, subtly stalking the local policeman, the person whose job it would be to sign our residency papers. Bumping into him in the post office, casually like (i.e. following him in), one morning, making sure to post nothing that looked like a vacationer's postcard. Seeing him again later that day as he was off buying a few groceries. 'Imagine-the-coincidence!'-ing him that same evening as Jason was in the café having an evening beer.

The idea is that if you have all this time to hang around town, then you must live here, a fact in direct contradiction of any common sense. For a start, if you live somewhere, you have to work! Only on holiday do you have time to mill about drinking endless coffees and reading newspapers in public places. But so be it, these were the rules and by day three, Jason was getting acknowledging shrugs of the head and even the odd '*Buon giorno*' from the unsmiling policeman.

Sooner or later this casual acknowledgement of Jason's existence in a world called Loro Piceno had to be converted into a form signed by said policeman. Popping the question of asking for this signature was a delicate art. It needed to seem so obviously a formality that it was almost tedious – 'You and I both know I live here, I'm sorry to have to bother you with this little bureaucratic detail of signing my form.' But at the same time it was also important to demonstrate that you had sufficient respect for Italy, for the local *comune*, for rules in general and for the rules of this policeman in particular – and that you, therefore, took the obligation to prove your residency very seriously.

I'm sure Jason did it perfectly. The policeman's response was straightforward. '*Va bene. Basta solo che vengo a trovarvi a casa vostra nei prossimi giorni. Devo controllare che ci sono l'acqua, l'elettricità ... niente ... per la dichiarazione ... è tutto sarà a posto.*' ('That's fine. I just need to drop by your house in the next couple of days and check you have running water and electricity for the formal declaration and we'll be all set.')

Jason could only say '*Meravigliosa. Grazie mille.*' Great.

But his stomach was churning. We didn't live there to be around for an impromptu 'drop in'. The water didn't run or even drip. And

69

there was currently not even an electricity line to the house, let alone a light switch.

The first problem was the easiest to solve. By now, having been the policeman's shadow for a week, Jason had a pretty accurate idea of his movements. He was always around town in the morning and in the evening, but seemed to disappear between about 11 a.m. and 4 p.m. Obviously, 12.30–2.30 at least was lunch so the most likely times for a home visit were 11–12.30 and 2.30–4. Jason would just have to make sure he was at the house during those times – and hope for the best.

The water was a problem. He went to the house, Rosie asleep in his arms, and asked Fivebellies when the plumber was due to come. Fivebellies had no idea but did have a number for him. 'Is there something the plumber could do if he comes now?' asked Jason. 'Well, sure, the boiler could be put in,' said FB. 'Could you possibly call him and ask him if he might by any chance be able to come and do it for the next couple of days?' asked Jason. Then, seeing FB's puzzled expression, he took a gamble and added, 'The policeman is coming to check I live here.'

It was like the code word in a heist. 'I see,' said Fivebellies with a conspiratorial wink. 'I'm sure we can get the plumber over.' And he was straight onto his phone, prattling away in unintelligible dialect – the only recognizable element the tone of complicity – to the plumber, who would, of course, be happy to come and eke out the job on the boiler.

Two out of three. Next up, electricity.

The electrician was a local Loro lad who appeared to be still in his teens and had the sort of slightly unhinged look that made one worry about him playing with high voltage. Fivebellies, now on a mission, called him, too, and told him to make sure he was on call to do some high visibility wire fiddling.

Two mornings later, the policeman showed up. It was 11.45. Jason had been on the lookout and was outside ready to meet him and overwhelm him with a charm offensive. He pointed down to the olive grove, talked about our plans to make olive oil, told him how much work we planned to do to the grove and what a crime it was when people let olive groves go to rack and ruin.

The policeman was attentive but unmoved.

Then Jason spotted that there was a small child's car seat in the back of his car and he cheered inwardly. There is no Italian man who doesn't have a weak spot when talking about his offspring. And this time he struck gold – the policeman had a little boy, aged two a half, who actually had just been rather ill. 'Oh how awful,' said Jason, gently asking for more. It was nothing serious, just a fever here and there 'this terrible winter', 'how the little ones suffer'. Jason shared the pain of a father's worry over the health of a child, recounting a story of how we'd taken Rosie to hospital one night because she had just gone completely limp with a raging tempera-ture. There was nothing more frightening, they agreed, cooing and empathizing like two old grannies. Then at the perfect moment, Jason said, 'Well, we must introduce them, I'm sure they would get on, Rosie would love a playmate … you never know, they might even end up getting married! Stranger things start this way.'

And so that was it. Jason had traded our only daughter for our residency permit. The policeman, smiling properly for the first time, came into the house. He nodded to the plumber, who shrugged his shoulders in a way that obviously meant 'Still working on this darn tap, water any minute' and then bang on cue the electrician ran in, puffing under the weight of multicoloured wires and fuse boxes in his arms, muttering something about the 'usual problems' with Enel the electricity company.

So there was no water and there was no electricity (and no beds, no table, no oven, no chairs). But there was virtual water and virtual electricity. And a virtual future marriage of toddlers. And this all somehow meant the right games had been played and the right scenes acted out.

The next day, the policeman surprised Jason while he was having a coffee in the bar. He handed over the signed residency form.

'*Benvenuti in Italia*' ('Welcome to Italy'), was all he said.

We were round at Mike and Gavanndra's house in Brixton. They had fairly recently come back from spending a year living in the middle of nowhere in France and were wholehearted supporters of our idea to move to the middle of the Italian nowhere. But they are both writers so are probably more used to the idea of being lonely than the normal people we consider ourselves to be. And I can't help feeling (though Jason would disagree with this and even tell me off) that they are maybe a little hardier than we are, that they would relish an evening heated only by the occasional warm breath from a candle and fed only with a piece of dried bread rubbed with some mint picked from outside the freezing window. We like the idea of liking the idea of that sort of thing. But in reality we both, and Jason in particular, really hate the cold. And for some reason living in the middle of nowhere and being cold seem to go hand in hand (what better advertisement for city living?).

Anyway we were round there, all nice and warm in their nice warm flat, being treated to a deliciously cheering butternut squash risotto, so all this was very far from our minds when Becky, another writer friend who was there, told us about this amazing present idea she'd found for her dad. It was called 'Adopt a Sheep' and was a scheme run by a farmers' cooperative in Abruzzo. The idea was that you'd adopt said creature, receive a fulsome flow of cheese and wool and wotnot for a couple of years – and then, Godfather-like – a sheep carcass would land on your doormat. Wow. That is a modern gift. Not just the gift of life but death presented in gift form, too. It seemed a little macabre, the adoption concept conjuring images of nurturing, naming, taking under one's wing – and then wallop – there's a cadaver for you. But hey ho, it's fashionable to know the provenance of your food and it doesn't get a lot more personal than that. We applauded her creative gift giving and hoped her father would enjoy his temporary foster pet.

Later on, on the tube on the way back home, Jason brought up the subject of this adoption thing again. Being vegetarian he wasn't so interested in the idea of dead sheep, but he 'had been thinking'. 'You know how we've talked about trying to make our olive oil unique, about needing an original idea,' he said. 'Well, how about we let people adopt our trees? The oil they buy is that from their own tree.'

To give a bit of context, we'd spent most of the week sniffing out our potential competition in Selfridges and Harrods and Harvey Nichols and Waitrose and Divertimenti and umpteen little independent delis – and had become somewhat disillusioned. There were just so many olive oils on the market. Cheap oils, mid-priced oils, exorbitantly expensive oils, prettily bottled oils, rustically bottled oils, angularly bottled oils, Italian oils, Spanish oils, Greek oils, Australian oils, tall thin bottles, short fat bottles, bottles in boxes, bottles in tubes. Lots of them were a bit grubby and had slightly wrinkled up labels which suggested they weren't exactly flying off the shelves. It was pretty hard to think of anything which would set us apart from this myriad bunch; we were suddenly struck by images of having sad, desperate conversations with buyers from these sort of shops, conversations in which we'd be made to feel like lower life forms than Hollywood agents.

But maybe this adoption thing was the answer? It certainly felt good to be able to say something about our future life that was a bit different from 'We're going to Italy to make olive oil', which still didn't have the taste of credibility in our mouths. Partly because we didn't yet know how we were going to make it, partly because of the sheer nerve of a couple of semi-clueless Brits going to Italy to try to do what the Italians have perfected over centuries, but more than any of this because we were really unsure how we'd ever get anyone to buy it. And it sort of felt right, this adoption concept. The British seem to be intoxicated with Italy, so the notion of their being able to own a little piece of it seemed to have a certain romantic sense. It put people directly in touch with the provenance of their food, with good, properly made untampered-with food. And more crudely, it would probably offer a better potential for us to make some money than schlepping round all these shops that were already overflowing with oil, begging them to take ours at ever discounted prices.

But even though this really was, with hindsight, our 'Eureka moment', we didn't treat it as such at the time. We talked about it a bit, and thought yes it seemed a good idea – but we didn't leap up and down saying, 'That's it! That's it!'

More fool us.

The next few weeks saw us, and especially Jason, working through the daunting 'to do' list. We had a nascent business plan and an accountant whose surname was Italian for chestnut grove, which somehow felt auspicious. We had bought computers, registered websites, chosen a name for the company, and Jason had started sniffing out suppliers and getting his head around scary new concepts like VAT and import/export regulations. We'd also been working closely with Madeleine, who had come up with some bottle and tin designs and also a company logo, all of which we really loved and which made the whole plan seem real. It's useful having a design genius in the family.

It was maybe two months later that we sat down for the first time with our website designers Andy and Noam. They said they'd find it really useful if we could describe a bit about the company and what we planned to do so that they could start to get a clearer picture of what we'd need from a website.

We started down our now quite well-worn address about how we were going to make olive oil from our own trees to sell, but how that was just the start and in the bigger picture we were going to use our position of physically being in Italy, and in a relatively unknown region, to sniff out other local produce as yet unfamiliar to Britain and become the exporters of it to the UK. We were also en route to becoming organic and would want gradually to make any of our suppliers also go down that same path. So we'd be Italian organic food importers to the UK. We'd chosen the name 'Nudo' which is Italian for naked, to convey the idea that all our produce would be pure and unfiddled with – and, of course, because we thought it sounded a bit cheeky.

None of it sounded that inspiring in terms of an innovative website and it showed on Andy and Noam's faces.

'So what did you imagine in terms of a website?' they asked.

Well, we liked the idea of making the grove more personal, hav-ing lots of pictures of the different lovely views and of the trees, descriptions of the process of making oil and so on. But it all needed to be done in such a way that we'd be able to add other products as and when — in other words so that the site could expand and grow as we expanded and grew.

Then Jason mentioned the adoption idea and the room changed.

Noam was particularly smitten. 'That's brilliant,' he said.

From then on, the ideas started to run much more freely. We could have a map with each tree marked on it, and you could click on each one and see a photo of it, and so choose which one to adopt. Maybe it could have a 360 degree thing so that you could stand in the virtual world under your tree and see the view in all directions. We would have an 'adoption-o-meter' which would count how many trees had been adopted and how many remained 'orphans'. We could have GPS coordinates on each tree so people could see their tree on one of those satellite maps and count the olives on it. We would have names for each tree, or at least every bit of the grove. Things like a description of the life cycle of a tree immediately became personal because suddenly it was *your* tree we were talking about, not some dry botany textbook one. We could have pictures of the people who helped us prune the trees, those who helped us press the olives, the man who came to make sure we were being organic.

At the end of that meeting, it was obvious that we had hit on something.

But still we weren't whooping and hollering with delight. We thought, 'Well, let's see what they come back with' and 'I'm worried that it's sending us too much down that route, we know we can't make enough money to live even if all our trees are adopted' and other generally rather uncelebratory things.

Noam felt differently. And when we met up with them again a couple of weeks later, he showed us the first page of the website and it only had five words on it. Those words were:

NUDO – Adopt an olive tree

Roasted butternut squash risotto with home-made pesto

Risotto di zucca al forno

Ingredients for 4 people

For the pesto:
Pine nuts – 100g
Basil – 100g
Parmesan – 100g
Extra virgin olive oil – 150ml

For the risotto:
Butternut squash – 500g of flesh
Garlic – 20 cloves
Butter – 2 large knobs
Chicken stock – 1 litre
Shallots – 10
Flour – couple of tablespoons
White onion – 1 big one
Risotto rice – 400g
Parmesan – 100g grated
Buffalo mozzarella – 300g

Mike and Gavanndra are the king and queen of risotto making. First of all their rich, caramelized butternut squash risotto was the brain food that stimulated the idea of 'Adopt an Olive Tree'. Secondly, I lived with Mike as a student and his carefully prepared risottos lined my stomach for many nights of debauchery. They are just great cooks and always make delicious unusual things, often with freshly picked vegetables from their allotment.

There are many elements to this dish but as a short cut you can buy some good quality pesto and/or ditch the garlic. But for those who want to go the whole hog, first make the pesto – toast the pine nuts and blend with equal amounts of the cleaned basil and grated parmesan. Add the quality olive oil to moisten and cover.

Preheat the oven to 180°C /gas mark 4. Seed, skin and chop the butternut squash into medium-sized cubes. Coat them with olive oil and put in the oven for 30 minutes or until they are starting to brown. Shove them around and turn them over halfway through.

Peel the garlic, heat half the butter in a pan, brown the whole cloves then add about 100ml of chicken stock and let it bubble away until the cloves caramelize. Slice the shallots finely, coat in them in flour and deep fry until they are crispy. Put them aside on some kitchen towel.

Finely chop the white onion. Heat the remaining butter and fry the onion until it's translucent, then add the rice and coat it well with the butter. Add the remaining chicken stock, ladle by ladle, until the rice is *al dente*, letting the rice absorb the juice each time. When it's done add the grated parmesan cheese, the butternut squash and some cubed buffalo mozzarella.

Arrange on plates with a sprinkling of crispy shallots and caramelized garlic, and with pesto on the side.

Cannellini humus with parsley

Ingredients
Cannellini beans – 400g tin
Garlic – a half to a third of a clove
Olive oil – 8 tablespoons of your finest kind
Salt – $1/4$ teaspoon
Pepper – several grinds
Parsley – $1/4$ of a cup chopped

Drain and wash the beans. Place everything in a food blender and blend. If it's too dry add more olive oil. Check for salt and pepper. Place in a dish and drizzle a bit more oil over the top.

Cannellini humus
with lemon and basil

Ingredients

Cannellini beans – 400g tin
Garlic – a half to a third of a clove
Olive oil – 6 tablespoons
Salt – $1/4$ teaspoon
Pepper – several grinds
Lemon – the juice of a medium-sized one
Basil – about 10 leaves

Drain and wash the beans. Place everything in a food blender and blend. This benefits from leaving it to rest for an hour or even overnight. Sprinkle olive oil over the top before serving.

Plum, peach and almond cake

with vanilla mascarpone

Ingredients
Plums – 300g
Peaches – 300g
Unsalted butter – 100g
Soft brown sugar – 100g
Eggs, large – 2
Flour – 125g
Baking powder – 1 teaspoon
Almonds, ground – 100g
Mascarpone – 100g
Vanilla essence – a few drops
Icing sugar – for mascarpone cream
and dusting

Make sure the fruit is nice and ripe so that it all ends up nice and gooey in the finished cake. Cut it all up into haphazard big-bite-sized pieces.

Preheat the oven to 190°C /gas mark 5. Grease a deepish cake tin – round or square – and line with greaseproof paper.

Cream together the butter and sugar until pale and creamy. Beat the eggs in one at a time, adding a little flour if it looks like the mixture will curdle. Fold in the flour, baking powder and almonds without knocking out all the air. Then fold in all the fruit and tip the whole lumpy mixture into the tin.

Cook for about 40 minutes or so, putting foil over halfway through if the top is browning too quickly. Take out the cake and let it cool slightly before turning out.

For the mascarpone cream, add a few drops of vanilla essence and a sprinkling of icing sugar to the mascarpone and beat well.

Serve the cake while it is still warm, with a dusting of icing sugar and a generous dollop of mascarpone melting slightly on top.

6 Buon viaggio

We got up at six. Whenever I get up at that time I always say to myself, 'Why don't I get up at six more often, it's so lovely to see the world like this.' But if I did, the world would seem anything but lovely so it's just another thing I should shut up about.

Anyway on this day, it was particularly lovely. I mean on the surface it was horrible – wet and grey and chilly – but in spirit it it was lovely.

The day before we'd spent packing a huge white rental van to within an inch of its life. There was just room left for Jason in the driver's seat, wedged in by garden furniture and duvets. Rosie and I would be travelling in the Mini, which would be making the permanent move with us to Italy. The Mini was filled with treats to try to keep us going for the journey – well, Rosie at least. Little boxes of raisins, tiny juices with straws, funny squelchy packets of drinkable yoghurt that I've never seen before, packets of Hula Hoops and baby Cheddars, pieces of chopped-up carrots, pears and satsumas and bananas and cheese and well, we wouldn't go hungry before Dover.

There was also a supply of things to try to entertain Rosie during the long journey. That's quite a tricky thing for a one-and-a-bit-year-old as they can't really do very much – I mean there's no colouring-in or I-spy. So our entertainment came down to two tapes of songs – one, mostly nursery rhymes, sung by sweet precocious little children, and the other a collection of sort of modern songs like 'The Wheels on the Bus' and whatnot, sung by a lady who I hate and a man who J thinks sounds like Tony Blair. The man is OK, though I don't like to picture him, but the lady is a complete cow; whenever she has to sing a song together with some children, you can almost hear her elbowing them out of the way so that she and only she has domination of the mic. It probably goes without saying that Rosie loved this tape. Then there was a book called *Baby Classics* or something where there were some pictures and some electronic buttons which you pressed to hear horribly bastardized versions of things like 'The Flight of the Bumblebee' and Handel's Water Music – yeh, but it's all for the children's later appreciation of music, right (maybe it works – after this, anything would sound good). And finally there was a *Sesame Street* toy, in the shape of miniature ghetto blaster, given to us by 'American Kathy', which had maybe six different tunes and a button which if pressed went 'Boiiiiing'. Rosie had control over these last two items.

The Mini was loaded and was starting to rival the van for fullness. We had a last check around the flat to make sure we hadn't left anything, to take plugs out of sockets, those kind of old-fashioned dad things, had a check that the back door was locked. But hang on, what was that behind the back door? A baby pine nut tree, a symbol of the start of our new life. How terribly inauspicious it had been forgotten. There was no way it would fit in the van, there was not an inch of space even in the front let alone a four-foot-tree-shaped space. J managed to wedge it in the footwell of the front seat of the Mini, where it hung all over the snacks that I'd slightly pedantically put to hand on the front seat ready to pass back to crying child. It made me a bit grumpy, this plant all in the way, dropping its pine thingies all over my baby Cheddars, but I felt embarrassed to be grumpy about such a pathetic thing so I tried not to let it show.

At 7.30, as scheduled, we waved goodbye to the 'village' or Marylebone High Street – goodbye to the shop with some forgettable French name that sold only stinky candles, goodbye to Rococo, the shop that sold only chocolate, goodbye to the shop (that to my pride I have never gone in and that to my greater pride I can't remember the name of) that appeared to sell bourgeois yoga-related products, goodbye to your sickliness Cath Kidston, goodbye, with sad heart, to the lovely bread shop, and goodbye to Waitrose, alternately loved and cursed.

Goodbye all you lot. We were off to live in Italy.

Travel day one

The journey was like a proper old-fashioned adventury adventure.

The fact we were in two separate vehicles was in one way a shame but in another way more exciting. A convoy, no less. We even had walkie-talkies. Never mind that they slipped out of range as soon as the hire van edged more than fifty metres back, we had walkie-talkies and we felt like we were in a movie. It helped that Dover was our point of disembarkation from the mainland – it is somehow still such an old-fashioned feeling town, with everything faded; you even feel the petrol you've just put in might be a bit 'gone off'. The service station hasn't been tarted up and the staff still, resolutely one almost feels, understand the concept of a cup of tea a lot more than that of a cup of coffee. No overpriced Londonccino here.

In our keenness, we were early for our ferry so got to hang out with big lorries for a while, to Rosie's delight. On the journey so far, we'd only been round the nursery rhyme tape three times (marked by the appearance of 'The Grand Old Duke' – now what's his story?) so spirits – well, OK, mine – were still high. We had barely dented our treat mountain.

In this blurry half-place on the road to our new life, everything formed a moment all its own. We bought our last English newspaper.

We drank our last cup of tea. We put our English change into one of those spherical charity things where the money goes round and round and round like an astronomy demonstration before disappearing into the abyss. We wanted to act like we were going somewhere far and wild and different where we would be denied contact from home. We wanted the feeling that everyone was looking at us thinking 'Wow, adventurers.' We wanted it to be a time before mobiles – a time before the present in which anyone could spoil our game by phoning to ask, 'Where are you now?'

Parked up and loaded aboard, we sat in a quiet part of the ferry by a big, big window. As it started pulling away from the port, we suddenly didn't have to pretend any more. This really was an adventure. Even without any buckles to swash or trunks to be met by horse-drawn carriages, we were heading into an unknown future. We had given up our jobs, our income, our home, left our families, our friends, our training, our city, our country, our language, our habits – in fact, pretty much everything we knew we'd left, except for each other. The feeling of smallness in the world in the face of it all was exhilarating and made us want to whoop. I think maybe boats are good like that.

We made a friend on the boat, as one does with children; *they* make friends and then what are you going to do? We were all in the children's play area, sitting slightly awkwardly on bright inflatable cubes. Pete was a policeman and he was with his daughter, Natalie. He was one of those parents who are very tough on their own child and very doting on others, something for which I'm sure there is a sound psychological explanation. He was the personification of a good, honest, normal bloke. Off on holiday with the family for a week in France, he was playing with his daughter to give the wife a bit of a breather. He was really interested in what we were doing and particularly the fact that we only had a one-way ticket on the ferry. There's something poignant about a one-way ticket. And we heard the sort of things that we have heard a hundred times since starting to hatch our plan. He was so jealous, wished he could do something like that himself, thought we were really brave, what a life we would have. It's like a knee-jerk thing; we say we're moving to Italy and before we have even mentioned the wheres and the hows and the what-we-plan-to-dos, this stream of sort of admiring envy comes out. It's addictive to hear but puzzling to analyse.

I thought about a scene from *The Sopranos*. Christopher has discovered that Adriana has been spilling the beans about his dodgy dealings to the Feds and he faces the choice of a life in hiding or a continued life in crime, but with his long-term girlfriend ahem – erased. He has all but decided that love beats all and that he should go with Adriana and her Houston safe house scheme, when he stops at a gas station. As he's filling up with gas, he sees a family at the next-door pump – two leery kids, and a dad with that uniquely parental permanently put-upon look. They are in a station wagon. The dad is wearing beige. The kids are yelling about nothing much. The dad is just trying to do his gas thing. Nothing happens. It is just a pure vision of the terror of normality. Terror of the nothing happening.

In the next scene, Adriana is being taken to the woods to be executed and it is clear that love might believe it conquers all – but it hasn't a hope against the dread fear of being boring.

And so it was that we headed off the ferry, signed up to our version of life with the Camorra.

France was rain, rain and rain. We were OK in the Mini but Jason was a bit up against it in the hire van, which had the kind of windscreen wipers that only ever clear half the windscreen and even that not well. And with an overpacked van on skiddy roads you have to have your wits about you.

When people get weepy-eyed about the picturesqueness of France they sure as hell can't be talking about these grey, flat, bare, occasionally industrial swathes of inconsequentiality of northeast France? I was unprepared for the grisliness of it all, obviously having imagined a beautiful postcard of a journey blazed in sunshine from start to finish. It was worse than Norfolk. Oh, I mean Norfolk has lovely bits, of course. In fact, maybe I mean Cambridgeshire. Just lots of it but nothing much there. Sorry France and sorry Cambridgeshire but I was really surprised. The highlight of a four-or-so-hour chunk of motorway was a display outside what I assumed was a Smart Car factory of lots of Smart Cars all piled on top of each other like a totem pole.

Occasionally I would slow down or stop to change Rosie's nappy or something. That would give Jason the chance to catch up and for a while we would travel together, in walkie-talkie range and everything. Naturally, every time I used the walkie-talkie Rosie wanted to 'talk daddy', too. Her delight at the miracle that daddy could be talking to us, albeit crackled, from that van all the way back there almost made up for the fact that she always held down the send button so long that the batteries got flat.

The first French service station reminded me of what inspired John Major to start his motorway initiative. That speech where he overshared what seemed too intimately drawn from personal experience by telling us how awful it is how long one sometimes has to go between pees on the M4? And how in France and the rest of Europe they have it so much better because they can stop and pee or drink a cup of tea every few miles. And how when you do decide to stop and pee the experience is good because the facilities are clean and nice and the food is good and not ludicrously overpriced (as it is in England, presumably because the infrequency of services means people are desperate enough that they'll pay the sky for a bite of their BLT).

As I remember, it was shortly after this that Mr Major started manning the cones hotline and continuation in office became impossible.

Well, he had a point. The French service station was almost the sort of place you'd go for a day out. Even though today was pouring with rain and we couldn't play on the extensive outdoor child playground, they'd had enough climatic foresight to build another one inside. So we had a really nice break, where Jason and I sipped good French coffee, commenting, of course, that we hadn't seen anything yet and just wait till we reached Italy, and Rosie played happily with other children in the maze of Day-Glo balls.

We got to Reims as it got dark and even though we could have driven on and on we felt that nearly twelve hours in the car for Rosie, and twelve hours of 'Boiiiiing' and the 'Flight of the Bumblebee' in one day, was probably enough. We found a Travelodge-type place and prepared to settle in for the night.

We nearly had a hiccough when we tried to drive the van into the underground car park before even my amateur sense of height told me that that van wasn't going to fit under that roof. Max headroom. Remember him?

So J went off for what felt like hours, trying to find somewhere to leave a van where we wouldn't wake up to find it empty or gone.

Eventually he settled on somewhere right outside a church, he claimed coincidentally, but I'm sure he was thinking that we were adventurers and God would protect us if we gave him some clues about where to look.

Back in the hotel, we were starving, as was child. We thought we'd try the hotel restaurant but a glimpse inside and a word with the richly stereotypically French head waiter suggested otherwise. Anyone who can reply 'We have liver' to the question 'Is there anything on the menu for a one-year-old?' is either French, childless, sadistic or all the above.

So we set out into Reims, in the drizzle. Around us, it suddenly seemed the only others were adventurers who had somehow fallen foul of their adventures. Drunk men lying in shop doors, lots of young hippy hairy men with young hippy hairy dogs – people who seemed like they'd maybe come one day for some concert or just for an adventure and never managed to leave again, though the party had long since ended. We looked at lots of menus on lots of restaurant doors, with repeated disappointment – as the combination of finding a menu which holds appeal both for vegetarians and for carnivorous one-year-olds in France is fraught. Then like a beacon on the horizon we saw the red, white and green clue to an Italian place on the other side of the square. Of course, children were welcome! Of course, they had a baby seat! Of course, they'd be able to prepare something for 'le végétarien'!

Minutes later, we were all throwing ourselves into delicious freshly microwaved plates of lasagne and *melanzane alla parmigiana* which bore as little resemblance to Italian food as is possible to imagine unless you live in New York. It was French-American-Italian food, huge cheesy portions with a gherkin on the side. I think we might have kissed the chef on both cheeks when we left.

Travel day two

The next day involved a lot more rain. It's funny how worries change – as soon as J found the van was there, we stopped worrying about whether the van would be there and immediately put our worry eggs into a different basket. Now we'd worry (or at least complain a bit) about the rain instead. I wondered if this was what our new life was going to be like? Was there a fixed amount of dissatisfaction we modern humans were predisposed to have? Would we just exchange the worries and dissatisfactions we had had in London for a new list of worries and dissatisfactions? Was that maybe all we really wanted? A change of things to worry about? I knew that for me one of the things that made me feel most miserable was having the same complaints as everyone else. While celebrating things together with other people was invariably a joy, shared moanership was nothing but gloom. Not only were you moaning, a bad enough habit in itself, but you were boring because you were moaning the same as everyone else. You deserved to moan, you loathsome creature. Find your own moan. When, or rather if, you watch those TV shows about people who chuck it all in to move abroad and have a new life, they actually all end up moaning about the same things, too. The septic tank is usually high up there. Being cold is another one. Is that somehow more honest? Are these moans at least about some sort of fundamentals? Or are all these people – and God forbid, us too – just joining a new moan demographic? And actually, they also moan about how many other English people there are in *their* bit of France/ Spain/Italy, too, which is anything but an honest moan.

Well, at that moment, we were having a moan about the weather, a good traditional moan as English as trifle. Because that day the rain actually started to get a bit boring. I think it was because we could see that around us the classic Swiss landscape filled with blue, blue lakes and snow-tipped mountains would be really pretty if it wasn't for all this fog and rain. In northeast France we hadn't lost much but here we knew what we were missing. And that's never a good thing.

We ate something called *Reisenkalbsschnitzel* that night in Switzerland. Do they really need to have so many consonants? Rosie couldn't believe that so much sausage-type stuff could exist in the world, let alone on her plate. How far she had come from milk.

Travel day three

We went through the longest tunnel in the world (blissful rainlessness) and, suddenly, we were in Italy. Oh my God what have we done? We are coming to live in Italy. I tried saying out loud 'Ahar … home' and things like that to see how they felt but it reminded me of that feeling when you're in a school play and your ego really wants you to be a great actor but your body and mind are like 'What the hell are you doing? You look like an idiot.'

So instead I slowed down, waited till J was in walkie-talkie range and said, 'Coffee?'

We wanted to seem like locals from the off. We failed. We went to the counter and asked for *'due cappuccini'*, feeling rather clever to know that because there were two they had to end in 'i' not 'o', only to be swiftly deflated by the bartender pointing to the sign telling us to get a receipt first. That's how it works in Italy. You decide what you want and pay at the till then you get a receipt which you take to the bar and say it all over again. I'm sure there is some psychological reason for this ordering of things – along the lines that people are happier to queue to pay for something when they are still heady in its anticipation rather than satisfied by its delivery. So this pre-queuing thing has been invented to control people who are living in hope – a necessary control for a populace not predisposed to queuing. Next they might even master the idea that the queue should be an essentially linear phenomenon.

So we queued and got our little chits, which must have some use that we will hopefully learn because everyone religiously takes them and no one throws them straight in the bin like we do. And we drank our first Italian cappuccino – or 'cappuccio' as they seemed to call it here (we'd be saying that the next day, for sure) – and our first Italian cappuccino was good.

As we hit Italy proper and got towards the coast, I had strange feelings. Not pure excitement, though certainly some of that – but also a sense of slight anticlimax. The idea 'it is better to travel hope-fully than to arrive' kept going round in my brain like one of those cursed nursery rhymes. I had loved this trip – this promise, this on-the-wayness, this queue before the *cappuccio* – and now I found I was a bit afraid of the arrival. What if, what if, what if? I thought how brilliantly corny it was that the sun came out for the first time in three days within one minute of passing the sign welcoming us to 'Le Marche'.

I looked around and sort of became aware that everyone was now driving like a madman. I was in the slow lane, but even there there was someone driving so close he could probably hear the 'Boiiiing'. Why? Why do the Swiss drive nicely and the Italians nas-tily? Is it because the Italians have a religion which means the next world is a better bet so what's to lose, while the Swiss are stuck on earth to make the best of things? There must be a book on this somewhere. I wanted the answer but I didn't want to spend too long thinking about Italian driving as I wanted our interest and understanding of the country to be a lot more profound than these things tourists say. Wow, I've really got issues, eh?

Within a couple of hours of this mad driving, we found ourselves turning off the S78 and up the hill towards … towards home.

Our driveway is enough to make a visitor change his mind. There is a sharp join between the road, made of tarmac, and our drive, made of an ungodly mixture of gravel and rocks and bits of protruding metal prongs which testify to the last attempt to systematize things. The lip of the join is so lumpy that if you take it straight on, there is a good chance the underbelly of your car will get stuck, and you will be left see-sawing on your chassis, with all four wheels off the ground, as cars fly round the blind curve in both directions, probably honking their horns. Instead, as you learn from experience, you have to take it at a very, very steep angle, sideways on – steep enough to give the uninitiated the sense of being about to fall sideways down the bank into the field below.

So, ever practical, even at this time of heightened emotion, both of our first thoughts on arrival at our new life were, 'We must fix that driveway.'

We meandered down the driveway to the house. The next shock was that there was no view! The hedge, which had been a modest short sort-of-Italian-privet number a couple of feet high, had grown to an impressive couple of metres with the result that a motorway could have been built in the middle of our view and we wouldn't have even known. This was an early lesson in the unforgivingness of nature – you might think you're ahead, but nature doesn't stop for weekends or holidays – so ultimately, if you want a life which does have such decadences, you're going to lose.

So our next thought about our exciting new life full of possibility and adventure was, 'We must cut that hedge.'

We tried to cast away the spectre of these impatient 'to do' lists and concentrate on the job of crossing the threshold of our new home. It seemed almost impossible that these virginal keys we were clutching, that had been stashed away in a drawer in London and now carried halfway across Europe, would really turn in the lock of this house. But turn they did.

My first thought was that this house just seemed too big and grown up for us. Although it was our house in the legal sense, I couldn't imagine it feeling ours in the heart. There was just so much space, so much unbreathed air. The kitchen alone would have eaten up half the flat we'd just moved from. We walked around the whole place, commenting on little things we hadn't yet seen like the light switches – and the peculiar fact that they all operated the light opposite from the one you'd expect – the left one doing the right light and so on.

We felt like visitors. In fact, we half looked at the house in the way you'd look at a holiday home you'd booked on the internet and were seeing for the first time in the flesh, nervously excited, wanting it to be all you hoped but anxious that you might have misunderstood. The other half of our looking was a 'to do' list. There were boxes everywhere, sofas covered in black tarpaulins, furniture still wrapped in brown paper, suspicious mice droppings tumbling from furniture too long left. We had shipped all our worldly goods from

LA straight to the house when we left there two years ago. So there were things here, possessions that had formed part of our daily lives, which we hadn't seen for years. There was a strange familiarity of the old mixed with the uncertainty of the new.

I don't think we said very much, certainly nothing profound. I think we were both (not very) secretly terrified and overwhelmed, so our conversation revolved around do-able practicalities. We fed Rosie (pizza we'd picked up en route and car snack fruit leftovers), assembled her cot (propped up with a pile of five spare tiles we found in the cellar to substitute a broken side slat), gave her a bath (boiled water from a kettle, since the boiler wasn't plumbed in yet, poured into the big sink in the kitchen). These practicalities are like small gifts of distraction at times when things are too much to take in. The parallel that comes to mind is of funerals, though that seems a bit unnecessarily dramatic; but they do serve a great purpose of distracting our heads and so buying our hearts a bit more time to cope.

It was later, after we had eaten our first meal in our house – in our *home*, that we dared to ask each other how we were feeling.

'I just keep thinking about all those really awful boring-looking places we drove through and that we made a good decision to choose this place,' Jason said rather unconvincingly. 'But it is really quiet.'

I said, 'I just feel bewildered. I can't help asking myself why we have come here. Not in a bad way. But just, well, why? It seems so strange. We had a really great life, lots of friends, a nice home, good jobs, money, everything. It's not like we're running away from something. It's a bit bonkers really … I think we're doing it because we have a fear of being boring.'

And along these lines our chat continued as we tried to match the right slats to the right beds so that we could have a horizontal spot to lie down. Things from the journey had all arrived unscathed; I think thanks to being so firmly wedged there was simply no chance of movement. The stuff that we'd shipped over from LA was a little worse off – it'd now been sitting around for a couple of years, moved by impatient builders and squatted alternately, it seemed, by maggots and mice. At least someone'd been feeling at home.

We dug out toothbrushes and toothpaste and some sheets and blankets from various bags and boxes and managed to make a bed which looked very welcoming, despite being surrounded by boxes and other symbols of emptiness and transition. Lying in bed, neither of us could sleep. It was so quiet that we could almost hear each other's thoughts. I wanted to put a tape on with noises of the city. Nothing fancy, just a bit of hubbub, something to give my subconscious some clues that there were more people than just us alive in the world. And maybe a video with the odd flash or bit of traffic light reflection or something, because the dark was also quite spooky. With the shutters closed, you could put your hand out in front of your face, like right there, and only your powers of proprioception would tell you it was there. Can this be natural? I mean it's obviously natural in the sense that once upon a time we lived without any of this stuff, but not in my lifetime. It didn't feel natural for me, it felt strange and uncomfortable.

I lay there awake, so did J, but neither of us spoke. I thought about how many times we'd been here on holiday, not actually to this house, which wasn't yet finished – but near here, to places equally quiet and equally dark. And that gave me my first whiff of the difference between being on holiday somewhere and actually living there. The difference between what is an escape from normality and what is normality. The difference between how one copes with novelty when in experimental holiday mode and how one copes when one is seeking comfort.

I lay there and tried to think that we were on holiday. After all, most of our friends secretly or openly thought we were coming here on a huge extended, endless holiday, where the light would be permanently dusky and there'd always be a glass of delicious cheap local wine in our hand and where working would be something to do if we felt like it, and where we would be spared all the worldly worries of the train being late and interest rates going up and your boss asking you to work the weekend. Imagine if they were right – we were on holiday – we were on holiday for an unspecified amount of time. Lucky old us. I tried to look at the light a bit differently and to hear the quiet a bit differently and to fall asleep with optimistic thoughts. And it must have worked, because the next thing I heard was a small person with a loud voice saying, 'MILK.'

Pear, parmesan and rocket risotto

Risotto di pera, parmigiano e rucola

Ingredients for 4 people
Olive oil – 2 tablespoons
Butter – 25g
Risotto rice – 350g
Onion – 1
White wine – ¾ of a cup of Verdicchio
Vegetable stock – 1.5l
Salt and pepper
Parmesan – 50g
Rocket – 100g
Pears – 2 ripe ones, cut into small cubes with the skin on

Pears are a real Rosie favourite. But thanks to her gorging on all the other journey treats, we had a couple of slightly dented ones left over by the time we arrived at our house.

All our pots and pans were boxed up except one we had brought from London, but we had a spanking new kitchen to play with. These two factors could only lead to one unlikely sounding conclusion: pear risotto.

Heat the oil and butter in a saucepan over a medium heat. Add the rice and the chopped onion and coat in the mixture, then stir for a couple of minutes over a lower heat until the rice becomes translucent. Add the wine and continue cooking until most of the wine has reduced and absorbed. Add a ladleful of stock at a time, adding more as it's absorbed. Cook until the rice is tender, but still has some bite, then add a couple of pinches of salt and lots of pepper, stir in the parmesan, then the rocket and then at the last minute the pear. Serve immediately.

Oven-roasted tomatoes

Ingredients
Tomatoes – 1kg
Garlic – 6 cloves
Brown sugar – 1 tablespoon
Maldon sea salt – couple of pinches
Basil – a handful of whole leaves
Extra virgin olive oil – 6 tablespoons
Balsamic vinegar or sapa – 2 tablespoons

Home is a well stocked fridge. Not just your basic foods, but also things that it's nice to have knocking round. We nearly always have a jar of oven-roasted tomatoes. We usually make a whopping great tray of these and put the ones that don't get eaten immediately into a preserving jar with several glugs of olive oil on top. The oil has to cover the tomatoes otherwise they'll grow mouldy after a few days and anyway, once you've scoffed all the tomatoes, you can recycle the yummy tomatoey oil in your cooking.

Preheat the oven to a low heat, 150ºC / gas mark 2

Cut the tomatoes into quarters (or half if they're small), trying to cut out the stalky bit as you go. Put them in a ceramic or heavy bottom dish, so they're no more than one layer thick. Add the thinly sliced garlic and sprinkle on the sugar and salt. Throw in the basil, torn up a bit. Glug on the oil and liberally apply the balsamic vinegar or sapa. Mix it all up a bit with your hands so that everything is coated with the juices.

Put the dish in the oven for about an hour, while you have a nice glass of wine and give the tomatoes the odd stir. When the hour's up, turn off the oven and leave the tomatoes to cool down slowly inside. Or if you want to eat them straight away and hot, they're delicious like that, too.

Marinated aubergines

Ingredients
Aubergine – ¹/₂kg
Dried mint – 1 heaped teaspoon
Red chilli – 1
Garlic – 1 big clove
Olive oil – 160ml
Capers – 1 heaped tablespoon
Salt and pepper

Cut the aubergines into 5mm thick slices (lengthwise if they are long and thin, sideways if they are wide enough). Chuck them in a colander, sprinkle with salt, put them in the sink and find something heavy to rest on them, to squash them a bit. Leave for 30 minutes and make the marinade.

Get a big bowl and put in the dried mint, finely chopped chilli and garlic (spend a few extra seconds chopping the garlic up really fine), two-thirds of the olive oil, the chopped capers and a bit of salt and pepper.

Wash and drain the aubergines. Heat up a heavy-based, non-stick frying pan. Blot dry the aubergines. Brush each side with olive oil and fry them in the pan. Once both sides are looking brown and slightly burned, add them to the marinade, making sure each piece is coated. Continue with the rest of the aubergines. You can eat this straight away, but it's much, much better to wait a while so that all the flavours coalesce.

7 Putting down roots

It seemed we'd barely arrived when Jason was off again. He'd to drive back to the UK to return the hire van and would then fly back out a few days later. I was torn between wanting him to go really fast so that he'd be back quicker and not wanting him to drive so fast that he'd break his neck in the dodgy hire van – which would potentially, unburdened of its load, go like the bloomin' clappers.

We had a last breakfast of something quite un-Italian like Weetabix, and Rosie and I waved him, skidding in the mud up the drive, off into the fog. The silence of the house was crushing.

A few hours later I was waiting with Rosie on the platform of the train station in Macerata, our nearest local biggish town, for my mum and dad to arrive. We could have been in the 1900s. The station was old in architectural terms and even older-feeling in terms of upkeep – even the grime felt old. So when the 13.55 train pulled into the station, it was hard to believe that this tiny train in this strange place could really contain two people so familiar. True to Hollywood form, they were the last of the dozen or so passengers to disembark, shrouded, in my mind's eye at least, in a foggy cloud of spent steam.

We bundled into the Mini and set off for that place we'd started trying to refer to as home.

It was a relief to have third parties see the house and gasp and gawp with excitement. Mum had been here before, one time when we came out during the building phase – but for Dad it was the first time he'd seen anything other than photos.

He couldn't believe how big it was. The *proportions* were as he'd imagined from the photos but the whole thing was scaled up to almost twice the size. He started plotting a mezzanine for our towering kitchen/living room. The right noises were made about what a good job we'd done and how transformed the house was from the mouldy, unloved half-wreck that we'd bought. But there was no room for comfy complacency.

You see, Mum and Dad, like me (i.e. I'm their fault!), are people who like to get on with things rather than sit about wondering. And it didn't take much looking around to see that there was an awful lot to get on with.

Dad took on the job of the 'library'. We all decided this was a perfect Dad job and he certainly rose to the occasion – unpacking all the thirty or so boxes of books and putting them on the shelves, *in subject order*. He was disappointed not to have made subdivisions into alphabetical order, too, but even as it was the job took nearly two days.

Mum started ripping into boxes like a wild coyote and set about doing every job it'd never have occurred to me to do and that, even if it had, I would have found an excuse not to do anyway. This basically meant working on all the items of furniture that had come from Grandpa Jack. The assembled stuff which we now had in the house was all the stuff that had come from London, plus all the stuff we'd shipped from LA, plus all the stuff that we'd inherited from Jack and the twelfth-century castle he used to inhabit in Dublin. So there was slightly used LA stuff, there was brand new London stuff and there was centuries-old Jack castle stuff. And it was all this ancient stuff on which Mum set her eyes. She spent hours cleaning frames of paintings that hadn't seen a cloth since Michael Collins was in town, she got into the tucked-under chassis of a brass coal scuttle that only the brasssmith had previously touched, working away on everything with her super-duper magic cloth. Then she sliced her filthy dirt-clogged hand open with a large knife.

This seemed a good moment to call work off for the day and head to the local restaurant for dinner.

Thank heaven for food. J always says, quoting someone I think, but I can't remember whom, that the greatest gift that humans have been given is their hunger. Every few hours there comes this gnawing need to fill one's belly. Which means that every few hours, there is the potential to re-enjoy the feeling of satiating that gnawing need. It is true. And as we drank red wine that was literally cheaper than the water (1 litre of fizzy water 80 cents, one litre of red wine 75 cents) and ate (the ladies) delicious tagliatelle followed by delectable grilled lamb and oily chicory and a gorgeous zingy *tagliata* (Dad), the world was suddenly OK.

A few days and plenty of rain and fog later, we realized there was something seriously wrong with our utilities.

The first clue came when the tumble drier took eight hours to dry a sheet. I'm not expecting sympathy for this minor inconvenience, but it was our first sign. There were more.

Dad started to piece together some clues:

Clue 1. When the tumble drier was on, the boiler turned itself off and there was no hot water.

Clue 2. When the oven was turned on, all the lights dimmed to Victorian gas lamp levels.

Clue 3. The oven took approximately one hour to reach temperature.

Clue 4. When the washing machine was on, the clicky thing that starts the gas on the kitchen hob (which by now, of course, we have resorted to because of the life-ebbing time taken to heat the oven) was clickless.

Clue 5. Everything electrical kind of didn't work very well or very quickly.

All of this led us to the conclusion that … we had an electricity problem. How rustically chic of us. How end of part two 'Join us after the ad break to see if sparks will ever start to fly for Jason and Cathy' … 'crackle' … in the TV documentary that thankfully we aren't making.

We did some research and spoke to some folk. It seems a normal electricity supply would be about 3kW. In fact, the legal minimum is 3kW. Our electrician came out. He seemed suspiciously young. Like fourteen. Is that legal here? Anyway, he looked at boxes and stated rather enigmatically that our supply 'should' be just under 3kW. I think it was 'should' but I'd been letting the grammar lessons slip lately.

He advised calling out someone from Enel, the electricity people. We did. Someone came. He wasn't so young, which was good. He looked at the same boxes and his eyebrows went squiffy but it was before lunch so not the grappa. He said 'Beh', which means 'Well …' He said 'Beh' again. Which still meant 'Well …' but slightly more emphatically. I gave him a look and a bit of noise which started life as 'dunque' (which means 'so …') but then got embarrassed – too big a word for too small a thing, so it ended up more as a 'duh' coupled with a puzzled expression. The international language of communication told him that I wanted answers. But instead of answers, he started reciting a poem! The village was old. The line was long. The hill was steep. The hill went down. The hill came up. We were at the end of it. The electricity leached out along the way. Oh hang on, not a poem. This was our life. There was nothing he could do. They themselves wanted to upgrade the line because every winter it breaks (oh great) but they can't because lots of the people whose land the lines go through won't let them in. Really? At the very least a novel excuse. Was there nothing else we could do? 'Get a generator,' he said.

This, it seemed, was to be our electricity fate.

Meanwhile, Jason was back. He'd only been gone four days but it felt like weeks, and it was time for Mum and Dad to head back to England. Bet they were glad to be heading back to fully functional heating, phones with phone numbers you understood and the ability to bake a potato at the drop of a hat. Next time they came out, I was determined that we'd have sorted out all these glitches.

A few days later, we turned on the tap of the kitchen sink and nothing came out. 'Hmm', I discovered, is a noise that uncontrollably comes out of you when you turn a tap and nothing comes out. It's as if it's making up for the water deficit with the arrival of at least something – a little sound. I tried another tap. A dribble then nothing. Upstairs the same. Everywhere the same. No water. It was a Saturday evening and we had spent the day burning the wood from the ten-foot hedge we had lopped down to two feet. Surviving the fire was a feat since it took place in a patch between the overhanging trees and the gas tank, set about with its *VIETATO FUMARE* (no smoking) signs. But surviving it meant we were doubly nasally repellent – our sweat from the work and the soot from the fire. Nice. We had just put our new duvet cover on our bed and actually couldn't bear to pollute it with our filthy if sleep-deserving bodies, so made back-up plans to hole up in the spare room.

But before that, we called the *idraulico* (a tough job given that the word's almost impossible to pronounce for anyone of Anglo-Saxon origin) and told him that the water had stopped and could he come. Rather surprisingly, 7 p.m. by this time, he said he could. Jason answered the door and showed him to the nearest tap.

He turned it on and said, surprised, 'Ma non c'e aqua' ('But there is no water'). Jason, equally surprised at his surprise, retorted, 'But my wife told you there was no water.' To which he said words similar to 'Well, what do you expect me to do about it, I'm just the plumber' and suggested we call the water company. He was kind enough to stand over me as I battled with their suggestion that maybe tomorrow night they could come, doing my best (i.e. hopeless) impression of a desolate Italian mama with a filthy baby in need of a bath and a terrifying Corleonesque husband in need of his two-hourly shave ... and couldn't it be perhaps please by any chance sooner? They said call again in the morning if there was still no water.

I decided to quiz the unpronounceable one once more. He was a slightly creepy man, an unfair statement because he'd done nothing to deserve it, but he had a shifty half-smiley look and a squashed face. But I vaguely remembered him talking about a water problem before, back in the days when we could afford not to be that interested. I asked him directly to his squashed face whether this had happened before during the building works, and he admitted that yes it had, twice. The answer had lain with a big house up the hill which 'had turned off our water'.

How could this be possible?

'Non dovrebb'essere'' ('It shouldn't be'), he said. But that was his suspicion. We were a bit further down the hill than them, we had gravity on our side, we got good water pressure, they didn't, they got fed up, they turned us off.

He left; we made a cup of tea with the last of the kettle water and climbed stinkily into our borrowed bed.

Next morning, phone calls, more pleading, eventual agreement to come and even more long-winded mobile exchanges for the fellow to find the place. They use mobiles like walkie-talkies. The man looked as if he had just woken up, as he probably had. It was Sunday morning and we wouldn't have been up if we hadn't smelled too bad to stay in bed. He had that knack that so many here have perfected, of having a cigarette permanently hanging from his lip, always there and always about half burnt through even though you never saw a cigarette packet, a lighting moment, a throwing away of the butt, any of that. He looked at our controls and confirmed that we had no water. Then he drove off in his car for long enough that I started to be sure that he wasn't coming back. After all, the plumber had referred to the big house up the hill. This was just the sort of conspiracy you hear about, admittedly mostly from France, where newcomers are edged out by subtle psychological acts of war just like this one. The image of this big mansion house on the hill, all-powerful, all-seeing, resenting these young pretenders having the cheek to come in and take their precious water, water that their family had worked for over generations, water from a well they'd probably dug themselves by hand, was more than enough to conjure up a conspiracy theory involving Mafia, horses' heads in beds, kidnapping of first-borns and so on and so on. But, of course, we were far too scaredy-cat to go up to the big mansion house and confront them, politely, to ask about their relationship with our waterless state – God only knows what could result. I asked J was it stupid of me to think that maybe the water company guy had been up to the top and found a hate note about the stupid English who use too much water and so was scared off and left?

J (kindly) said yes.

The water company guy reappeared. *'Provatelo adesso'* ('Try the water now'), he said. Jubilation! Schhhhhh! The explanation? He was keen to get away. Muttered about the 'house up there'. I wanted more. He wasn't giving it. J mentioned Jean de Florette. I was trying to hang on to the rustic chic side of that story, too.

I can't even bring myself to start on the story of our non-existent phone line. Suffice to say for now that we might well have been the first web-based company that has no means of accessing its own website.

A month later, we were starting to feel a little more settled. I'd even go so far as to say we'd had moments of feeling that one day we might even feel we belonged. One day, we might even even be able to refer to this as home, without it sounding translated.

We had a nursery for Rosie, we were registered with a local doctor, we'd had some orders for olive tree adoptions, we'd met our first neighbours and, possibly best of all, Jason had found out the name of the person at Telecom whom we needed to harass on a daily basis to get our phone line put in.

The origin of most of this success was discovering the local *'comune'*. This institution is something without a direct equivalent in the UK – it's sort of a local council but with more power and, I suppose our being in a small village, much more of a local touch. We went in thinking that we'd have to introduce ourselves, but came out realizing that they already knew things about us that we weren't even sure of ourselves. They knew where we lived, how old Rosie was, what car we drove, the date our residency application had been approved, how much rubbish we threw out, how many olive trees we had – everything that mattered in this new world of ours. This could have been spooky of course, but for now it was reassuring. It was a simple sign that, even without pay cheques and work colleagues and friends to drop in on, we existed.

As well as registering us for various acronyms – nearly all of which turned out to be different taxes to pay, disguised in catchy jingles of letters, ICI, IMPS – the lady in the *comune* could advise us on anything we threw at her. She told us where to go to get a medical card – the key landmark in getting there being 'the traffic lights', which she emphasized in a way we only understood the significance of when we realized there is only one set of traffic lights within a twenty-mile radius of Loro Piceno. When Jason asked if there was a local football team, she told us with puffy pride that yes there was and that her son played for it – doing training almost every night. She said Jason should just go along one evening to the local sports ground.

As for nurseries, there were no council-run ones – 'Scuola materna' starts when children reach the age of three and Rosie was only a year and a half. But there were several private ones in the area. They were called 'asili nido', which translates literally as 'asylum nests' – a close to perfect description of the chaotic caring of borderline lunatics that is a room full of under-threes. We looked up 'asili nido' in the yellow pages, and found that there were three within a ten-minute drive from our house. I plucked up the courage to phone the first one, having practised some key phrases like 'asilo nido? I have a baby, eighteen months … any places available?'

It didn't go according to plan. The lady replied with a torrent of I'm-not-sure-what, it sounded like questions but I couldn't really understand, not least because there was a loud screaming noise in the background which was making me nervous.

Going along to places in person seemed more likely to produce results without trauma. The lady in the *comune* had said that the one in Mogliano, the next village along the crest from Loro Piceno, was particularly good, so Rosie and I went there first. It was in a sort of side building of the elementary school, in the grounds of the local playground which was green and nice. I rang the bell and waited and rang the bell and waited some more. I peeked through the window but there was no sign of life. I said, '*C'e qualcuno?*' ('Is there anyone there?') quite loudly round the side of the building but all was silent. As I turned to leave, a little shrivelled lady appeared wagging her finger and said, '*Chiuso*' ('closed') '*pomeriggio chiuso.*' I eventually realized she meant it was closed in the afternoon, which wasn't a great sign as we had planned on leaving Rosie in some whole days.

So it was off to the next one on my list, our nearest, with the slightly unusual name of '*Titti*'. I couldn't help wondering if it was a reference to tearing the child from the mother's breast, until I realized from the sign that '*Titti*' is the Italian for that little bird cartoon creature we call 'Tweety Pie'. Well, in Italian it's titty pie. I rang the intercom and said something along the lines of 'Mother, baby eighteen months, future? *Asilo nido*?' It was a strange feeling to go from a job in which communication was your livelihood to being thrust into a child-like pre-linguistic state where the promise of even a stilted conversation seemed a distant dream.

Someone came to the door and I guess the combination of my

hopeful expression and a baby in my arms said more than my inter-com ramblings ever could. I said, 'Any places?' and the smiley lady said something I didn't quite understand about numbers but which definitely didn't sound like 'yes'. But she let me in, showed me to some blue paper shoe covers to put on, and led me in, looking like a nurse going into the operating theatre, to a little room. There were about eight children playing around on climbing toys and pre-tend stovetops and whatnot. Rosie immediately dashed off to join them and the lady – Debora – sat me down to explain a bit about the asylum.

Although many of her words went over my head, the chance to sit and observe was worth more than as much. The children seemed happy and stimulated. Debora excused herself for a moment to admonish a child who had taken a toy from another, making the child apologize and return it in a way that was kind but emphatic. It inspired confidence. Rosie was immediately at home among these children and brightly coloured squishy bricks and baby slides and I had little surges of excitement about the prospect of putting some pieces of our new life together.

Debora handed me a load of forms to take home and look at, and managed finally to make me understand that yes they did have space but that they only liked to introduce one new child a week as it could be quite a to-do. So Rosie wouldn't be able to start for another six weeks or so. As I managed to coax Rosie away, Debora led me to the door where she showed me the piece of paper on the notice board which had the costs of the nursery. It was 215 euros per month full time (full full time being from 7.30 in the morning until 6.30 in the evening if you really want rid of your little treasure) and 150 euros part time (just mornings or just afternoons). Then lunch cost an extra 2.5 euros a day, which you paid by lunch vouchers that you got from the post office. The monthly cost, including food and even if she went full time, which she probably wouldn't, would be less than it used to cost us for two days' nursery care in London.

After giving Jason the low-down, we decided to look no further and settle on this Titti place. I got the forms out and sat down with a dictionary to start deciphering them. The level of detail in the questions about Rosie and her abilities and preferences was startling. It involved everything from allergies and comfort toys to her level of sphincter control (*'controllo sfintere'*). We filled it in to the best of our linguistic ability and level of Anglo-Saxon embarrassment. There was a menu. At the top it said that the nursery's menu repeated every month – or in other words, for thirty days they eat different things every day. A typical lunch goes along the lines of:

Primo: pasta in brodo di verdure (pasta in vegetable broth)
Secondo: pesce arrosto (roasted fish)
Contorno: zucchine (courgettes)
Frutta: pera (pear)

Jason asked whether we could get extra vouchers and all eat there.

Registering for a doctor turned out to be even easier. We located the famous traffic lights, from where it was a quick left turn to the health centre. There was a simple form to fill in – and bingo! We were given medical cards, a choice of doctors (we chose the one with the surname we liked the best – Silauri – having no other basis for deciding), and before we had blinked they had also checked that Rosie had had the right vaccines for her age. There was one missing – for 'antihaemophilo influenza B' – but if we came back any Tuesday morning between 7.30 and 9.30 they would happily stick a needle in her arm. I even managed to scribble down the numbers of the emergency services that were on a pinboard and wrote them on our blackboard in the kitchen at home as a sort of security.

The next day Jason went off with the laptop to an unsecured wireless connection we'd found in Tolentino. We had managed to launch our business on the internet, we could take payments, we had mapped out the grove with every tree represented on line – but with no phone for the foreseeable future and even a temporary internet connection not sorted yet, we couldn't even look at the website. It was comedic that the owners of this exciting new website-based business called Nudo had to drive ten miles, park in the car park of 'Punto Sma', get out the laptop and hope that 'Miriam 2002' hadn't decided to secure her wireless network, even to be able to see if they had an order. But this time the trip was worthwhile, as five people had adopted trees. By the end of our first month here, that meant we had a grand total of twelve olive trees adopted. Yes they were mostly by friends of friends but it was a start and, thanks to our positive mental state, we allowed ourselves to feel a modicum of chuffedness.

As part of getting to know our locale, we decided it was time to get out a bit more on foot rather than always jumping in the car. You see so many more things at the slower pace and it was probably part of our training to slow down. The first thing we discovered was that although we didn't have a local pub, we did have a local *oleificio*, the place that presses olives to make oil. A jolly man turning the leg of a chair greeted us as the proprietor.

We'd like to ask him about the press, we said.

'*Ma prima prendiamo un caffè*' ('Not before a cup of coffee'), he said.

He had a leg withered with what we later decided was either polio or a war wound or maybe both, and it took him a good five minutes to get to the house, which was twenty metres away. Luckily there were lots of animals en route to distract Rosie so it didn't seem like we were dragging it out. He shouted to a lady to make the coffee and she duly obeyed, appearing a while later with coffees for both of us, a goodly dose of Varnelli (the local aniseed tipple) in each and a Kinder Egg for R.

We talked a bit about the press – which opens up November to January every year for the olive season – and of which they were obviously both very proud. We definitely felt a bit of *contadini* bonding in that when we said where we lived, they already knew about us and had seen the work we'd started doing on the grove. It was a crime, they said, that a beautiful olive grove should have gone to the dogs.

Their house was full, full, full of a lifetime and more's worth of stuff. J asked about a photograph of a rather beautiful woman on the wall, thinking they would proudly announce their daughter, but no, it was the woman herself, years ago. They didn't have children because they were not married (gasp!). They were not married because they were brother and sister.

There was such sadness about their relationship – like a couple grown too familiar but somehow worse because they both seemed to feel deprived, in this land of families, of families of their own. Maybe that was why the house was so full – of dwarfs, animals, trolls, coral, china dolls, all sorts of tiny pretend people – to make up.

At one point the lady asked if we would like a cat. We were well down the default road of polite acceptance of anything proffered before we stopped … 'A what?' 'A cat. We have lots of cats; perhaps the baby would like one?'

We thanked them both and said we'd see them soon, when it was time to press our olives.

Buoyed up with our sense of local integratedness, I decided to pluck up the courage to do something I'd been meaning to do for ages and phone our neighbours. We didn't have many people we could really call neighbours as there were no other houses in sight of ours, but these came the closest. There's a restaurant come function/banqueting place called 'Il Maniero' whose entrance is just opposite ours on the dangerous curve of the road at the top, and they're the ones I suppose we'd have run to had we cut an arm off before we knew an emergency number. More ominously, they could also have been the ones the plumber had referred to when he talked of the people in the 'big house up the hill' – the ones who'd supposedly sabotaged our water supply. So we could have been about to introduce ourselves to the local Corleone family and never be seen again.

Undeterred, I phoned them up and said that we were the English people who lived opposite and there was what seemed a very warm response at the other end of the line – they said that they had been meaning to phone us for ages, too. Since the day was a bank holiday (we'd wondered why it was even quieter than usual) why didn't we come up at about twelve? Of course we said yes.

We weren't quite sure what the invitation was for, as I hadn't really understood quite what was said. And we didn't have anything to take with us, being too embarrassed to take a bottle of cheap wine to a place probably swimming in vintage deliciousnesses, and with the short notice, I hadn't had time to make a cake or get flowers or anything. We didn't even have any unopened packets of tea to play the fallback English tea card.

The place was an amazing warren. It was like a modern castle, with thick walls, and a hundred different entrances. Actually, that's probably the last thing a right-thinking castle would have. We picked one at random and walked into a darkened room filled with antique pieces of furniture and paintings all over the walls – all over, from the ceiling to the floor. All kinds of paintings, paintings of still lifes of flowers, paintings of monochrome geometric shapes with blurred edges, paintings of numbers embossed in gold with strange hieroglyphics up the sides. We went uncertainly along to the far end of this long entrance room, giggling as we said '*Buon giorno?*' in too quiet voices. Then two very smiling faces came to greet us, with the names 'Guida' and 'Daniele'.

They hustled us in and put a glass of Prosecco in our hands and we did our best to answer their questions. By now, we'd repeated the speech about what we did here (growing olive trees, making olive oil, having a scheme in which British people – or people from anywhere else for that matter – could adopt an olive tree for a year and in exchange would receive the produce from it) enough times that it came out in reasonable sounding Italian. Not only that, but we'd noticed that when we described our scheme to Italians they were always fascinated by it – a mixture of a national admiration for original ideas and an even more potent admiration for anything seen as '*furbo*' – or crafty. And to them, the idea of selling olive oil for more than you normally would because people ostensibly 'owned' the tree it came from was the pinnacle of cunning.

We asked them about the Maniero and what sort of place it was. Mostly, they explained, they opened for large functions – weddings, baptisms, charity events – but the restaurant could also be booked for just a normal dinner. Guida was the chef and Daniele was the debonair master of everything else, including creator of many of the paintings. As we chatted, bits of food kept appearing – delicious little pieces of pizza, panzanella and bruschetta with tiny pieces of salami or tomatoes and pieces of pecorino cheese with honey drizzled on top. The food was brought in by two younger men, who we wrongly assumed were Guida and Daniele's sons. They were in turn introduced to us as Marco and Luca – Luca spoke pretty good English, which was a relief as an emergency get out – and both of them were very charming and talkative.

Before long other people started showing up – Daniele's mother, a friend from Civitanova Marche with his wife, and a couple of others. I could see that behind us was a table set for a number of people which seemed to resemble the one that we now constituted. Sure enough, a moment later, Daniele said, '*Mangiamo?*' ('Shall we eat?') I stutteringly, stumblingly tried to say, 'Oh no it's too much trouble, we'll leave you in peace, we'll come back another time …' being all English and embarrassed. Daniele smiled and said, 'I didn't think you understood on the phone. We invited you for lunch.'

There was no refusing this invitation. Even though we'd timed the energy of our Italian speaking and the quantity of our pizza eating to an hour maximum, we had quickly to rethink. As bowls of steaming lentils with pancetta appeared, Jason had then to confess his vegetarian status. If Guida felt any twinge of 'bugger' it didn't show on her face – instead she disappeared into the kitchen for five minutes and reappeared with a different terrine, still lentils, but 'without the flesh'.

It was delicious. Even Rosie thought so, and we made another schoolboy error by saying yes to seconds. I say schoolboy error because by now we should have known that if you were invited to lunch, and on a bank holiday, and by the chef of a restaurant, you were looking at a good five courses of food. It's a marathon, not a sprint, and pacing is key. We'd blown it before we'd even reached the pasta course. But the pasta course, too, was divine – just simple fusilli with zucchini and saffron but somehow out of this world. We ate and ate.

The next course involved a large plateful of tongue. I've never done well with tongue. I can't get round the feeling that I'm eating my own mouth. Luckily by this stage Rosie had itchy pants and so I had the excuse of running around after her to explain the food still left on my plate.

By about 4.30, we really felt it would be good manners to leave. We managed to coerce our fat bellies out of our chairs to say our very gratitude-filled goodbyes. As we walked home, we talked happily about the fact that we had managed, for the first time, to sit and have a long lunch speaking almost entirely Italian (except the odd desperate resort to English with Luca). Better still, we had discovered that our very-next-door neighbours were lovely interesting friendly people who we felt at home with. Even better still, we wouldn't have to cook again for at least a week.

Lentils from Castelluccio

Lenticchie di Castelluccio

Ingredients for 4 people
Carrots – 2
Celery – 1 big stick
Onions – 2
Olive oil – for frying
Sage leaves – several
Small green lentils – 400g, ideally
Castelluccio lentils but any small green
variety will do
White wine – a glass
Salt and pepper
Passata - 5 tablespoons (optional)
Mentuccia or marjoram

What are the chances of moving to the middle of nowhere in rural Italy and living next to a top Italian chef? Boy was I happy when we met Guida Stacchietti, our new next-door neighbour. She's elegance personified and was good enough to give us recipes for some of our favourite dishes.

Finely chop the carrots, celery and onions and cook in olive oil until they are softened. Add the chopped sage and lentils – there is no need to soak them if you get good ones. Add the white wine and cook on a medium heat until the wine has evaporated off. Then add enough cold water to cover the lentils times one and a half, some salt and pepper and a bit of tomato passata if you fancy it. If you can't find really good lentils boost the flavour by using stock instead of water.

Cook very slowly for about 60 minutes, until the lentils are cooked but still have a bit of bite. The cooking time will vary depending upon the type of lentil.

Before eating, drizzle some good olive oil on top and some mentuccia or marjoram to season.

To make this a more substantial dish, you can use the lentils as a bed for two or three large ravioli (filled with ricotta and spinach), with a sage butter sauce. Or simply eat it with some pieces of lightly toasted bread as a delicious lunch.

Panzanella

Ingredients

Dry or lightly toasted bread in slices
White wine vinegar
Salt
Tomatoes, cut into tiny cubes
Marjoram or mentuccia
Olive oil

This is one of the poorest of the *cucina povera* (the cooking of the poor), making stale bread rather tasty. In the really poor versions, even the olive oil is omitted. You can hardly call this a recipe it's so simple.

Sprinkle a bit of water on the bread and toast lightly. Then pour on a tiny bit of vinegar, and add the tomatoes, herbs and salt and finally the olive oil. If you can find really tasty tomatoes, this is a perfect light appetizer that takes half a minute to prepare.

Fusilli with courgette and saffron

Fusilli con zucchini e zafferano

Ingredients for 4 people
Red onion – 1 large
Courgettes – 300g
Olive oil – 3 tablespoons
Large sultanas – 40g
Fresh fusilli – 400g
Pine nuts – 40g
Saffron – a good pinch
Single cream - 2 tablespoons
Pecorino – 60g
Thyme to garnish

Finely chop the onion and slice the courgettes. Fry the onion in the olive oil till soft then add the courgettes. Once they've softened and are almost ready, add the sultanas.

Cook the fusilli in some salted water. Lightly toast the pine nuts. Soak the saffron strands in a little cream.

Just before the fusilli are cooked, add the saffron and liquid to the courgette pan.

Then mix the cooked fusilli with the sauce, serve and sprinkle on the pine nuts, the grated pecorino and some finely chopped thyme.

8 It'll be so good when ...

With this new life, it seemed that with the ups inevitably came the downs. A comfortable easy life doesn't have many ups and downs – it has a lot of being 'fine'. A brand new, shockingly new life, full of excitements and terrors, has the Himalayas. As typically quite well-adjusted and level-mooded people, we'd begun to realize that we were not immune to this lunge and lurch of emotions.

The house still had lots of little annoying unfinished bits, a wire hanging out here, a hole waiting for shelves there. There was still no sign of a telephone line, and it became rather pathetic trying to run a company with neither internet nor phone; we couldn't start pestering magazines about press coverage, we couldn't start research into local suppliers, we couldn't phone Carlo, a regular seasonal worker with us, to quiz him about where we'd find a trac-tor – we were tied to having physically to go everywhere in person to ask even a simple question. In one way it was very Italian, but it meant wasting hours and hours. And we still felt frustrated with our-selves on a daily basis about the state of our Italian – surely we were meant to start being fluent by osmosis by now?

So we had passed through the phase of feeling all is right with the world to a phase of not feeling all is right at all. Instead of wak-ing with feelings of deep wholesome contentment as we'd hoped, we woke with feelings of disquiet and confusion and anxiety.

I did not quite know what we had imagined this life would be like, maybe we had not thought about it too much – but I'm sure if we had, we'd have thought that at least occasionally we might sit back and feel slightly smug about how clever we'd been to throw our whole life into chaos, then land back down in a splendid place.

We hadn't been having a lot of that feeling the last couple of weeks.

It was for this slight disappointment at the temporary lack of splendidness that we coined a catchphrase: 'It'll be so good when …' This catchphrase served to address the paradox that YES we felt we had made a good decision and were right to be here but NO it didn't feel quite nice yet. BUT IT WOULD! And it would, just as soon as some of these little things had been done.

Our list read: 'It'll be so good when …'

…It stops raining

…The house is clean and we don't have to wipe our feet before getting into bed

…The electricity has been fixed so that we can have combinations like oven and lights or oven and heating or heating and washing machine *at the same time*

…We have a really successful company

…We have an internet connection

…We have found a friend for Rosie so she doesn't get fobbed off by us all day

…We have put all the pictures up so we aren't faced with huge white lonely walls

…The fog clears so we can see our view

…We can walk about feeling like glamorous, well-dressed Italians

…We own two dressing gowns between us

…All our clothes are in one place and contained within some kind of clothes container like a wardrobe

…It isn't the mosquito season any more (and hang on, it's already October)

…The gravel has come so it isn't muddy everywhere

…We know there will be a tractor for the harvest
…We have lots of lovely Italian friends and are constantly being invited to interesting places
…We can speak Italian properly
…All the packing boxes are gone
…Our company is making enough money to support us and get us treats
…We have a bank card
…We have made some friends to invite round to sit at our huge empty table
…We have bought some insect repellent to kill all the flies
…We aren't cold all the time

Every other day or so we also wrote a new 'to do' list. It had everything on it from 'buy stools high enough to sit at the kitchen counter' to 'work out how to be happy'. That was a stupid thing to put on a 'to do' list because even if you achieved it, wouldn't you feel too superstitious to put a tick next to it? But I suppose it was to remind ourselves that we were still on the way to something, rather than at it yet.

The truth was that once you'd thrown away what seemed like pretty much everything you knew, there was more scope than ever before to change still more things. Suddenly everything was up for grabs. You were in control of making your life the one that you wanted to live. How terrifying was that? No one to blame but yourself. No boss working you too hard, or children getting you down, or house too small or job too meaningless – it was all up to you to make your life the way you wanted it. And if you didn't, it was your own fault.

No wonder that, even though everyone said they'd love to do something like this, relatively few people ever actually did it. And most who did tried to keep some sort of link with home – a granny flat so their parents could come every other weekend, a part-time job still working for their old company in the UK, selling holiday homes to Brits – things to lessen the blow. Personally, I thought you had to go into something like this with your eyes closed. If you thought about it too much you'd almost certainly not do it, because there were just too many reasons not to. Rather, the only thing to do was jump in and then take a peek at where you'd landed. I wondered if many people did that and landed with an immediate smile? Weren't there just too many new bewildering things to make simple happiness a realistic possibility?

So we wrote our 'to do' lists and our 'It'll be better when' lists and tried to keep some sort of momentum going towards having the life that we thought we wanted to have. Secretly, we both realized that the really hard part was *knowing* what sort of life you wanted to have, but that was too big for a list.

One morning, to cheer ourselves up, we decided to take a walk up to San Lorenzo again, our local hamlet where the *oleificio* was. We liked the idea of getting a coffee on foot, as we had done when we had lived in cities. The walk turned out to be in fog so dense that we had to leap into the bushes if we heard a car for fear of being blindly run down. When we arrived – after a mile of car-dodging – the one tiny café looked closed and we were about to turn for home when a thin man appeared behind the darkened doorway, turned the key and opened it up. It was '*quasi chiuso*' ('sort of closed'), he told us, but if we just wanted a coffee then that was fine.

The inside of the bar was dark and sparsely furnished and didn't have quite that warming effect and coffee stench of a wintry London Coffee Republic-type place. But it was nice to be warmer and out of the fog and we put in our order for two cappuccinos. With this information, a bead of sweat appeared on the forehead of our new barman friend. We put it down, as we put everything down, to the stress to others of understanding our Italian.

We both kept a sharp eye on his technique. As our first coffee of the day, this was one of life's highlights and something not to be messed with. He performed the espresso-making part effortlessly enough – the click to dispense the right amount, the all-important tamping down and the confident twist to put the silvery caskets into the machine. But then things started becoming weird. Firstly, horrif- ically, he brought out a carton of long-life milk from the cupboard. Long-life milk! Then he fiddled with the steam valve awkwardly, causing milk to splutter and spray over the counter. Obviously unsure whether he should be moving the milk up and down or holding it still, he struck an inelegant balance between the two, uncomfortably jiggling it every now and again, like a childless uncle trying to burp a newborn. After a few minutes, the awaiting coffees were getting cold while the milk was still as thin as when it started – though with a few spittoons of froth here and there and possibly a degree or two warmer.

The final 'cappuccino' was barely drinkable, UHT-milky, luke- warm and the spittle of what looked like marine scum floating on top, a poor excuse for foam. Our man watched us cringing with discomfort, as we forced the revolting liquid down. Keen to leave, J took out his wallet to pay. But no way. Our man said he absolutely couldn't possibly charge us for that horror. He was terribly sorry.

'When the others do it,' he said dolefully, 'it looks so easy.'

Sometimes the only way to cope with the overwhelmingness of how much there was to do was start at the top of the list and plough down. For some time, our number one thing had been this cursed internet connection. The schedule for the phone going in meant that we couldn't wait that long, so we had been exploring other options that people had told us about, including a marvellous sounding thing where you plugged your mobile into the side of the computer and magically dialled up. It certainly sounded like it warranted further investigation.

'TIM' is the name of one of the biggest phone companies in Italy. They had this great theme tune in their ads. It had this cheeky whistled tune, then had fully grown men singing 'dum di da, da da di da di da di dum-di da'. Enchanting.

'Centro TIM' in Corridonia put forward a different face. Well, for a start it was not in Corridonia, which sounds rather poetic. It was on an industrial estate opposite a closed-down bed shop. The smell of it greeted you about two metres from the door – a smell of very strong aftershave. Someone must have taken the Lynx ad 'the more you use the better it gets' (or some such perfidy of truth) to heart and I thought I knew who. Inside, you were greeted – if a head angled an extra 2 percent to the vertical from completely parallel to the desk constitutes a greeting – by a straggly boywire-loving teenager sporting an overadorned shell suit with words like 'energie' and 'I love it the power' scrawled all over it in pseudo-urban pseudo-English *gold* graffiti.

Now by way of background and fair dealing, I should point out that tackling a. mobile phone issues and b. computer issues were two of my least favourite things in my homeland and mother tongue. And they were two things I had largely been spared thanks to the benefits (and it was a growing list) of working for a biggish company, big enough to have had someone who dealt with temperamental computers. We would have been in trouble even at home. Here there were at least, and thank God, two of us. In theory, I was there to do the language part and J was there for the boy-wire/wave part, so on paper at least we were giving it our best shot as Mr and Mrs Jack Sprat.

In practice, of course, a half understanding of a language and a half understanding of a technical issue were the worst of all worlds — because there were so many possibilities for wrongitude. The wrongness could have been to do with the part of the language we didn't understand, or the part of the technical problem. Or any combination of the two. There were so many possible problem recipes that existed in that dual half world. Or, it could have actually been that there was a problem that existed *quite outside the extra problems we had created for ourselves*. This, in a way, was what we lived for — because to have those problems was to live the normal life of an Italian citizen. They had to queue, to manoeuvre through annoying mechanical-voiced operators, to have computer packages that were temperamental — so to have those problems was in a very real (i.e. very much the stuff of everyday life in all its tedious detail) sense to live like a native.

On this our first trip to Centro TIM, we encountered no such problems. Our problems were entirely down to the more tedious and predictable ones of language and technology. Misunderstandings to do with the vagaries of mobile phone tariff deals and the amount of giga or mega or kilo bytes one typically needed in a day in the olive oil office. Not facts we had to hand.

The manager was brought out to assist the lanky boywire (maybe he needed plugging in to recharge) and any mystery about the excess of Lynx fell away. The fug that had pre-empted him brokered no doubt. He was Mr Lynx. He was living it. He was surly, he was swarthy, he was sanguine; everything you might want from a Lynx man manning a mobile telephone shop. He wrote things on pieces of paper and said 'giga' with a charming accent and sold us a double whammy of packages – one for the daytime (very few geegah) and one for the evening (many, many geegah). Sold and slightly overcome by fumes we left, very excited at the prospect of being able to check e-mail using a mobile phone dial-up, in the comfort (bar leaking roof) of our own home.

It worked for a bit. This strange set-up where we put a mobile phone card into a little plastic holder and slotted it into the side of our innocent and unsuspecting laptop to get e-mail. It worked. A wonder really. We read e-mails and even did a bit of non-essential web-browsing. Then we got excited and started doing some proper work like e-mailing press releases and sorting out a merchant account and updating bits of the website. Then a day or so later, it stopped working and we were back to Centro TIM and the fug.

This time (Hallelujah) a problem not of our own making. Though none the less tedious for it. Apparently it was possible to go into 'minus credit' on your SIM card, even though it could only be paid for by real money and never on credit. It was like pay as you go but when you hadn't paid it still went, at least for a spell. It shouldn't have happened because we had paid a set tariff in advance, but sometimes 'it just did', with the result that even a few cents in the red could shut down our whole budding internet business empire.

So we got a new card and played the same game again. A couple of weeks later, it stopped working again and we went back to see Mr Lynx. The same thing had happened. A minus credit of some 85 cents had screwed our state-of-the-art 'home office'. We asked if maybe there was a way we could put some extra money on the card to stop it happening, but no, that wasn't how it worked. We also asked if we could set up an account where we automatically paid our tariff every month or whatever – so that we didn't have to wait for it to run out (because we'd always forgotten our run-out day) and then drive half an hour to do it in person, but no, that wasn't how it worked either. We wondered how Italians coped with a life where everything had to be done so long-windedly.

But at least we had internet access, creaking and rusty though it was. We reminded ourselves of the old days and how we had had to drive to a car park to borrow someone's wireless signal. And we really felt that, though it felt tortuous and slow, we were making progress.

When all the tedious dealings with life's practicalities got too much we had a way out … We sweated.

There was only so much sitting in an office waiting for orders to come in we could do. Especially when they came in at the rate of about two a week, or roughly one every eighty-four hours. We had come here, partly, because we had wanted to do some physical work, work that wouldn't mean sitting in front of a bloody computer screen all day.

The day before, we had taken a stroll to one of the most remote parts of the grove. Even though the harvest would be our next major concern, we had also needed to start work on trees that would hopefully be harvestable the following year or even the year after that. To get to this remote part, we had to cross a hundred metres or so of the next-door farmer's field, below which was the dreaded gulch. Ridiculous as it sounds, it was the first time we'd actually been over to work on this part of our land.

It was in a right state. Many of the trees had been snow damaged and had broken trunks and branches, and they were all covered in brambles and bindweed so thick that it was only when you were right up close you could even see there was an olive tree under-neath. To even get into this part of the grove meant hacking away at dense brambles which ran in a thick and unwelcoming line all along the border of the farmer's field.

As soon as we'd seen this poor ailing area, we'd both wanted, needed, to fix it. As soon as possible. So we'd phoned Elmedine, the daughter of the nice man who had done the tiles on our then very nearly finished house; she'd been a couple of times to babysit in the evening and now we'd requisitioned her for the whole of the next day for babysitting – the six weeks of waiting for Rosie to start at the nursery were a killer.

The satisfaction of making a small bit of the world a little better was deep and pure. After about two hours' hard work, we had uncovered six olive trees between us – nearly the whole of the first row. The trees were a little wonky and a bit battered-looking but there were six discernible olive trees in a nice straight line – which it felt like we had created.

The bell on the campanile had donged ten higher-pitched dongs and two lower-pitched ones, which meant it was time to crack open our thermos of coffee. We sat among our damp cut-tings, trying to avoid the bramble spikes, tuned the cheap radio to something which sounded vaguely like music and drank the nicest cup of coffee you could imagine.

Another great side effect of physical work is that it warms you. For the first time in ages, we hadn't been cold *for the whole day*. We had spent the hours slashing and sawing and dragging huge piles of brambles away from the trees. We had discovered that if you rolled brambles up you could make an enormous ball – as tall as us – which was much easier to move around. We got scratched all over our arms, we got scratched all over our faces and in our eyes. Jason managed to get a huge gash in his leg and even he didn't know how.

I'd never imagined that to make a place look beautiful would involve so much murder. Sometimes it felt that all we had done to nature since we had arrived was kill it: trees encroaching on our grove and blocking light from the olive trees, hedges that had grown too tall, pine tree branches that blocked the view, brambles that were growing where we deemed they were not welcome, bindweed that fought death like a witch – all of them were mercilessly slaughtered and burned. And it felt good. It brought out primitive instincts. Those olive trees were our livelihood and we would have done almost anything to protect them. If a few competitors had to cop it en route that was a tiny price to pay. We were happy to kill for our new babies.

The bonfire grew and grew, the flames leaped to twenty feet. Brambles burn with screams. All the more satisfying for it. And so our massacre continued all day, with breaks for a sandwich, olives and fruit at lunchtime, and chocolate and water in the afternoon. By the time we got back to the house, filthy and bleeding and happier than we'd been in days, to find Rosie, her hair in eight spiky plaits, being taught how to shake her ass by Elmedine to the sounds of Kelis's 'Milkshake', the world seemed perfectly, messily, complicatedly all right.

Sliced steak on a bed of rocket and tomatoes Tagliata

Ingredients for 4 people
Sweet vine cherry tomatoes – 500g
Rocket – 100g
Extra virgin olive oil
Balsamic vinegar
Salt and pepper
Sirloin steak – 1kg, about 2cm thick
Parmesan cheese – 150g shaved

You could go to Locanda Locatelli in Mayfair and eat a perfectly cooked steak tagliata and pay an arm and a leg, or you could go to the Innamorati family restaurant, L'Approdo, and pay 6 euros. L'Approdo was five minutes from our house. So we went there, thanks. They also did a mean porcini tagliatelle which was better for us veggies. Mamma Fabiola confided in me that she'd use frozen or jarred porcinis in the off season, but never dried.

Roughly chop up the tomatoes and cleaned rocket. Mix in a bowl with a good dose of olive oil, balsamic, salt and pepper.

Heat a cast-iron skillet and cook the meat over a moderate heat for 2 minutes on each side (or according to how you like your meat done). Remove the meat and cut at a slight angle so you get strips about $1/2$cm by 1cm.

Lay out a plate for each person. Pile some salad on and arrange the cut meat on top. Sprinkle the meat with salt and olive oil. Add more of the salad on top of the meat then the shaved parmesan. Give it to them and watch their eyes light up.

Tagliatelle with porcini mushrooms

Tagliatelle con funghi porcini

Ingredients for 4 people
Fresh porcini mushrooms – 500g (or similar quantity of bottled or frozen)
Extra virgin olive oil – 2 tablespoons
Garlic – 1 medium clove, whole
Salt and pepper
White wine – $^1/_2$ glass
Fresh tagliatelle – 600g (or a similar quantity of dried pasta)

Wipe the mushrooms clean and cut off the ends of the stalks if necessary. Cut up into $^1/_2$ cm chunks. Into a deep pan, pour the olive oil and over a moderate heat fry the garlic then remove it. Chuck the mushrooms and some salt and pepper into the garlicky oil. When the mushrooms begin to colour pour in the white wine and cook till it evaporates. If you can be bothered (it is worth it if you can), take a fifth of the mix out and blend in a food mixer – it gives a richer pasta dish.

Cook the pasta as instructed on the packet (or by your fresh pasta maker). Mix everything together and serve.

Grilled lamb

Agnello alla brace

Ingredients
Lamb chops – 4 small per person
Olive oil – 3 tablespoons
Lemon – 1
Rosemary, thyme and oregano
Salt and pepper

Nazzareno Innamorati does this *alla brace* style, over the flame grill, but he came up with this recipe which works fine at home without the flames. In a bowl mix the oil, juice from half the lemon and all the herbs finely chopped. Then with your hands massage the mix into the chops. Leave covered for an hour.

Warm a grill pan over a medium heat. When it's hot push the chops firmly onto the pan and cook for a couple of minutes (longer if they are thicker). Turn over and sprinkle salt and freshly ground pepper over the cooked side. Cook for another couple of minutes. They should be eaten rose pink with a couple of wedges of juicy lemon.

Oily chicory

Cicoria saltata in padella

Ingredients
Chicory – 1 kg
Garlic – 3 cloves
Olive oil – 3 tablespoons
Chilli – 1 small
Salt and pepper

Cut the bases off the chicory and cook in boiling salted water for 5 minutes. Drain well. Slowly heat the olive oil with the whole peeled garlic until it is browned. Add the chicory and whole chilli and cook for another few minutes. Take out the garlic and chilli, season with salt and pepper and serve with a drizzle of olive oil.

9 Liquid gold

We'd first met Antonio that spring when we were still living in London. The lovely Alfei, Barbara, supremo of the pruning course, had given us a list of registered olive tree practitioners in Le Marche. These were all people who knew which bits to cut off an olive tree and who would at least consider doing it for a living. By luck, the one on the list who had lived closest to us was Antonio and we had made his acquaintance when we were looking for some help with our pruning.

Antonio was one of those people who inspired confidence. He had hands as big and strong and out of proportion as someone in a Caravaggio painting and was completely without bullshit. If he said it would take five days to prune 500 trees it would take five days. If he said you needed to cut that branch off to let the others grow better, off that branch came. And if he said, 'You are infested with *la mosca*,' then you worried.

It was the end of October and we had barely been here a month. One foggy day, Antonio came round as we'd phoned him for advice about the harvest. It would be our very first harvest and we were not sure when to do it, or even more fundamentally, how to do it. There was nothing that would make us happier than knowing that Antonio was with us to keep an eye on things.

He had already explained that he would probably not be able to help us with the actual harvest. With the terrible weather, he was going to be pushed to get his own trees picked on time, never mind others. It was only because it was foggy and wet that he'd been able to come all the way from Fermo on that day. But he was happy to have a look at our olives and give us some harvesting tips, though he kept saying there was nothing simpler and even a child could do it. We looked at each other sheepishly.

We set off down into the grove, Rosie in arms. Antonio started looking at the trees with those eyes that you knew wouldn't miss a trick. Up at the top, the trees in Il Fico looked to us to be ready to pick – some were already laden with black olives. But it was strange because others were almost completely green still while others were speckled. I suppose it would be fair to say they were in some sort of transition. Antonio had a roughness that only those with great confidence in their trade have. He picked an olive from the tree, squished it between his fingers and sniffed it. He took another and sliced into it with his fingernail to see the purple fleshy interior.

'*Beh* ...,' he said. 'Let's go down to the other part.'

'The other part' referred to the part of the grove where the majority of the trees were. The ones down there were generally slightly behind Il Fico in terms of restoration as they were a year or so behind in the whole cycle of pruning and reshaping. Il Fico, simply by dint of being nearest the house, had had the first doses of any TLC that was going around. Down in 'the other part' were about 650 trees, in the groves Madalena, Immacolata, Furbo and Gruffina. We'd named all the groves after people who'd helped us in our exploits thus far – 'Madalena', after my sister Madeleine, who'd done all the Nudo design work, 'Immacolata' for my friend Veronica, whose birthday fell on the day of the Immaculate Conception and who had wielded a giddy array of menacing gardening implements with us. Furbo after Jason's father, a cunning fellow, and Gruffina after my mother's nickname.

Down in this 'other part' were all the Piantone di Mogliano trees; they were a more delicate variety of olive than the Leccinos which made up the major part of the grove. The Piantone olives were smaller; the trees were tinier and spindlier and seemed like

Leccino's slightly pernickety cousins.

The Piantone di Mogliano olives, unlike the Leccino, never went entirely black. Instead, as they ripened, they turned from green to amazing shades of pink and purple and even red. They produced oil more buttery and delicate in flavour than pure Leccino oil. Monovarietal Piantone commanded a much higher price locally. But Jason and I both preferred the more earthy tones of the Leccino.

The first grove we came to was Madalena, which was made up of 80 percent spindly Piantone trees which cut a dash in silhouette against the dusky hills. The olives were already starting to turn purplish in speckled blotches.

Antonio again gave his speedy scrutiny of the tree with a twisted expression. He plucked an olive and again sliced into it with his grimy fingernail.

'Mosca,' he said.

I thumbed through my mental dictionary of Italian words meaning 'good, great, delicious, wow, lovely trees' and so on. Mosca wasn't there.

'Si si, mosca. Dovete iniziare subito.'

We had to start straight away! What, the harvest? A wave of sickness went through my innards. We hadn't found anyone yet to help us. We had no childcare for Rosie, we had no tractor, we didn't even know what other stuff we had to get – but obviously at the very least we needed nets and some sort of containers to put the olives in. I felt queasy.

It sounds ridiculous that we were so unprepared but we hadn't thought the harvest would start so early – everyone we'd talked to before had told us late November, early December would be the time – and that the presses all stayed open until the New Year. In our mental schedule, we were to get sorted out in the house and the office, have Rosie settled in the nursery, have a bit of time to get our act together preparing for the harvest, then start in a nice, organized, planned sort of a way. Now instead it looked like it was going to be an unseemly scramble.

What was this stupid *mosca* anyway? Apparently, Antonio told us, it was the tiny larva of a fly that could burrow into the flesh of the olive when it starts to become ripe. It gradually eats away the flesh of the fruit and moves on to the next one.

'Is there nothing we can do to stop them?'

'Yes, you can start harvesting. As soon as you can. As soon as this fog clears.'

'But we don't even know what to do,' I said, pathetically.

We walked back up to the house, the word '*mosca*' ringing in our ears. I tried to stop myself thinking about how this bad news would be a really good bit in the documentary we were not making, and wished I had had the privilege of being on the film-maker's side of the fence – the side where drama was just drama and you were not implicated.

We stopped at one of the two trees on either side of the front door.

'I'll show you on this one,' said Antonio.

He whisked out a huge green net from the back of his van. It was square, about eight metres by eight metres, with a slit cut up one side to the centre. Apparently we needed to get a net like this, and cut and sew the slit – this would be where the trunk of the tree went. He gave one end to Jason and we started laying out the enormous net around the tree.

'Obviously when you are working "down there"' (he gestured to Mosca Central) 'you'll need to peg the net up at the bottom.' He grinned, looking at our bemused expressions, 'So the olives don't roll down the hill.'

He then took out three strange-looking bright yellow plastic combs from his van. They were like claws, a bit bigger than hand size with a short stubby hollow handle. He handed one to me and one to Jason. He stepped towards the tree, took an olive-heavy branch in his hand and started raking the comb thing through it, *really roughly*! This was Antonio and of course he must know what he was doing, but it seemed so violent – these were our precious olive trees! I said, 'Gosh, that's much more forceful than I was expecting,' to which Antonio looked slightly offended, and I wished I hadn't said anything. I mean the effect was the one that we were after – all the olives fell into the net below and the branch was left intact. And when I looked at each olive close up it was obvious that no damage had been done, as there was no sign of a bruise or even a dent.

Recovering from the slight shock, I felt a wave of something a bit like relief; this unassuming Afro comb thingy was actually an 'egg of Columbus', a simple solution to a complex problem. I had imagined that picking by hand literally meant picking each little olive off one at a time with pincered fingers. Looking at the number of olives on a tree and the number of trees, this thought had been overwhelming. But now, with our new plastic friend, it was all going to be OK.

This plastic friend had another trick up its sleeve. Antonio asked us if we had a broom handy. We did. He undid the broom bit and just took the handle – and we saw that the yellow miracle fitted perfectly on the top of it! So even those out-of-reach olives were now within our grasp. Wasn't technology wonderful?

That had really been it, so far as the harvesting lesson went. We did the whole tree and it was true that it became obvious how to do it almost as soon as we'd started. One of us would work around the outside of the tree while the other climbed up onto the inside – with a ladder so that our boots didn't scrape the bark – and worked from there. Antonio told us that some people would even take their shoes off to climb on the tree to avoid the slightest scratch. I invented a story for *Vogue*, with accompanying photos, in which I insisted on harvesting only in Dolce and Gabbana gold ballet pumps.

That evening as we ate our pasta we alternated between desolation and optimism.

'I don't even see how we can start with Rosie still at home. We'll have to do it one of us at a time while the other stays at the house with her'.

'Maybe we can do the near bits of the grove together while she has her sleep in the afternoon. Or get Elmedine to come some days.'

'But she costs a fortune! I worked it out, if we leave Rosie at the nursery for ten hours a day, I know we won't but just say – that works out at less than 1 euro an hour. We pay Elmedine seven! It'd be cheaper to buy olive oil.'

'And where on earth are we going to find someone with a tractor?'

'Well, it's all hypothetical anyway as long as the fog keeps up.'

We got up early and headed off, all three of us, to the *consorzio*. Every village had one of these places – it's a sort of corner shop for the *contadino* (Italian farmer) and sells everything from wheelbarrows to ant killer to dried pasta for feeding the dogs. It was one of those quintessentially 'honest' places – consumerism that didn't feel like consumerism because it was all good honest stuff for good honest poorly paid outdoor work. It was one of those places that made us feel good about the fact that we had somehow gone from English bourgeoisie to Italian peasant folk. What a strange world.

It felt a bit like a miracle to see the yellow Afro combs exactly like Antonio's for sale there – like little pieces of the world joining together. Better still, they only cost 49 cents. Antonio had advised us that the cheap plastic ones are much better than the slightly more expensive (2 euro) metal ones and we looked on very smugly as we saw a German lady come in, hold one of each in her hands, then buy two of the metal ones. Oh, the pleasures of being on the inside of the peasant gang.

The *consorzio* – even the name sounds vaguely communist - also sold the nets for harvesting – in great big rolls so that you could choose the dimensions you wanted. We opted for a generous ten metres square, because some parts of the grove are so steep that we figured we'd need the big area to stop the olives rolling off the net and straight down the hill. When we saw it laid out we wished we'd been a bit more modest. Ten suddenly seemed a lot of metres. The net alone made the task feel daunting.

Next on the list was a ladder – a tall one and ideally one that didn't weigh too much. We'd found a couple of Italian picture postcard wooden ones (gnarled wood, no right angles, one missing step) in the outhouse but they weighed a tonne and were only about five foot high – not much better than standing on tiptoe.

Again there were a hundred choices, of different heights, different metals, different stability levels depending on how agile you thought you were. The cheeky-grinned *ragazzo* who was helping us suggested that if it was our first harvest we could go with the heavier, more stable one, at which we both immediately and defensively proclaimed we'd go for the other one, and yes, the tallest one you have please.

We had a cursory look at the crates to collect the olives in, but Antonio had given us a tip for somewhere we could buy them straight from the manufacturer – at 'a fraction of the price'. They only seemed to cost 5 euros as it was, but it would have felt treacherous to ignore Antonio's tip-off so we left them.

The *consorzio* lady asked us if we were starting the harvest already. 'As soon as the fog lifts,' we said. '*Mosca*,' we added, knowingly.

'Ah,' she said. And added, 'Take care won't you? There are a lot of bones broken at harvest time. If an olive is out of reach, maybe it is better left on the tree.'

'Yeah right,' we thought. 'Yes of course,' we said.

We headed off to the secret place to get the olive crates. It was true they were cheaper – a full 15 cents cheaper. And that's even with the foreigners-price-hike that we are coming to expect. We bought twenty. And with these crates stuffed into the back of the Mini, we allowed ourselves to imagine for the first time that we really were going to have crates filled with olives that we really were going to turn into our very own delicious olive oil. We celebrated the feeling of our imminent advent with a cappuccino.

It turned out that crates and combs were very easy to come by compared to hands and legs. We talked to everyone we could think of about helping with the harvest, asking them if they could help, or if they knew anyone who could. We would pay well, we said. But no one wanted the work. The young people weren't interested and the old people were pushed enough just getting their own trees done. And to be honest, I would have felt nervous sending someone twice my age and half my height up a ladder. And the terrible weather meant this year was worse than usual – the work was even more unattractive to the *ragazzi* and there was even less time to get it all done.

There was also the problem of insurance. Almost everyone we talked to had some horror story. My friend/neighbour/relative was helping me with the harvest x number of years ago and they fell from a tree. They broke x number of bones and of course I was responsible – it didn't matter that they were doing it as a favour or that it was their own stupid fault, it was my land so I was responsible for them on it. It cost me a fortune.

There were also stories of heroic evasion of this 'accident on land = fault of landowner' rule.

'Oh, Gianfranco, he's a good guy. You can trust him. He had an accident at my place, but he managed to crawl home to his house before he called the ambulance. Yeah, he's a good guy.'

This harvest was starting to sound less like an Italian idyll and more like a bloodbath by the minute.

But even the good guys weren't interested. Was it because we were foreign, we wondered? Were we doing something wrong? Asking in the wrong way? We were pretty sure we were paying OK, as we'd asked Antonio about it. But it just seemed implausible that in the middle of the agricultural heartland of Italy we couldn't find a couple of people for a couple of weeks to do a bit of olive picking for us.

Next year, we swore, we were going to get it all sorted out weeks in advance, with a team of eager and fit young bodies, wherever we had to get them. I mean there were people in London who would *pay* for a holiday doing this, weren't there?

Meanwhile there was the other pressing problem of finding someone with a tractor. Finding someone with a tractor, that was, who wanted to lend it to us.

Without a tractor, we had to face the thought of carrying 20-kilogram crates of olives by hand up our hill. From the bottom of the grove to the house is probably 500 or 600 metres and the hill is about a 1 in 3 incline. It's the sort of thing they'd check out as a potential testing ground for the Special Forces – but then decide it was 'a bit much'.

Jason valiantly went off on a mission. He set off to the local village – hardly even a village – called San Lorenzo, which was full of people whose job involved tractors. He stopped at the first house he saw with a tractor in clear view and, trying to placate the mad barking dog in his best canine Italian (without great success not least because he always got the words for up, 'su', and down, 'giu', muddled), went in to enquire.

At the door was a lady in the obligatory Le Marche rural uniform of knee-high beige pop socks and a patterned sleeveless overall over her clothes. Her suspicion lifted a little as it became clear(ish) that Jason wasn't trying to sell her anything and instead she gestured towards the local bar, where she said he would find her husband. It was a slightly vague clue given that every bar in every village was filled with wizened men, usually playing cards and drinking unspeakable liquors – any one of whom might have belonged to her.

Jason headed off anyway. He was greeted by the hunter, another 'anziano' (old man) whom he vaguely recognized because he came and killed animals on our land. Even this flimsy connection seemed to help enormously and suddenly Jason's request to find someone with an available tractor was met with half a dozen chattering men racking their brains for someone suitable. One man took Jason under his wing. *'Andiamo a trovarti un trattore.'* 'Come on,' he said, 'let's find you a tractor.'

They knocked on some doors and the man spoke an unintelligible dialect with whoever answered. Invariably it was a child or a mother or a deaf grandma, none of whom were really able to help. There was waving and gestures towards tractors but no result. The bad weather had affected everybody, so any day there was a half chance of us harvesting was also a day when there was a half chance of overdue tractor chores being done.

After about three hours, Jason finally returned home, proudly proclaiming that he had found a guy called Patrizio with a moody wife and a four- by-four Fiat Panda who was prepared to help.

There are three types of farm tractor in this world: the Massey Fergusons, the John Deeres and, best of all, the Fiat Pandas.

Now that we were ready for anything, we set the alarm for sunrise. We both slept in that strange way you do when you really need rest but also know you have to get up early and are worried about oversleeping. Not well, in short. Jason jumped out of bed and went to the window to see if it was picking weather. He could hardly see past the shutters – it was a thick fog, so heavy you could see the wetness of it. And cold cold cold. We went downstairs and out into the world. It was like being inside a cloud. As well as the fog it was actually drizzling a little. We couldn't pick in this.

The no-harvest-when-wet rule was not so much for the pickers, it was for the trees and ultimately for the quality of the oil. We'd been doing our homework. Scraping away at trees when they were wet meant that the bark could easily be damaged, which was like giving the tree lots of little wounds. Wounds into which, if it was raining, infection could be carried. Forget the idea that rain is nice and clean – it's actually a very efficient carrier of disease. Shocking isn't it? And oil quality wise, you don't want a lot of damp olives piled on top of each other all starting to fester – or the mouldiness could be transferred to the oil. This last problem, I felt, was a minor worry for us in that we planned to press at the end of each day, so there was very little time for any festering to go on – but it was our first year, so we didn't want to break any rules.

The hardest thing was being all psyched up to work and then not being able to do anything. The plan had been that Jason would pick in the morning and I would do the afternoon picking, and whoever wasn't picking would stay at the house with Rosie and do important support activities like making lunch and bringing down thermoses of coffee.

Instead, we were reduced to looking at the weather forecast on the TV and doing menial chores while we hoped that the fog and the drizzle would lift.

We couldn't help but feel frustrated with it all. In our previous jobs, we had been used to making schedules that would be stuck to no matter what. Working to nature's erratic whim was a skill of patience and adaptability we had yet to master.

Three more days went the same way, each evening expectant, each morning disappointed. On Thursday night, the military-uniformed forecaster was so confident that the next day would bring a break in the clouds that we phoned Elmedine in preparation. That way Jason and I could both work all day and claw back some of our lost picking time. But we woke up to the sound of big gloopy raindrops on the skylight window in Rosie's room next door and had to call Elmedine off.

With every day that passed, the olives still hanging tauntingly on the trees, we thought about that word 'mosca' and Antonio's face as he said it.

On Saturday, we decided to throw centuries of olive-picking wisdom out of the window and pick anyway, rain or shine. Or, as it transpired, fog and hail. It was a really foul day, dense fog, constant drizzle and the occasional entertainment of a hailstorm. Our plan was to pick as carefully as we could, to minimize the bark problem – even doing it by hand if it seemed the combs were doing extra damage. Then we carried each crate as we filled it up to the house, where we tipped the olives out onto big tarpaulin sheets laid out in the cellar. That way, the olives weren't in damp piles that could get mouldy, and laid out one layer thick we hoped they'd dry out. It was also important to keep the olives cool so the acids couldn't build up – but that was fine because our cellar was bloody cold whatever time of year it was.

Jason cut a hilariously English, miserable picture heading down into the fog, thermos in one hand, yellow claw in the other, ladder on one shoulder, net under an armpit, wellies, a QPR hat and the best lightweight anorak-type affair we could find. This wasn't the olive harvest idyll we had pictured in our daydreams. Despite it all we were both excited and when Jason, just before disappearing from view, turned and waved with a smile, I felt so happy that I grabbed Rosie and we did stupid dancing around the room to Basement Jaxx.

We had no idea the speed at which the crates would fill up, but as half an hour turned to an hour and an hour to two, I thought Jason must have changed the plan to bring them up one at a time. It couldn't take two hours to fill a single crate, could it? Eventually a damp figure came up the path by the house, raindrop on nose, with a crate filled to the brim with olives of every hue. They looked rather beautiful, all plump and shiny. We rushed them down into the cellar as if every second more in that crate was an affront to their dignity.

'It's bloody slow,' said Jason. 'By the time you've chosen your tree, laid out the net – that net we got is far too big – pegged it at the bottom, clipped it at the top, you've taken ten minutes. Then doing the tree isn't too bad, except sometimes when there are some olives really out of reach. Then I was going through, picking out any olives that have any sign of *mosca.*'

'You're picking through each olive one at a time? Please tell me you're kidding.'

'I'm not; we don't want bloody maggots in with our olives.'

'But Antonio said it was fine, they're only bad because they eat the olives, not because they do anything to the oil.'

'Well, I, don't like the idea.'

'But J, we're never going to get enough to press at this rate. Look, it's already nearly half past nine, it gets dark at five. At this rate we'd have five crates, that's only just over 100 kilograms – we need 300. Minimum. Else we can't press them.'

'I know.'

We decided to call Elmedine and see if she could come straight away. By good luck, she had been told that she wasn't needed at the hairdresser's where she was apprenticing that day so she could. I loaded Rosie into the Mini to go and collect her while Jason headed down to the grove again, with a slightly grim 'I'm at the bottom end of Immacolata.'

I left Rosie, distracted by some Italian cartoon on TV and thankfully unresisting, with 'Dina', and moments later, I was looking as sensational as Jason in my wet-weather harvesting garb.

It was true about the net — it was huge and even with two people seemed to take an age to get it into place under the tree all laid out flat. And we were doing a steep part of the grove — well, it's all steep, but this part particularly so — so there could be no short cuts in putting our home-fashioned tent pegs in. Without the bottom of the net pegged up, our booty would be off down the hill, straight into our nightmares.

There followed a period of that specific calm one gets when doing a satisfyingly repetitive job. Harvesting turned out to be more like hairdressing than anything. The branches were like big hairdos, with layers and layers of knots. You had to take each part of the branch in layers, lifting it separate from its knotty pals, and gently comb through it so that all the knots — the olives — fell out into the net below. You then moved on to the next layer until you'd cleared that patch. You quickly learned that the less you moved your feet the better, as every move risked squashing some of the precious olives already on land.

You also quickly learned that it was impossible to leave an olive on a branch. The disproportionate time you spent getting that last single olive, on the furthest out twig of the highest up branch, defied all logic, particularly given the rush we were in, but it was somehow impossible to leave. I thought about the lady in the consorzio saying maybe the ones you can't get you should leave — but it just didn't make sense. She'd either never harvested an olive tree or she had

had generations of her family wiped out in olive harvesting fall injuries to have talked like that.

The rain had the decency to stop after a while, and it was just the fog which seemed to plan to stay all day. We'd temporarily avoided arguments about what to do about the *mosca*-affected olives by starting on trees that weren't affected. Really it was because we knew arguing was time-wasting and we couldn't face it. We both satisfied ourselves with the reasoning that picking the ripe but *mosca*-unaffected trees was important in that, left, they might have soon turned into affected trees.

Carrying the crates by hand up the hill called upon levels of inner strength that one didn't necessarily want to test. The Fiat Panda was out of the question because the rain meant everything was so slippery – even the hardiest tractor didn't stand a chance on the slopes in this.

Each crate weighed over twenty kilograms and their shape meant there was no easy way of carrying them – out in front was the only option, hands round the far side and elbows gripping the near side, the bottom bit balanced on a hip bone if you could find one. We'd walk 100 metres or so up the hill then pause, resting the crate on our thighs, as we contemplated the next chunk of hill. It was steep and slippery and you had to do a kind of snowplough shape with your wellies to avoid falling over and watching the olive jewels disappear for ever. One time I suggested we try the wheel-barrow – that way, maybe one of us could push up two crates at a time while the other carried one. Hopeless. The wheel skidded around and the heavy weight meant it nose-dived into every dip – and there were lots. Also with two crates on top of each other it was very top heavy and at one point the unthinkable happened, with the top crate falling over, luckily not completely, but enough to tip a quarter crate of olives into the mud. We rummaged on our hands and knees and picked each one up, one at a time, and had to hose them down when we and they finally reached the house. After that showing, the wheelbarrow was abandoned for good.

We filled the last crate in the sort of semi-darkness you can only see in if you've been in it from the transition from light. The olive leaves were starting to look like olives and vice versa. By the time Jason carried the last crate up the hill, it really was pitch dark, but he somehow managed to do it by conjuring a vivid mental picture of the route and sheer bloody-mindedness.

By the end of the day we had eight crates, about 160 kilograms. Not enough to press.

We called Corrado at the press. 'We have 160 kilograms,' we said.

'*Per fare il vostro da soli, avete bisogno di almeno trecento kili*' ('You need 300 kilos to do your own press'), he said. 'Did you want to put them in with the communal ones?'

We didn't, we couldn't. This had to be our own oil, for our adopters. We couldn't mix it in with a bunch of other olives of unknown origin. But we really wanted to press them today, we had promised ourselves we would, we had set our hearts on it.

It was the first time we'd had to admit defeat.

'Can we book in for tomorrow,' J said, 'as soon as possible after dark.'

Luckily it was still early enough in the season that the press was quiet and we could still choose our slots.

'Eighteen hundred hours?' said Corrado.

'Great. See you then,' we said.

That night we tucked up our precious olives in the cellar with more care than we did Rosie. We made sure they were all only one layer thick – so they took up the whole cellar floor. We even took an electric fan down there to help them dry off. We said goodnight and closed the door.

The next morning was foggy again. We were up before it was light, creeping around already in our thermals, hoping not to wake Rosie up. I was just contemplating the risk of going out and starting on the bit of the grove closest to the house while she slept on when the 'MUMMYYYYYYYY' cry came out and my cover was blown.

We had a problem. Elmedine couldn't come that day but we needed both of us harvesting for at least a good chunk of the day to get to our 300 kilogram target. We didn't know anyone else to ask to help at such short notice so there was nothing for it but to take Rosie down with us. We bundled her up in as many clothes as would fit, packed up the travel cot and as many toys as we could carry and went off into the grove, a very unlikely picture. We set her up on the flattest bit we could find, propped against a tree so the cot wouldn't tumble down the hill, gave her bananas and little packets of raisins and drinks in fiddly distracting containers, put the radio on and prayed that she would play ball for a while.

Children can be good at rising to occasions like this. She must have played with her bricks (these really strange ones we got in Italy that are *perfumed*) for a good three-quarters of an hour before there was even a peep. God bless her. We then bought another chunk of time getting her to 'sort the olives' into ones with leaves and ones without. There was a certain amount of wastage this way as she decided some were 'naughty' ones but we were so grateful to her it didn't matter.

At about 11.30 it started snowing.

There was nothing to do but laugh. The picture of us holding our lurid combs, in our big wellies and silly hats and Rosie in her cot, all in the middle of an olive grove with snow falling around, was just too ridiculous. We laughed and laughed, all three of us, that laughter that is borderline madness and no less satisfying for it.

The snow didn't last long – it was just a shower really, just something to give us a boost. And it really worked. We had been to the most impossible point and now we were climbing out the other side. By the end of the day we had twelve crates of olives in total – all full to the brim.

By some miracle Jason managed to fit them into the Mini, but there was no room for me and Rosie. We were not going to miss our first olive press trip! So Jason drove to the press, which was about twenty minutes away, dropped the olives off, then came back to collect us and – luckily we remembered at the last minute – the barrels to put the oil in.

We got to the press just in time for the weigh in. Everyone's olives were weighed before going into the machinery, as the charges for the olive press are per weight of olives processed. That's the reason why you see the old timers arriving with crates without a single leaf or stalk in them. Their wives have gone meticulously through each one, making sure that they won't be spending their precious pensions on having olive leaves crushed.

Ours weighed in at 293 kilograms, seven short of the 300-kilogram minimum. Corrado gave us a grin. 'I think we'll let you off, shall we?'

We then watched the process of turning olives into olive oil. Our now tiny-looking crates were emptied into one huge crate which fitted onto the forklift truck. It was taken to the first staging post of the press, where the olives were tipped into a pit. Then gradually they were scooped up onto a little conveyor belt where they were carried uphill through a shower to wash them off. Once they came through this, the olives all fell into another waiting pit.

This was the stage just before crushing, and they stayed there until the olives of the previous occupant had finished in the stone grinder. Once they were out of the way, the olives were vacuum-sucked into this metal container. What had seemed vast quantities of olives now looked so insignificant. Then the machine was turned on and three giant granite wheels started to move, each one angled slightly differently so that no olive was spared. The olives were crushed, stones, skins and all. These granite wheels were about a metre each in diameter and must have weighed hundreds of kilograms each. They just went round and round as they proba-bly have done for centuries, turning green and black and purple shiny olives into a greeny-mauve lumpy paste.

The olives stayed in there for about fifteen minutes then passed on to the next stage – this time a horizontal closed-off tube with a giant corkscrew inside it. This stage was to emulsify the oil, so it formed first tiny droplets which then got bigger and bigger the longer the churning went on. All of this was done at room temper-ature and without any chemicals or anything being added – it was, as the label of any good olive oil will tell you, a purely mechanical process.

The paste stayed in the dark tube for about forty minutes, long enough to nip to the bar across the road for emergency crisps for Rosie, before going on to the more invisible process of centrifuging. This meant whizzing the paste around at high speed, so that water was spun off in one direction, oil in another, and the solid matter in yet another. The centrifuging was done two or three times to make sure all the water had gone. The pulp was discarded onto a big pile out the back – though actually our pulp was of a high enough quality that it could be reprocessed, this time heated up, to produce a lower grade oil. Some of the bigger producers bought the pulp from first extract extra virgin producers to make their own lower quality oil. But we were only interested in the best.

And the best was about to come. After all this processing, which had taken nearly two hours in the machines, but for us several years in the planning, we were about to taste our very first drop of our very first, very own olive oil.

Some *oleificios* had bits of bread lying around to taste your oil with but Corrado was a purist. He had tiny little plastic cups, usually used for espressos, which you dipped momentarily under the flow of oil to get a tiny thimbleful to taste neat. The taste was an intense version of the smell that was all around us – incredibly fresh, incredibly *olivey*. And not at all greasy – just smooth, grassy green and with a lovely bite, a sort of peppery kick, after you'd swallowed it. Tasting proper olive oil like this, as fresh as can be, was like drinking your first proper coffee when before you've only ever had instant. It was a completely different thing – you felt there should be a different name for it. And as you tasted it more, and let the oil stay in your mouth for a few moments, you really found extraordinary flavours appearing – artichokes, avocados, a hundred other things that you couldn't quite name.

Corrado said the idea was to have a taste, not drink the whole lot. But you could see the vicarious pleasure on his face at seeing the joy of our olive oil virginity being lost.

After about another quarter of an hour, all the oil had come through – though we wanted to crawl inside the machinery to scrape out any last drops. We weighed in at a grand total of thirty-six litres of olive oil – so just one of our barrels was more than sufficient. We drove it home at a pace so slow it was almost suspicious and carried our precious fluid down into the cool cellar.

Then we realized we were utterly, completely shattered. We practically threw Rosie into bed and fell ourselves almost immediately into a deep, deep contented sleep.

Having the first press under our belts felt like a major achievement but it was really a drop in the ocean. To do it, we had probably only harvested about forty trees, out of a total of 800. Even if we were going to ignore the ones with too many *mosca*-infected olives, we had a hell of a way to go.

But some things got easier.

Rosie was finally allowed to start at nursery – tentatively at first, an hour on the first day, two on the second – as they got her acclimatized. Actually I think the acclimatizing was as much for them, as she seemed happy from the off. To be around lots of other small friends, singing songs and having different exciting toys to play with and painting to do – I mean what's not to like? In fact, I secretly fancied that most adults would enjoy a spell in nursery school doing painting and gluing and pouring different coloured sand into pots. By the end of a week, she was allowed to stay for the whole day, which meant mounting the twin towers of having lunch *and* having an afternoon nap. All the tiny lined-up nursery beds looked like something from *Snow White and the Seven Dwarves* and sure enough the first song she came home singing was an Italian 'hi ho'. The words had been adapted though, to make them more about food.

Nursery made things much easier. And we also got quicker at the netting and collecting and pegging, so each new tree didn't seem quite such a faff. And we found a lovely helper – 'little Carlo' we called him, to differentiate him from the other Carlo we already knew who was probably only a centimetre taller. We'd been given his number by Antonio – what finer start – as he had done a bit of work with him in the past. He was currently still a student, training to be a maths teacher, but in all his spare time he loved being outside and doing healthy physical things. We had plenty of those to offer.

Every day we made an early morning telephone call/weather report so Carlo knew whether to set off or not. Working as a three-some was so much more satisfying – and, of course, also meant that we spoke Italian all day. And Carlo was an excellent teacher in that he relished teaching us quirky little words – explaining what a song lyric on the radio was saying, or telling us the slang word for the piece of bread you use to swab up the juices on your plate – even though in polite company you shouldn't, of course, do this. And since we ate lunch together every day, we also learned a lot about the rules of Italian cooking; we were particularly keen to crack those about which pasta shape goes with which sauce – for example, why do you always see 'penne arrabbiata' but never 'spaghetti arrabbiata'. When we asked Carlo this particular question, he looked at us as if we'd asked 'Why don't you sometimes wear your socks on your ears instead of your feet?' and we realized we had a way to go.

In return, we taught him curious English expressions – the 'silly bit' of food left at the end of the meal which hardly merited the trouble of putting in the fridge, or when it was time to 'shake a leg', or

Clockwise from top left –
A Loro Piceno local demonstrates the
village's pace of life. Antonio shows us
how to harvest an olive tree. Two thousand
is a lot of tins to label by hand. Local
butcher 'Pepe Cotto' shows off his
dinosaur sculpted from animal parts.

Clockwise from top –
Cathy harvests our first olives. Corrado
and his mum – who own the local olive
press. Rosie, Jason and Cathy in the
snow. Cathy versus secateurs.

Clockwise from top left –
Sunflowers in the field next
door. 'The Hunter', Stella
his dog and friend. Our
front door. The
delicious Guida Stachietti.

Clockwise from top –
Jason and the local football
team. Jason gathering up the
olives. Jason harvesting in the
rain. Welcome to Loro Piceno

Clockwise from top –
Morning mist in the grove.
Our new dining room and
kitchen. Rosie helps pack up
our old life. Oil barrels await
their booty.

Clockwise from top left –
Our first olives roll through
the first stage of the olive
press. The window of a
pasticceria. Gigia, queen
of vincisgrassi, assembles
her creation. Rosie gets
serious with some seafood.

Clockwise from top left – Choir buddy Nicoletta serves osso bucco and risotto. Cathy gets a lesson in correct butchering of osso bucco. Freshly pruned olive trees take in the view. Rosie, as lion, cuddles kid goat.

Clockwise from top left -
Rosie inspects our very first extra virgin ultra
delicious olive oil. Rosie and Jason contemplate
our new life. Misty morning view from our house
A sprinkling of Apennine snow over the grove

trying to explain what the 'hang the consequences' he'd spotted on our website meant. The giggling and banal chatter jointly managed to pull off the impressive illusion of halving the length of our working day.

And when it was done, we'd pick up Rosie from nursery and all sit and have tea and cake together.

But there were some things that didn't get any easier. Carrying the crates up the hill felt a more biblical task by the day. Each time they were heavier. Or maybe our psychological tricks of self-distraction (trying to remember the words to a long-lost Eurovision Song Contest entry or counting backwards from 18,744 in threes) were starting to wear thin. Patrizio and his willing steed the Fiat Panda were still, in theory, available. The trouble was that there were never more than a couple of days without rain – which meant that our steep mud-covered hillside would be too treacherous to tackle, even in that superstar of off-roadery that is a four-by-four Fiat.

The pleasures of the olive press didn't lessen. The satisfaction of doing a job where you walk away at the end of the day carrying the product of your labours was immense. And we were becoming friendly with all the regulars now. Corrado's mum loved Rosie but for some reason Rosie always got shy or squealed when she came near. Old nonna didn't hold it against her though.

'È normale. È perche sono vecchia e bruttissima' ('It's because I am so old and ugly'), she said, as if it made perfect sense. Then there was the man who we had never seen without his broad smile, uncluttered by teeth – a stalwart of the olive press, driving the fork-lift, fixing broken machinery, tapping the last olives out of the corner of the pits with his all-purpose stick – knowing that he would incur the wrath of a contadino if he missed a single one. And

Corrado was nearly always there keeping an eye on things and looking distinctly greyer and older as each week went by and his accumulated sleep deficit mounted.

We developed a little routine of seeing our olives through to the corkscrew part, then nipping across the road to the bar for a glass of wine instead of waiting, hypnotized, for the coiling to end. This behaviour was not something the locals would approve of. The in-built suspicion of Italians – and of peasant stock Italians in particular – made it impossible to leave your station even for a moment. Only if you watched your oil for every microsecond of the process could you be sure that there was no funny business and that your oil really was your oil. We, perhaps naïvely, seeing our olive paste into a hermetically sealed container, took a more relaxed view.

One evening, unusually, there was another young couple there. I say young but it's all relative – we were normally half the age of anyone else and these people were only a bit older than us. We struck up conversation – Mirella and Gianni they were called (though for some reason those names never lodged and from the start we referred to them as Hansel and Gretel). In true Italian style, Gianni's opening gambit to us was the 'revelation' that a percentage of everyone's oil was being siphoned off into secret vats somewhere hidden away. When we laughed and said we trusted Corrado, he laughed back in a way that eloquently but firmly said a kinder version of 'Oh you funny little foreigners you know nothing.' They both seemed really nice and we were sorry to say goodbye when we were both whisked in separate ways to fill in our oil transport documents.

But the next day we received an e-mail from Mirella. Gretel. She'd tracked down our e-mail by looking up our adoption idea on

Google – I didn't even remember talking to her about it – and finding our website. She wrote to say that she hoped it wasn't presumptuous but would we like to go round for tea one day?

We decided we liked this olive oil business a lot – not only were we starting real production of real produce for a real business, but we were picking up friends along the way. That night we went to bed with that warm feeling again, that everything was going to be OK.

As the season went on and more and more people had started their harvest, it was harder and harder to get a slot at a reasonable time. And the press by now was working almost around the clock. Jason did one stint which was the last press of the day which started at 1.30 a.m. and finished at 3.30 a.m. I did another where I was booked in for the first press of the day at 4 a.m. The best bit was relishing drinking my first cappuccino of the day, chores completed, with the surprisingly numerous others who frequent coffee bars at six o'clock on a Sunday morning.

And when the days were too foggy and wet, we made up our minds not to let ourselves get miserable about it but instead to work on the business. Even after such a short time here, it was clear that a business that relied on constantly battling with nature was going to be tough tough tough. We loved the adoption scheme, but thought there were also other possibilities – for example, getting involved with other local food producers and working with them to get their products sold in the UK. Le Marche was still quite behind in terms of its international marketing – just think how many people have heard of Tuscany by comparison – but it had an awful lot on offer. And we felt that we would genuinely have something to bring to the table as, if nothing else, we knew English and we knew how to deal with English people.

This thought had barely leaped across the synaptic fluid when there was a cry of '*Buon giorno,*' from the side of the house. A large jowly man appeared a while after his belly, with a big smile on his face.

'*Voi siete gli inglesi. Fate olio e fate anche il projetto di "adozione"?*' ('Are you the olive tree adoption people?'), he asked, most improbably.

'*Si,*' we replied, baffled as to how he could possibly have known.

'*Buono,*' he said.

He then embarked on a series of questions so detailed that we could only think he was planning to thieve our idea. We were cagey and eventually asked him why he was asking. The reason for his curiosity, it transpired, was crafty but not in the way we'd imagined. He was trying to sell a house to an English fellow and, having heard of our scheme, thought the gift of a local olive tree would be a perfectly cunning persuasion tool, something '*per rendere piu facile la sua decisione*' ('to help facilitate his decision-making').

But there was another reason he'd come over. '*Questo, questo ... dovete assaggiarlo*' ('*You have to try this*'), he said, whipping out a very moonshine-looking, unmarked bottle of liquid. I got a couple of glasses and he poured some out. We tasted it, me feeling slightly naïve about having to report to the police how we had willingly drunk down the drug before this stranger burgled the whole house, and it was rather delicious – sweet and fiery.

'You will never guess what it is made of,' he said.

We hazarded enough guesses to humour him into saying, with great pause and relish, '*Le foglie degli ulivi*' – olive leaves.

So there it was: bizarre Nudo product number one – a highly intoxicating liquor made from the offcuts of our pruning labours. Dandy. We said we'd have a think and get back to him. His card told us that he was a shoe design technician – and he was gone.

On more sane business development routes, Jason had tracked down a fellow called Buccolini (hard not to say Berlusconi) who had a company, SIGI, which made delicious condiments, vinegars, jams, all sorts. Jason had got in touch with him and had found his ears very open to the idea of a partnership to help him into the lucrative foreign market. That day we thought we'd take advantage of the bad weather to go and meet him face to face.

He'd given us directions, as so often happens, to the nearest café. This habit derived half from a desire to help people find places more easily and half from the desire to be always drinking coffee. And so it was that we were sitting in the strangely named Peter Pan café waiting for 'Mr SIGI' as we had christened him.

He arrived, literally twitching with – nerves? Excitement? A neurological condition? We couldn't be sure – and bade us follow him to his place a couple of miles away.

His place turned out to be a large house with a small factory in the garden. In the factory, there were workers buzzing about wearing white lab coats and white hats and white gloves. Everything was pristine and the air was full of smells from steaming vats of this and that. Beyond the factory were the fields from whence many of the steaming things originated – orchards of fruit trees, an olive grove, several vines in perfect rows.

Mr SIGI took us to the tasting room, where there were maybe 100 different products all scattered about. If we hadn't stopped him, Mr SIGI would have had us taste them all. Every time we tasted a new one, the room would go silent and he would stare at us intently waiting for our reaction. There were *zucchini* under oil, there was *agro dolce*, there was apple and bergamot jelly, there was a special jam 'for you English' made of lager and there was sapa. Like a delicious, sweeter, less acidic balsamic vinegar, it was rich and caramelized and tasted sort of ancient – in the way mead does. Could this be our very own Le Marche balsamic vinegar, soon to be adorning shelves in every right-thinking British kitchen? Mr SIGI suggested myriad uses for it – as an ingredient in biscotti and broths, as a surprise treat in polenta, or simply drizzled on anything from pecorino to duck breast to *gelato*.

We left with smiles, promises of further discussion and fistfuls of goodies. And a skip in our step that came from feeling like we had just pulled off a coup of pretending to be business people *and* in a foreign country.

Silvano and his sacred sapa

I like people who are passionate about food. Silvano Buccolini has passion with a liberal sprinkling of obsession. His hands trembled when he talked about his beloved sapa and its luxurious caramelized taste.

Sapa has about 1,000 years of history in Le Marche, Silvano told me. In times of famine the Marchigiani people would turn to cheap polenta. When they could afford it they would drizzle some rich, sweet sapa on the polenta with a few shards of sharp, aged pecorino. To make the most of these luxuries mamma would spread the steaming hot, soft polenta out on a large wooden pasta board in the kitchen and make a few small pits at equal distances from the edge. In each pit she'd put a bit of sapa and a bit of cheese, so the family could sit at the edge eating their way to the cheesy sapa bits.

Silvano's version of this is simple but without the extra pressure of the biting poverty.

Polenta with sapa

Ingredients for 6 people
Water – 1.3l
Polenta – 200g
Olive oil – glug for frying
Aged pecorino – 130g
Sapa – 20ml
Salt and pepper

Bring a pan of salted water to the boil and slowly whisk in the polenta. When the water is boiling again turn the heat right down and put a lid, slightly ajar, on the pan. Cook for 45 minutes, stirring every now and then.

Once it's about cooked (like the consistency of thick treacle), lightly oil a clean surface (like a bread board) and pour over the polenta. Smooth it out till it's about 1cm thick. After 20 minutes it will be set. Now get creative and cut it into any shape you like, then fry for a few minutes on each side in some olive oil.

Grate your cheese and squash a good mound of it onto your fried polenta, then drip some sapa over the top. Season with salt and pepper. Eat quickly as an appetizer or afternoon snack and remember how lucky you are.

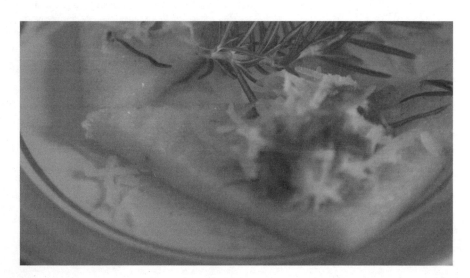

Sapa and pecorino

Sweet and tangy. Drizzle some sapa over slices of seasoned pecorino. Actually, to be honest, I think sapa goes even better with really good strong mature Cheddar but I wouldn't dare say that round here.

Or try mixing young, runny honey with sapa and drizzling the mixture on cheese or prosciutto crudo.

Sapa with ice cream

The *gelateria Incicco* in San Ginesio makes sapa ice cream. According to Silvano it harks back to old days when the poor farming kids would collect cups of snow and run back to mamma, who would spoon in a few drops of sapa as a treat. To treat his own kids Silvano will drizzle a generous serving of sapa, over vanilla and strawberry ice cream.

Sapa with strawberries

Rumour has it that sapa is much better than balsamic vinegar with strawberries. I agree. It's to do with the low acidity of sapa which settles better with the acidity of the fruit.

Onion and sapa tart

Ingredients for 4
Onions – 800g
Butter – 50g
Olive oil – 2 tablespoons
Sapa – 10ml
Puff pastry – 200g
Parmesan – 60g
Thyme – couple of sprigs

Cathy also came up with a delicious tart which uses sapa. It will also work with a good balsamic, if you can't get hold of any.

Preheat the oven to 180ºC /gas mark 4. Peel the onions and cut into thick rings. Put them in a pan with the butter and oil over a low heat for 20–30minutes. Near the end add the sapa.

Lay the pastry over a flan dish. Cover with ovenproof paper weighed down with some baking beads (or any dry beans you can get your hands on), and whack in the oven for 10 minutes.

When the flan is back out of the oven lay down a base of shaved parmesan and then add the onion mix. Sprinkle some chopped-up thyme over the top and cook for 15–20 minutes at 180ºC /gas mark 4.

Penne all'arrabbiata

Ingredients for 4 people
Garlic – 2 cloves
Fresh chilli – 1
Olive oil – 6 tablespoons
Chopped tomatoes – 550g tin
Salt and pepper
Ribbed penne (rigato) – 350g
Parsley – a handful

'Why is it always penne with arrabbiata sauce, why not spaghetti arrabbiata?' we had asked little Carlo. It was to do with matching the consistency of the sauce with how it hangs on the pasta, he told us. It was about the gooey, rich tomato sauce oozing up the inside of the pasta tubes and clinging on in sticky lumps to the ribbed outer surface. Ah, that explained it.

Penne all'arrabbiata means angry penne on account of the chillies. I like my penne really quite cross, so I will use as much chilli as I think Cathy and Carlo can handle.

Peel the garlic and chop the chilli. Gently fry both for a few minutes in the oil. Add the tomatoes, season with salt and pepper and cook for a good 20 minutes on a low heat. Take out the garlic cloves.

Cook the penne in a large pan of water, with salt and oil, till *al dente*. Drain and mix so the gooey tomato sauce sticks to the ribbed pasta. Sprinkle over the parsley before serving.

10 Learning to be Italian

It was hard to believe that we had only been here three months. Three months in our old life could pass in a snap, one week blurring into another. But here with every day presenting a new challenge, a new setback, a new triumph, even a new word, time seemed extended beyond measure. And as well as all the things we were consciously experiencing, there was a whole host of others which we were experiencing by osmosis, simply by existing in a different culture. Most were extremely puzzling.

There was an expression that we heard, without exaggeration, at least once every day. It was 'piano piano'. It literally means 'softly softly' but was used to mean anything from 'Hey don't sweat it, calm down' to 'Gently does it' to 'Life is impossible; the only way to cope is to take things a little at a time.' I said the words, too, to try to fit in, but I didn't mean them yet.

I didn't mean them because even though our bodies had made the move here our minds hadn't yet. We were not believers in 'piano piano'. We still had Sunday night feeling – that grey ache that started in school days which descends at around 5 or 6 p.m. on Sunday evening to shroud you in a calm dread of the week ahead. We shouldn't be dreading the week ahead, should we? We should be embracing it, enjoying our new challenges and all that? We had CHOSEN this week ahead!

It was clearly harder than we might have predicted to desist from constantly driving ourselves in that London/career sort of way. We had to start early. We didn't feel satisfied unless we had worked hard all day. Even then we worried that there was so much to do that we hadn't done enough. We felt relief, lightness of being when the weekend came around again. We wondered why it was that when we told people at home what we had decided to do (give up successful well-paid TV jobs in Hollywood for a life of uncertainty running an olive farm in Italy) everyone declared their jealousy. But what were they jealous of? Why did everyone declare a wish to do something like this? People mentioned things like a 'stress free life'. Ha! What was stress free about having to be fully responsible for every euro you earn when you were used to being paid every month no matter whether you had achieved greatness or mediocrity in the preceding weeks?

If you decided to live in a blissful relaxed place where everyone else was 'piano piano', where opening hours allowed for being closed on Monday mornings (a brilliant answer to 'Sunday feeling'), Thursday afternoons, Sunday all day – and other miscellaneous times when life was just too wearisome to open up shop – that didn't automatically enrol you in the school of stresslessness. We put our own stress on ourselves. Even though we were neither Catholic nor Protestant nor Jewish, we still suffered this work ethic-induced guilt. The fact we did it to ourselves made it even more annoying! So would we have succeeded in this new life when we could say 'piano piano' and understand the sentiment, the ambition, the pace of the statement and not just the words?

More prosaic concerns about language were also constantly out to get us. As a vegetarian Jason had, from way back, a stock phrase that he used in restaurants to clarify this. This stock phrase is 'Sono vegetariano; non mangio ne pesce ne carne', which means 'I am a vegetarian; I eat neither fish nor meat.' We had noticed, but not thought too much of it, that this stock phrase was sometimes met with a slightly bewildered expression. We assumed that the expression was to do with the strangeness of meeting a real live vegetarian in these parts. But it turned out to be something else …

There were two pitfalls in this phrase. The first was the word *'pesce'* which if pronounced with a hard c, means 'peaches' rather than 'fish'. The second was the word *'carne'*, which if pronounced without the obligatory rolled r (an r unattainable by Jason's unaccustomed tongue) means 'dogs'. We fell into both of these pitfalls, with the result that for the previous three months or so, Jason had been advising all the local restaurants that he was a vegetarian who enjoyed neither dogs nor peaches.

Another strange thing was that people kept offering us cats. Was it a coincidence or did it mean something? And if it meant something, did it mean something profound about us being British and them being Italian or did it mean something banal like nobody got their cats 'done' here and there were armies of kittens running loose?

Our new life was full of these questions. Questions about what the 'anti-slip socks' which formed part of Rosie's Titti 'essentials' list were. Questions about why you couldn't put your spinach on the same plate as your meat. Questions about why, when you went to a florist, it was clear that the uni-bunch — one big bunch of the same type of flower — was considered the height of vulgarity. Questions about why so many Italian men over the age of thirty and even forty and even fifty still lived with their parents and had their dinner cooked by their mum every night. Questions about why, whenever there was an advert for a food festival, the boast was always of the *'antichi sapori'* ('ancient, traditional flavours') that would be on show to experience and never, ever of a new flavour or experimental taste to sample. Questions about why parents bundled up their children in a million furry layers on a mild autumn day because they were terrified of them catching cold; and then put them on the back of a scooter without a helmet. Questions about why nobody else seemed to have noticed the comic marvel that was the fact that the man who runs the 'second-hand' shop in Tolentino only has one hand.

I also tried to get my head around Italian popular musical tastes. My main research tool had been the radio, and a range of stations united by jingles so awful that they almost make you glad of Chris Moyles.

Our extensive listening had shown that Italians seemed to be in the grips of an '80s love affair so intense that it far exceeded any affection there had been for the '80s first time around. Simple Minds, Propaganda, Yazoo, the Thompson Twins, Boy George – there was no end to it. Of all the strange predictions people had made about our life out here, 'You will listen to an awful lot of Culture Club' was never among them.

Other cultural divides were still more mysterious: only now were we realizing the depths of something as apparently straightforward as gift-giving.

I remember years ago, studying anthropology, learning of a famous tribe who on the outside appeared to be pacifists because they never engaged in violence, or bloodshed, or killing in the way that many of their tribal contemporaries did. Rather, they had developed a way of waging war that involved no weapons, no armour, no attacks in the dead of night, but something much more subtle and much, much more deadly. Presents.

The gift-giving rituals they entered into were as complicated in the planning and execution as any war and the message always much the same – basically, 'We wipe our arse on you.' The explanation, or as I vaguely recall it from Malinowski, was all to do with power. If I give you a gift that I know you do not have the means to reciprocate, I either bankrupt you trying (i.e. I win), or I humiliate you by you having to admit the fact that you cannot reciprocate (i.e. I win). It is a simple power equation that anyone who has spent a family Christmas in England should be able to comprehend with ease. In this tribe's case, the gifts would become sensationally gigantic – their entire herd of goats, for example, or all the females in the village. Handing over such a stash of booty said, 'You are the son of a devil and your sons are sons of devils' so much more eloquently than words ever could.

I feared we were involved in a modern Italian version of such a ritual.

The key players were us and 'the hunter'. It had all started one day in our olive grove when we met him first in the shape of some clues: a range of red, blue and green rifle shells, a tiny battered Ford Fiesta parked at the top of our driveway, a stinky dog, a hat. Then finally the hunter himself, rifle in hand, dog at side, hat on head (car still parked up top because our rickety drive was too much, evidently, even for the hunter).

Jason is a vegetarian and loves animals. I'm not bothered about animals but I do love Jason. Between us, we both felt we didn't quite like the idea of someone coming and shooting things in our olive grove. In our lukewarm, half-hearted greeting of the hunter, we liked to think that our complex moral objections to the taking of life came through via a facial expression which gently but clearly said, 'We are delighted to be your neighbours and are indeed very keen to fit in with most of your incomprehensible country ways and rituals and we both have a keen need to be liked and accepted so are actually quite prepared to swallow our pride in many respects;

however, if you could keep the rifle sort of in the back of the car when you're in our manor, that would be really nice, thank you and do come round for tea sometime, bring the wife.'

The hunter left and we thought little more of it.

Later that day, the hat and then the hunter reappeared, carrying something scarier than a rifle. A gift. A gift in the form of a bottle of home-brewed *vino cotto*. An exquisitely chosen gift, it said, 'I am a true local' (*vino cotto*, 'cooked wine', was the one thing that even people who lived more than 10 miles away would know our village, Loro Piceno, for); it said, 'I am privy to customs and traditions that you can only dream of'; it said, 'I have toiled with these honest grubby farmer hands to make this symbol of hedonism for you'; and finally and most damningly it said, 'You cannot make things, the best you can do is get drunk on my gift.' And no, thank you, he wouldn't stay to have a glass.

We were flummoxed, the more so as we drained the bottle. Was this a sign that he had understood our wordless objections and was apologizing for any offence caused? Or was he more simply and more probably saying, 'Thank you for allowing me to hunt on your land'?

The Ford Fiesta and the stinky dog were already in situ by the time we got up the next morning. Jason was all for going and telling him outright, 'Get off my land,' but I thought we shouldn't be so direct. Not least because how would this country man who probably had enormous respect for animals and no experience of factory farming or the like understand an argument based on vegetarianism? And anyway, we were new; we didn't want to make enemies, so better to befriend him and then, once bonded, try to start explaining how we felt about guns and little tiny helpless animals and whatnot.

And so things trundled on for a while, him gaily massacring wildlife all over our land and us smiling weakly. Until one day, I hit on a brilliant idea. We should give him a return gift! I didn't know why it seemed so brilliant but I was as sure as any Malinowski-described tribe that it was somehow the right thing and would help restore the crooked balance of the power relationship. And we had the perfect thing – a bottle of *our* home-made lemon olive oil. It said, 'We might be foreigners but we can play at your local customs and rituals'; it said, 'We know that olive oil is the nectar of gods but see how we have dared to blaspheme and pollute it with lemons and to enjoy the results of our blasphemy'; it said, 'We have toiled with these clean media-savvy hands to make something for you to enjoy on a piece of barely cooked meat you have probably just slaughtered on our premises.'

We took it round immediately, and since he wasn't at home, left it with a little note by his back door. We returned home, satisfied. Our front door had hardly closed behind us when we heard the sound of someone outside. It was the hunter. We saw something huge in his hands and feared it was the rifle and that we had sinned. But no, it was a bottle, two, three, four times the size of any normal bottle; in fact, the largest bottle I had ever seen. And it was filled with *vino cotto*.

The hunter hoisted it onto the kitchen table, smiled fulsomely, said, 'Thank you for the oil,' and was gone into the night.

The Loro Piceno Shield

Our local butcher is eccentric, not least because he likes to be referred to by his stage name, PepeCotto. Last time I visited PepeCotto (and I visit unusually regularly for a vegetarian) he serenaded me with music from Fellini's *Dolce Vita*. He played it on a trumpet made of dried pig skin and cartilage. I had worn one of those grins that you have to hold for much longer than is comfortable.

Another time he showed me the dinosaur he had carved from fat, and another one a painter's palette he'd hewn from a shoulder bone, modelling the latter as if he were Raphael. But he obviously knew his meat. His locally famous creation is *lo Scudo Piceno*, the Piceno Shield. It is hard to get the exact details of how he makes it as he has patented it, but it is essentially the part of a cow called the chuck and the blade wrapped. He leaves the bits of muscles and tendons attached to it and stuffs them with salt, pepper, rosemary, thyme, bay leaf and some juniper berries. It's then wrapped in fat and covered in bacon. Apparently it tastes delicious – at least Cathy and Rosie and most of Loro Piceno think so.

Twice-cooked biscuits

Ingredients
00 flour – 300g
Honey – 200g
Eggs – 4
Almonds – 130g toasted and skinned
Dry yeast – 1 teaspoon

Our organic inspector, Tiberio, makes organic honey. He has to drive his beehives deep into the Sibillini Mountains so that they are at least three miles from any conventional farming. I guess somebody worked out that bees can't fly more than three miles. He's a lovely guy and gave me a recipe for honey biscotti. Biscotti means twice cooked, which refers to the fact that you cook them once, in a long chunk, then cut them up and shove them back in the oven to dry them out a bit more. They are even better, crunchier and drier after a couple of days. We eat them with tea but they're also great dipped in vino cotto.

Preheat the oven to 180ºC /gas mark 4. Combine all the ingredients and mix well into a gooey dough. Roll a flat cylinder about 4cm wide. Place on some greaseproof paper on a baking tray and cook in the oven for 20 minutes until golden. Cut into biscuits 1cm thick and put them back in the oven on the baking tray. Serve cold with a cup of Earl Grey every afternoon for the next week.

11 The 'other' press machine

Getting publicity is a necessary evil of any new business venture. I hate trying to get publicity. I hate it with such disproportionate passion that I think I must have had a past life as a press officer for a landmine manufacturer. I hated it when I worked in TV and I found that I still hate it just as much.

I'm sure the British press are worse than elsewhere. When we lived in America, it wasn't so bad because displaying enthusiasm is not against the law for journalists there. The British species, for some motive that I suspect is based on the quest to appear cool, maintain an air of determined disinterest. And that's even the ones who end up writing nice things about you. There's this ridiculous ritual which involves both sides trying to out-disdain one another. It's ridiculous because clearly this is a symbiotic relationship: we needed them to publicize our company, they needed us to fill their columns. Is it a hatred of this need that makes both sides so resentful?

Reflections aside, the fact was Christmas was looming large. And for any company selling what was essentially a gift item, Christmas was crucial. So far, fewer than thirty of our trees had been adopted, which was barely enough to cover the cost of a hire van to take the oil back to the UK. We needed something to happen to get the word of our adoption scheme out to lots of people. Which in turn meant swallowing this hatred problem and getting on with it. Which in turn meant raking through address books to exploit any contact past or present who might be able to help us turn our lovely idea into some bits of ink on a soon-to-be-thumbed page.

One such contact was the wife of someone Jason used to work with in TV. She was a freelance journalist who had been known to write for such publications as the *Observer Food Monthly*. THE *OBSERVER FOOD MONTHLY*! That was our ticket to the big time.

190

She said she'd have a word with the editor about our scheme as she thought it would be 'right up her alley'. We waited a polite number of days before following anything up – a casual e-mail asking about the children, the husband, before dropping in a throwaway question about whether she'd had a chance to mention anything about us to the editor of ... now what was it ... the *Telegraph*? Oh no, that *Observer* supplement, whatever it's called, wasn't it? The expectant wait for a reply was soon rewarded with a long e-mail detailing the extra-curricular exploits of the various children, and then at the end saying, 'Oh yes, I did mention it. She is really keen on you.'

Oh my God. The editor of the *Observer Food Monthly*, a supplement probably read by any person ever likely to adopt one of our olive trees, was really keen on us. Tra la tra la. We danced around the house.

A few days later, a timescale carefully judged to appear not too keen but equally (given the positive feedback from her at the top, and our loathing of journalists who appear unenthusiastic) not too blasé, we dropped said editor a line, outlining our scheme, sending pretty pictures, inviting a journalist out to help with the harvest, flattering her about her publication, getting down on all fours – you can imagine. We told ourselves that we didn't expect a reply immediately as, of course, she must be terribly busy – but we both twitched whenever the inbox pinged.

The inbox never pinged with her ping. We spoke to our mutual friend again about a week later, the questions about the children and the family becoming more cursory as we asked her for more clues about how precisely this editor's 'keenness' on us had been expressed and what might be a good next move. She proclaimed the silence to be 'most strange' and promised to try to give her a prod. Another week and another nothing.

In the meantime we had sent out more than 200 press releases to journalists and food writers. An obliging friend had given us his only-one-year-out-of-date copy of the directory of the Guild of Food Writers and we had worn it out. We had sent press releases to every national newspaper, weeklies and Sundays, and about forty magazines which had any sort of features of a food/style/ lifestyle/design bent. We spun our story as one of a radical new way of doing business, putting customers in touch with the provenance of their food, we spun it as a life-change story about two TV producers and presenters who'd chucked it all in to 'live the good life' (we crossed our fingers as we wrote that one), we spun it as a simple 'Perfect Christmas gift for the foodie who has everything' idea – there was nowhere off bounds. We hoped that our genuine passion for our adoption idea would come across no matter what the spin was – in the muck of the desperate press whoring, we had to keep reminding ourselves that we had a really great idea that we really believed in.

Writing press releases, sleuthing e-mail addresses and sending e-mails was all fine, I didn't mind that bit. The bit I really hated was when, inevitably, a week later not a soul (Out of Office Auto-assistants don't count) had replied and I had to get on the phone to chase them. I say 'I' because this job had somehow, despite my loathing, become mine; Jason said I was really good at it, something I think he believed, but which was also a clever delegational ruse.

I felt my tone faltering even in the first sentence. But then I heard an 'ahem' on the line and that offered enough encouragement; it

was going well! I carried on: 'Yes and the idea came to us when ...'
'... and we've already had lots of people adopt trees' ... 'I think
people like to know where their food has come from' ... that was
surely enough. I paused. 'Let me just put you through to editorial.
What did you say your name was?' Oh no, I had given my soul to
the receptionist again. And so it went on, being passed from one
person to another, with the occasional glimmer of interest, even an
order (birthday present for father-in- law), but nothing that felt substantial enough to base our future success on.

Then Jason decided on a different tack. He sent a photograph
of Rosie looking sad, with a note in fake child scrawl underneath
saying, 'I won't get any Christmas presents unless my mum and dad
sell some olive oil', to our friend Mike who was a journalist and
who probably already felt implicated, having been there at the birth
of our scheme.

The success of this approach showed me why politicians, even
knowing the pitfalls, cling onto babies with such gusto. There is
something in this formula that just works. Within a few days, our e-
mails had obviously done the rounds, and we had a call from
someone at The Times and one from someone from the
Independent, both saying they wanted to feature the adoption
scheme in pre-Christmas gift-related publicity.

Hallelujah! Santa Claus is coming to town!

Inevitably, post the huge 'up' of our press coup, came a down. I
think maybe we were just exhausted. The harvest had been going
on, on and off, for nearly six weeks, which meant early starts and
physical fatigue. And in the days in between harvesting we had
been relentlessly hammering away at the publicity, which resulted in

a completely different kind of fatigue — mental, emotional, life-questioning. At the same time, we were trying to make sure that Rosie had a nice life, so were also putting lots of energy into post-Titti activities for her that took us all till bedtime.

But the fact was, for the last week we had both been feeling pretty miserable. The constant, hopeless, possibility-less world of constant fog certainly hadn't helped, nor had the constant cold, and Jason and I had been taking turns to be narky with each other. We were gradually coming to realize that in this new life where we lived and worked together — and did both things under the same roof — there was little escape. Whereas before we had done our separate things and then enjoyed the time we'd come together, now we didn't have that luxury. Instead, there were a hundred roles we had to fulfil for one another: we were parents, lovers, business partners, co-workers, co-habitees; we were each other's bosses and each other's colleagues; we were each other's only real friends here; we were confidants, critics, encouragers, sceptics, chefs, sous-chefs, wind-down friends, rev-up friends; we were meant to inspire, improve, amuse, entertain, stimulate, fancy, challenge, support each other. No wonder we turned to Rosie for light relief and a chase around the kitchen on hands and knees.

Thankfully, we did manage sometimes to laugh at our plight. We imagined going to see a psychologist to talk about why we were feeling miserable and pictured the answer:

'Why aren't you happy? Yes, isn't it an unfathomable mystery? Only a couple of months ago you gave up your jobs and your security and a lovely flat in London, moved to a country where you don't speak the language, started doing a job that is completely new and which you have no skills for, with no promise of earning any money, and live in the middle of the countryside where you don't know any-one. You'd like to phone your friends and family at home but you can't really because you don't have a phone, so you think "Oh well I'll e-mail them instead" but your e-mail connection doesn't work. Oh, and you're cold all the time because the heating doesn't work. Hmmm. Yes I wonder why it could be. I think this will take us sever-al sessions.'

Fat chips
shallow fried in olive oil

Ingredients for 2 people
Potatoes
Olive oil – 100–200ml
Sunflower oil – 100–200ml
Maldon sea salt

There's nothing like an honest meal to bolster up the spirits. In London we'd nip down the Golden Hind on Marylebone Lane for some honest fish and chips. The friendly Greek chaps who run the place would do me battered feta in place of the cod. Loro Piceno isn't exactly overrun with chip shops, but feta is on sale at the big supermarket half an hour away. Time to cook up a greasy perk-me-up.

Cut the potatoes lengthways into thick angular wedges with their skins on. Place in a pan of cold water, bring to the boil and cook until par-boiled. This stage is very important if you're to get fat crisp chips with a floury cooked centre. Take them out before they are falling apart and drain well. Into your frying pan pour the 50:50 mix of olive oil and sunflower oil. The olive oil is for flavour and the sunflower oil is for its high frying temperature. Fry them, turning over occasionally, until they are crispy and brown. Transfer them to a sieve to drain or onto some kitchen towel. Sprinkle with Maldon sea salt and serve.

Battered feta cheese

Ingredients for 2 people
Flour – 65g
Salt – ¹/₂ tablespoon
Egg – 1
Water/milk – 100ml total
Feta – 200g
Sunflower oil – lots

Sieve the flour and salt into a mixing bowl. Crack the egg into the middle and gently beat it into the flour with a balloon whisk. Slowly pour in the liquid and continue to whisk to make a smooth batter. Cover it and stand for at least half an hour. Beat it again before using.

Cut the feta into long thin fingers (like 2 by 2 by 8cm or so, depending on the dimensions of the chunk you have) so you have about 8 (4 fingers each is about enough of this rich salty cheese). If your feta is like the stuff we get here and slightly wet, put some flour on a plate and roll each finger lightly in the flour.

Fill a frying pan with 1cm of sunflower oil and heat. Once the oil is just starting to smoke, dip the cheese in the batter and carefully place in the frying pan. Leave for a minute until brown and then turn over. If you have a deep fryer use that, if not, shallow fry like this and be careful. Once the batter is crispy and brown, take the feta out and place on some kitchen towel. You should be able to do this in a couple of batches. Serve as soon as you can.

Real ketchup
with Italian tomatoes

Ingredients

Tomatoes – 500g Italian vine tomatoes
Olive oil – 1 tablespoon
Balsamic vinegar – 1 tablespoon and 1 teaspoon
Sugar – 4 teaspoons
Garlic – 2 cloves
Basil – 10 large leave
Thyme – leaves from five 10cm stalks
Salt

Preheat the oven to 200°C /gas mark 6. Cut the tomatoes in half and place them, cut side up, in an ovenware pot. Sprinkle oil, a tablespoon of vinegar and the sugar over the tops of the tomatoes.

Roughly chop the garlic, basil and thyme and hide between the tomatoes.

Put in the oven, near the top, for 40 minutes. Take out of oven and add a teaspoon of balsamic. Blend in short bursts to get it going, then give it a good 40 seconds of continuous blending. Press the mixture through a fine sieve.

Artichoke and pea bruschetta

Ingredients
Young small artichokes – ¹/₄kg
Fresh or frozen peas – 100g podded
Salt and pepper
Parmesan cheese – 50g grated
Extra virgin olive oil – 2 tablespoons
Lemon juice – a few squirts
Bread

Even when the chips are down there is nothing more satisfying than buying food direct from the producer. No middle man, no excess food miles and you can see from the way they treat their produce how much love has gone into it. We bought a load of artichokes from a guy called Pepe, who'd driven about half a ton of them up from Sicily in his knackered old Suzuki van.

Rip off the outer leaves of the artichokes until you get to the inner part where the leaves are paler and tender. Then cut down the tops to just above the widest part. You should end up with about 100g of the good bits. As soon as each one is prepared, throw it in a bowl of cold water with a bit of lemon juice.

Boil the artichokes until they are tender when you stick a fork in. Pod the peas and put them in a pan of boiling water for a few minutes till they are cooked. They don't take long.

Put the drained and cooked peas and artichokes into a bowl, add salt, pepper, grated parmesan, olive oil and a squirt of lemon juice. Mash up with the back of a fork. Grill some bread, drizzle over a bit of olive oil, sprinkle over some salt and fork on a mound of the mixture. Serve warm.

12 Jingle bells

With the harvest finally over and Rosie about to break up, we had decided to go back to London about ten days before Christmas. We were desperately hoping that, by a miracle, we'd have a rush of orders right to the last Christmas Eve minute and would need the wonders of the post office to deliver them on time.

We'd pushed the limits of our Ryanair baggage allowance (admittedly not too difficult) not with Christmas presents like all our fellow travellers, but with olive tree adoption certificates and booklets. Jason and I always disagree over estimates of these sorts of things. I'd said let's take back 100 of everything, he'd said let's take 500, I'd said, that's ridiculous, he'd agreed that was maybe a bit much and we settled on 250. Given that our total orders to date, in two and a half months of business, had come to just over thirty, it was still pretty optimistic.

A few hours later we were unpacking our things into a miniature flat in London. When we had visitors to Italy they always went on about how we must just love having all this space, but our secret truth is that we must be half squirrel or something, because all three of us actually really like being cheek by jowl in a tiny cosy place. And the fact that in this flat we could turn on the only radiator and the whole place would be baking within half an hour felt like a wonder of modernity and luxury.

Jason was wandering around the flat carrying the laptop, stopping at different points for a while, then usually saying 'bugger' before moving on somewhere else. He was trying to find a friendly open-access wireless connection, there's usually one buzzing round here somewhere. Finally, with the bathroom window propped open and the laptop hanging halfway out, he said 'Yessss.'

It was always a toss up for Jason whether to look first for new orders or at the BBC Sports website. This time, the orders won. There was a pause. Too long a pause. Then the slightly forlorn but trying not to show it face appeared. 'Nope,' he said, ' nothing yet.'

The good thing about getting disappointing news when we were back in London was there were lots of gluttonish indulgences to cheer us. The thoughts of baked beans on toast, or halloumi stir-fried with harissa and ridiculously out of season vegetables, or even, gasp, a curry takeaway, were enough to make us swoon. So it wasn't long before we were eating ourselves out of trouble.

'We can't expect miracles,' said Jason, clearly meaning that he thought we should.

The next day I'd decided that doing a bit of Christmas shopping and taking Rosie to the park was a better bet than sitting in the flat, waiting for a decent interval (say, eight minutes) before rechecking the order situation. There was a fantastic park within walking distance, Coram's Fields, where they had ducks and rabbits and sheep – as well as the usual assortment of playground stuff. It made me think that if we could pull off a life that is in the countryside but with bursts of proper city (i.e. the city city, not the suburbs) then Rosie would be a lucky blighter. She'd have the excitement of visiting friends with donkeys and baby goats and sheep and seeing tractors farming fields and hay-baling – all things that children love in the country – and then get to go on the underground and double deck-ers and be among bustle and buskers and chaos – all other things that children love in the city.

We checked in with J from time to time, but there was no news. And after a while he even prised himself away from the computer. We spent a few hours just enjoying walking around London in the winter. It was a funny sort of a holiday though. First because it still felt more like we were coming home than being on holiday. And secondly because we really didn't want to be on holiday, we wanted to be rushed off our feet with orders and to be filled with adrenalin and panic.

The next morning, I went out quite early to go to a favourite bookshop in Marylebone. It's called Daunt Books and has an amazing collection of travel books. As such, it is always an interesting arbiter of Le Marche's growing stature in the world of the tourist. When we were about to make our first trip to the region, the best we could find by way of guidebook was one called *Tuscany, Umbria and Le Marche*. It managed a mention of Urbino, with a nod to its importance in the Renaissance – but not much else. Then the next time there was one which had Le Marche in as big a font size as the big guys. Then this time, to my excitement, there was a book dedicated to little old Le Marche all by itself. I could hardly have felt prouder if Rosie had written it.

As I left and was strolling down Marylebone High Street thinking about what an incredibly charmed life we had led there and wasn't it amazing that we used to happily pay nearly £2 for a cup of coffee every day without even really thinking about it, my mobile rang and it was Jason. Excitement twitched in his voice.

Have you seen the *Independent*?' he said. 'We're in it. I haven't seen it but people have been writing to tell us. And we've had eight orders already today!'

I looked at my watch, which said 10.45. I was most impressed at the efficiency of the weekending British public.

'I'll get a copy and come straight back,' I said.

The piece in the *Independent* couldn't have been more perfect. It was in a special supplement called '50 Best Christmas Presents for Men' and today was Saturday 17th December, so just a week before Christmas. It was perfect timing and it was the perfect target – inasmuch as if anyone else is like me that's the time when you've got all the easy lady presents and are just about to tackle the impossible men. And down there in print, 'Adopt an olive tree' seemed the perfect answer to the conundrum. They even said it was good value.

By the time I'd jumped on the tube and got home an hour later, we were up to thirteen orders and did a celebratory dance around the living room. Then Jason showed me some of the comments that people had made with their orders and it nearly made us cry. Anyone who had bothered to say anything said what a brilliant idea it was, or what a beautiful website or thank you for solving their Christmas present problems or how clever we were. We wallowed in it for a good ten minutes before thinking how we were actually going to do these orders.

Logging each order was a bit complicated because we had to take all the information from it off the website and put it into our master tree document. In doing so, we double checked postcodes, verified spellings of names for the certificates, confirmed which grove the adopter wanted, and logged where they wanted both the initial certificate and the later produce sent. All of which was fine if you concentrated, but that became tricky when the only way to do all this involved standing in the bath tub, leaning out of the window, scribbling down the information on a piece of paper to re-enter in the computer in the other room where there was at least a horizontal surface. Once *there*, Rosie inevitably wanted to have 'just one' go on the computer keyboard, which risked destabilizing the whole already fragile system. Finally, because everything was done by hand and with old-fashioned ink, we had to lay out all the certificates all over the living-room floor to dry.

We needed another solution. And we found it in the 24-hour internet café attached to the back of a corner shop up the road, the smell of freshly fried samosas filling the air. It cost £1 an hour to use one of their computers and meant I could get all the orders off the internet and into our uber-document in peace. Then at the end of the day, once Rosie was asleep, we could turn the computer document into the handwritten bundles ready to send out.

By the end of the day we'd had thirty-nine orders. More in a day than in the previous two months. That was why we whored ourselves out to the press; whoring paid.

The following day there was another small piece in the *Sunday Times* food section, and a sudden burst of orders from Ireland gave us the first clue that there was also something in the *Irish Times*. And so the orders just kept coming in, right the way up to Christmas Day.

And we really couldn't have been happier. Each evening, we'd finish dinner and get Rosie into bed, then clear the furniture into the corner of the room so that we had maximum floor space to lay out all the written certificates and envelopes on the floor. Once they were dry, we had the satisfying task of packing them all up and stamping them ready to go in the post first thing.

When the pile of certificates was starting to look a little low, Jason admitted with a grin that he'd stuck in an extra hundred of everything without my knowledge – except the little note cards which we had to hurriedly get printed at the Prontaprint place up the road. 'Told you,' he said. Thank God for his daft optimism.

By Christmas Day, 346 trees had been adopted. But more important even than the number of trees was the fact we felt that we had had an idea that people 'got'. Not just friends doing us a favour. This was an idea that people liked. An idea they would pay money for and be excited to give as a gift. An idea that just maybe we could earn a living from.

The Christmas turkey had never tasted so fine.

Back in Italy, with our clutch of Christmas orders, it was time to get serious about how to realize our promised packages of oil. Looking at all the 50-litre barrels of oil filling up our cellar was very satisfying, but there was still a long way to go to get that oil into some state to arrive on people's doorsteps.

Our 'to do' list for the few weeks ahead included:

Find out where to get tins or bottles for oil
Find out where to get labels for tins/bottles
Find out where to get boxes to pack up tins/bottles
Find out how to send boxes to UK
Find out about customs regulations
Find out about courier companies for sending packages out
in the UK

The daunting thing about all this was not that we'd have to have relatively technical discussions about dimensions and nozzle types and bottle shapes and inner and outer box measurements; we knew from our previous work that you could, with a bit of bluffing, a bit of nerve and no fear of looking stupid, find out pretty much anything. The thing this time was that we were going to have to do it all in Italian.

It became an art talking on the phone with a massive

Italian–English dictionary balanced on my lap, sitting back enough from my desk to make room to turn the pages as fast as an assistant on *Countdown*. I had a stack of words looked up in advance, all written on a crib sheet: the words for tins 'suitable for food', the words for different shapes, the words for lids, taps, inner, outer, cylindrical, square-based, round-based and so on.

Next stop, the *Yellow Pages*, which were familiarly, comfortingly yellow even in Italy. I looked up *'lattine'* (tins) but there was nothing there. I looked up *'bottiglie'* (bottles) but there was nothing there either. The thought crossed our minds that maybe all these things were made in China these days and that we were done for. But first a bit of lateral thinking. The Italian language likes to describe things in a roundabout way – it usually has long phrases where English has a single very specific word. Italian, for example, doesn't have a word for a dimple, instead it says 'little hole in the face' – that sort of thing. So I went to the categorized index at the front and thumbed through. There was something which said words to the effect of 'materials for enclosing merchandise' and I patted myself on the back.

I went through a lot of phone calls that morning. The deal was that Jason would keep the supply of coffee coming and say 'Well done' and 'That was brilliant' after each phone call (yes, each one) and I would make the calls. My Italian wasn't really that much more up to the job than his, but I had shed my pride a bit more. And Jason has always called me the 'chancer' with my Italian, in that I would go for a quite ambitious word on the basis of a bit of an understanding of which English words transfer, an added-on vowel ending and a bit of conviction in the delivery followed by a hope-filled pause. So 'intelligent' became *'intelligent-e'*, 'rectangular'

'rettangolar-e' and *'chromosomally inclined' 'chromosomamente inclinato'*. The danger, of course, given that this trick works better the more complex words you use, is that you can come across as far more proficient than you really are. You could go in after some simple tips about cooking a piece of fish and come out with a tract on Dante. But nonetheless it was usually worth a stab and with a bit of a trailing wind, I reckoned on about an 80 percent hit rate.

With this, I went into my list of *'imballagi metallici'* (metal packaging manufacturers). Like anything, a formula began to emerge after a while. Rather than going into our whole life story and trying to explain the adoption scheme (as I foolishly did in early calls, mistaking a puzzled silence for continued interest) I would ask three questions:

Do you make tins?
Do you make half-litre size ones?
Are they suitable for olive oil?

If the answer to any of these was negative, the call was over and we could all get on with our lives. If the answer to all three was positive, I would get so excited that I would start jumbling up my speech even more as I grabbed Jason to pay attention to the one-sided half-Italian bit of the conversation that he could hear.

The first time it happened with a nice man called Signor Perri and I was so shocked I didn't know where to go next.

'Er ... *eccelente* ... *quante costano?* ('Er ....great – er ... how much do they cost?')

'It depends how many you want. The price goes down the more you order.'

'Er ... we want about 2,000.'

'Two thousand units?'

'Well, yes, I mean, um ... is a tin a unit? We want 2,000 tins.'

'Ha ha.'

'I'm sorry?'

'Our minimum order is *una pedana* – a pallet – about 48,000 tins.'

'Oh ... And you couldn't do any less than that?'

'Well, not 46,000 less. I'm sorry.'

Oh, the crushing disappointment. I didn't want to let him go.

'What would be the really minimum minimum? We are a growing company. Soon we will be able to make bigger orders but for now we are just starting out. What would be the really minimum minimum you could do?'

'(Sigh). We could maybe do a half *pedana*, 24,000 tins.'

'That's very kind of you, thank you. Do you by any chance know anywhere that might do smaller quantities?'

'I think you will have trouble. Two thousand is hardly worth sending a truck.'

'Well, thank you very much. We will have a think and call back.'

'*Buon giorno.*'

'*Buon giorno.*'

'Well done, that was brilliant,' said Jason. 'You were brilliant.'

And I did feel a bit brilliant, for once. I was on a high. I had had a whole conversation in Italian on the phone with a tin manufacturer dude and I had understood all of it and he had understood me. The only tiny glitch was that he couldn't help us and thought there was quite possibly nobody who could. Mere details.

It made me realize something about our being here, that phone call. It made me realize that yes, we want to have a really successful company and to have ideas that people are enchanted by, and to be a good business in the sense of playing fair and not ripping anyone off – and all that. But we're also here for ourselves and to learn and to experience new things. And in a way it was as important that I could have a conversation in a new language and in a new world as that it delivered the desired end result. We were here as part of our desire always to be moving 'forward', to be gathering new skills and new knowledge, almost like gamblers addicted to their chips. When Jason and I worked in LA, often Jason would ask me at the end of the day, 'What did you learn today?' I dreaded that question and would often get cross with him for asking it and would answer facetiously saying that 'I had learned something about being able to buy a new dress with the money I had earned' or that 'I had learned that it wasn't important to learn something every single bloody day and couldn't we sometimes just have a day off.' But really it bugged me because it hit a nerve that said you do have to experience something every day. You have to end the day a bit more of a person than you started it or you might as well not have bothered getting up.

Back on the tin hunt, I spoke to another thirty or so places (come on China, there's work to be done here!). Mostly the answer was no – not that size, not that quantity, not suitable for foodstuffs – but by the end of a few days' phone calls, I had found four companies who seemed to do the right thing and who had agreed to send samples. At least I think they had. Either that or they were going to send me their champion, as the word 'campione' seemed to be the same.

We awaited the post with great excitement each day. Each day the postman was surprised but seemed pleased to see our eager faces as we leapt out to greet him to be handed an envelope of junk mail or a bill. On about the fifth day, he said, 'Are you by chance expecting something?'

Playing it cool was out and we admitted that yes, yes, YES! we were.

'I think there is a packet for you at the post office.'

Heart beat, heart beat.

'But, of course, it's closed now for the day.'

Oh my God.

It almost had to be a disappointment. We picked up a Jiffy Bag which contained one slightly dented round tin with a sticky up spout bit that looked perfectly adapted to pouring the oil into the engine of your car. But Signor Aristide from IMSIS still won points for being the first to deliver on his promise.

A week had gone by and we wrestled with whether to call and check on the other champions. Jason said we should definitely call. But, of course, he would since he wasn't the one making the calls. I put it off and put it off until a few days later when Jason was out and I called them in secret – or rather with it being my decision to call, not his command (yes, these are the pathetic office battles that go on when you work with just one other person and that person is your partner).

Of the other three places, two had obviously completely forgotten their promise (a case of different perspectives – what for us was an important life marker was for them a slightly tedious and very small chore) but seemed happy to replace it with a new one. The third place, while also saying that they'd still send a sample, sounded like really they had moved on to fresh pastures and I mentally wrote them off our list of hopefuls.

Within another two weeks (things were really flying now) two other tin samples had arrived, one rectangular but not a very nice rectangle, a bit too thin and tall (who says beggars can't be choosers), and the other a quite straightforward cylindrical tin with a hole in the top and some different coloured plastic lids thrown in to show how it would end up. One of the lids was an almost olivey green.

We had found our tin.

Jason came home one day with a skip in his step. He had been out on a slightly tedious mission to deliver some paperwork about setting up our Italian company to our accountant, so the skip was at first a bit of a mystery. But there was more to the story.

We had for the last week been trying to make some headway with getting hold of the boxes which would hold the tins which would hold the oil for our adopters and keep everything safe in the mail. This was a job which we'd been pretty optimistic about sorting out quickly. You see the main industry in Le Marche is the shoe industry – and if there's one thing which that means apart from the little leather fellows to put your feet in it's the little cardboard things you get the little leather fellows in. And the boxes we'd need would be much the same sort of size and shape as shoe boxes – we just needed a bit more robustness and an 'integrated lid'.

Sure enough, when I got going on research (the trusty *Yellow Pages* and a bit on the internet), I found company after company that seemed to be responsible for 'boxes for containing things'. I decided that, as a first pass, e-mail was the easiest method for determining out who was in and out. I composed a multiply checked e-mail in my best Italian that outlined our requirements of dimensions, materials, the purpose to which the box was to be put and the fact that it would have to survive the worst that Italian and British couriers could in combination throw at it. I said how many we would need, but that we understood the minimum order might be higher and that we could be flexible and wondered if they could be so kind as to let me know whether this was something they might be able to help with.

I sent out thirty-four of these small but (I thought) perfectly formed e-mails to thirty-four companies with exotic sounding names boasting their packaging credentials. Some of the names I even recognized from signs I'd seen by the roadside, interspersed among the ubiquitous 'Sexy Shop' advertisements.

I didn't receive one reply. Not even one. I couldn't believe it. These were all companies who had some sort of 'web presence', as I believe it's called — otherwise I wouldn't have had an e-mail address for them. But not one of them bothered to reply to my e-mail. Not even to say they couldn't help, not even to laugh at my Italian, not even to say 'Go Home English'.

But that day when Jason had gone out to drop off boring forms with our accountant, he had driven right past a company called, rather catchily, 'SIOS', which stands for Scatolificio Imballaggi Ondulati Settempedano so it's easy to see why an acronym appealed. We'd talked about them when I was sending out the e-mails, as we both recognized the name from signs we drove past every day — drove past but never twigged that 'Scatolificio' meant box shop. We'd talked about how nice and cosy it might be if our box suppliers turned out to be really local and how we'd feel better about not wasting yet more money and environment transporting goods halfway around the country.

So that day he'd decided to try the human touch. He'd approached a large automatic gate with an intercom at the side and, with a big breath, pushed the button. After a time, a voice greeted him with a questioning *'Buon giorno?'*

Jason replied, *'Buon giorno. Vorrei ordinare qualche scatola per piacere'* ('Good morning, I would like to order some boxes please').

The machine paused.

'Spiace', it said, *'ma le facciamo solamente al'ingrosso. Non vendiamo direttamente al pubblico.'* ('Sorry but we're wholesalers. We don't sell to private customers').

'Oh, OK,' said Jason, in a mopish English way. *'Grazie.'*

And he walked away disconsolately. But then he thought about it and realized, hang on a minute here, I'm not a private customer, we have a business, a business with the same name as our builder albeit, but we've got a P.IVA (VAT) number and everything now.

A few minutes later, he headed back to the metal voice. 'I'm not a private person,' he said when a wary voice said *'Buon giorno'* again.

'Oh, OK,' said the machine. And then it said 'Buzzzz' and he was in.

He was led up some stairs into a tiny meeting room filled with boxes of all different shapes and sizes. Eventually a lady called Fabiola came to meet him. Jason's Italian was not great at this point but she was patient as he managed to explain what it was he wanted. There was even the faintest trace of recognition as he mentioned that his wife had sent an e-mail a couple of weeks ago outlining our needs. Luckily with all those boxes lying around, he could deploy the old-style point and nod head or point and shake head technique of descriptive communication. It got trickier with more conceptual things like using recycled cardboard – something it's harder to point to unless you're in the know. Instead he described wanting to use 'material with trees cut down less please'.

Of course, Jason being Jason, he also wanted our boxes to be beautiful. He is unstoppable (I know because I try) when it comes to making that extra effort on presentation – well, on anything actually. Where I would have settled for pretty much any old box that fitted the tins well and which would mean they'd arrive intact, he wanted to have white boxes, in recycled card, printed on the side with the Nudo signature olive tree and the 'Nudo Adopt an olive tree' logo.

And so it was that he came away having made a friend in Fabiola. One thing we are starting to realize about Italians – and maybe it's more widely true of anyone who takes a professional approach – is that they like people to know what they want and they respect people who have exacting demands. It is common to see ladies in the butcher examining five different pieces of meat before they decide on the one that they will buy. This fussiness is seen as an essential part of the shopping process and I wonder whether the explanation for it lies in the recentness of Italy's peasant past. If you are a peasant, any parting with your money is treated with absolute seriousness, with no space at all for reckless consumerism. So fussiness is respected, shopping nonchalance is not. It's not just with food either. If you go into one of the many little clothes shops (round us there are no Gaps or Zaras or H&Ms, only tiny one-man-band clothes shops) and ask for a 'black shirt' you will be treated with a certain disdain, whereas if you say you are looking for a 'black shirt, with three-quarter-length sleeves, a collar that is slightly rounded at the tips but not so much as to be too feminine, tailored at the waist with darts not pleats and ideally with no more than five buttons' you will be whisked straight into the changing room.

And so it was with Fabiola and Jason. They were united in box

216

love and box detailing and he came away knowing that we were
going to get beautiful boxes made to measure. Hence the skip.

Halloumi stir-fried with harissa

Ingredients for 4 people
Halloumi – 400g
Red onion – 2 medium
Garlic – 2 cloves
Courgettes – 2 medium
Red pepper – ½
Green pepper – ½
Mushrooms – 200g
Olive oil – 3 tablespoons
Toasted sesame oil – 2 tablespoons
Lemon – 1 big
Chilli – 1 or more
(depending on how poky the harissa is)
Salt and pepper and any herbs you have handy like parsley
Rose harissa – 2 tablespoons of this or any other quality harissa you can find
Rice – 4 handfuls

Cut the cheese and vegetables into rough chunks and put in a big bowl. Pour over the olive oil and sesame oil. Squeeze over the juice of the lemon. Finely chop the chilli and any herbs you feel like adding and throw them in. Dollop in 2 tablespoonfuls of harissa. Add a couple of pinches of salt and several grinds of pepper, then mix it all up with your hands so everything is evenly coated. Leave for at least half an hour.

Bring a pan of water to the boil and cook the rice according to the instructions on the package. Heat up a wok (don't add any more oil) and throw in the cheese and veg mix, keeping back the juicy marinade you find at the bottom of the bowl. Allow some bits to get nice and crisp and burnt but generally keep moving the mix around. Once it's cooked put it back in the bowl and coat with the marinade. Drain the rice and serve a heap of it with a portion of the halloumi and vegetables on top and more harissa on the side.

Taverna Loro

Just when we were pulling our hair out at the limited local restaurant options, Matteo and Gian Paolo opened a new one in our tiny village. At Taverna Loro it's basically traditional cooking shaped by local availability and seasonal changes but with a modern kick up the bum. They even let me into the kitchen to see how they did a couple of our favourite dishes.

We Northern Europeans are big believers in measurements being followed to the letter, but as with Italian cooking in general Gian Paolo uses a substantial drizzle of intuition. His patient response to my insistent questions about specific quantities was 'al'occhio', 'by eye'. To satiate our Anglo-Saxon addictions I've filled in the missing gaps as best I can.

Focaccia

Ingredients for 1 loaf
Fresh yeast – 10g
Water – 125ml
Flour – 250g
Extra virgin olive oil – 25ml
Rock or Maldon sea salt – 10g

For onion and rosemary version
White onion – 1 roughly chopped
Olive oil – 1 tablespoon
Rosemary – 1 sprig

For black olive and oregano version
Pitted black olives – 100g chopped in halves
Olive oil – 1 tablespoon
Oregano – 1 tablespoon of chopped
fresh leaves

Add the yeast to the water, then add the flour and olive oil and mix until the dough comes away from the sides of the bowl. Now either turn it onto a floury surface and knead for 10 minutes or put it in a food mixer with a dough hook.

Put it back in the bowl, cover and leave to rest for half an hour in a warm spot (or by a radiator if it's winter), until it doubles in size. Mix your preferred toppings while you wait.

When the dough is ready roll it out till it's 1cm thick and put on a baking tray. Now the fun, messy bit: scatter the topping of choice over the top and use your fingers to press it into the dough at regular intervals. Then sprinkle over a couple of pinches of rock salt or Maldon salt. Leave it on the baking tray until it doubles in thickness, at least half an hour. There's no need to cover it.

Preheat the oven to 200ºC /gas mark 6. Cook the focaccia for 30 minutes, cut it up into strips and eat it as soon as it doesn't burn your tongue.

Pumpkin flowers stuffed with sheep's ricotta

Fiori di zucca con ricotta di pecora

Ingredients for 4 people

For the sauce:
Onion – 1 medium
Extra virgin olive oil – 100ml
Tomatoes – 250g
Basil – several leaves
Salt to taste

Sheep's ricotta – 400g
Sage – 10g
Parsley – 10g
Basil – 10g
Chives – 10g
Marjoram – 10g
Thyme – 10g
Courgette/pumpkin flowers – 12

This looks fiddly, but if you can get some beautifully fresh courgette flowers (try your local farmers' market in the summer) it's as easy, or even easier, than pie.

For the sauce, finely chop the onion and fry in a little olive oil for a few minutes, then add the chopped tomatoes, chopped basil and a pinch of salt. Cover and cook for 30 minutes on a very low heat. Add a couple of tablespoons of water if necessary.

While this is cooking mix together the stuffing for the flowers. Just put the ricotta and all the finely chopped herbs in a bowl and mix well. Cut the flowers away from their stems and slit them open along the side so you can roll them out flat. Gian Paolo then uses an icing bag to squeeze a neat, fat tube of filling into the open petals, but some careful spooning works just as well. Then roll the petals back up and place on a well-oiled baking tray. Preheat the oven to 200°C /Gas mark 6.

Back to the sauce – once it's cooked pass it through a food strainer (you could use a fine sieve and wooden spoon if you don't have a strainer) into a bowl. Then add the rest of the olive oil as you whiz the mixture with a hand blender, forming a slight emulsion.

Cook the stuffed flowers for 10 minutes. Place them 3 to a plate and pour over the sauce. Decorate with some fresh herbs and serve.

Potato soup with pig's cheek

Crema di patate con guanciale

Ingredients for 4 people
Olive oil – for frying
Onion – 1
Potatoes – 6 peeled and sliced
Vegetable stock – 1.5 litres
Guanciale/pancetta/unsmoked bacon – 200g

Heat the oil in a saucepan, add the sliced onion, cook for 5 minutes, then add the potatoes and cook for another 10 minutes. Season with salt and pepper and pour in the stock. Lower the heat and cook for 1 hour, when the potatoes will have broken up and thickened. Blend to a velvety, fine texture with a hand blender and check for seasoning.

Cut the meat into thin slices and fry in olive oil for 5 minutes until slightly crispy. Serve the soup with a small mound of crispy meat on top, drizzle on some extra virgin olive oil and garnish with a sprig of marjoram.

Strawberry pannacotta with balsamic

Ingredients for 6 people
Gelatine – 4 sheets
Strawberries – 200g
Fresh cream – 1 litre
Sugar – 220g
Vanilla – 1 pod
Balsamic vinegar – a few drizzles

Fill a small bowl with cold water; add the gelatine and leave to soak. Mash up 100g of strawberries. Mix together the cream with 170g of sugar, the mashed strawberries and the whole vanilla pod. Bring this to the boil over a low heat, stirring constantly. As it boils, immediately remove from the heat, take out the vanilla pod and stir in the softened gelatine sheets. Once they have dissolved strain the mixture. Pour the mix into individual ramekins and refrigerate for at least a couple of hours. They will keep for a few days.

To make the sauce, blend together 100g of fresh strawberries with 50g of sugar. Use thick balsamic vinegar (or better still, sapa) to add a pattern to the sauce. It's a bit 1970s looking but tastes divine

13 More to life than work

With business developing fairly well, it became clear what a gaping hole there had been in our extra-curricular life. That is to say, our *life* life. In a bid to start to enrich mine, I'd been asking around a bit about a local choir. I had sung with one in LA and even though I had been the youngest person by a good couple of decades, it had been fun and in that case a nice diversion from the obsessional world of TV and film entertainment.

Well, I had the urge to sing in a choir again, mostly because there was a specific thing that I missed which was the feeling of different voices singing in harmony together. It didn't matter whether it was in an indie band or a 100-voice choir, whether the harmonies had been self-invented or composed years ago – there is something simply uplifting about voices coming together in this way. More prosaically, I thought that an extra-curricular pursuit like a choir would offer a good and alternative way of improving my Italian, an excuse to get out of the house and a source of something new to talk to Jason about. One thing we were finding hard was the fact that we knew each other's every move. It was almost spooky – we spent all day of every day together, working together, eating together, sleeping together, socializing together, having existential crises together. Given that Jason is tone deaf, a choir was a pretty safe bet for a me-only activity.

Whenever I asked anyone within a twenty-mile radius about a choir, the answer was always the same. 'Try San Ginesio.'

And so it was that I was driving up a very wiggly road to a village that's only about quarter of an hour from us, but which I'd never been to before. It's funny how it seems to work that way in the countryside – some villages you end up going to all the time while others, equally near and equally equipped, you never do, just because there's no particular pull. And before you know it you sound like a narrow-minded, unadventurous yokel because you've, unbelievably, never even visited a village a few miles away.

A couple of hours earlier I had spoken to a man who talked very, very fast. I wasn't sure exactly who he was but he was obviously something important to do with the choir as he was the one who answered the phone of the number that the *comune* had given me. I'd asked about whether there really was a choir in San Ginesio (yes) and whether there might be a possibility of me joining it (yes) and what I should do (come along to the practice tonight at 9 p.m.). I had hoped for a bit of time, a couple of days at least, to swot up on choir-related vocabulary and do at least a bit of singing in the shower, but sometimes things don't wait.

It was a little nerve-racking as I had no idea what to expect, whether they would pray before singing (no one had told me if this was a church choir, would I be out of place as an infidel?), whether they would all be brilliant, slightly-sub-concert-soloists, whether I'd be able to understand what was going on and so on and so on. The fact that the practice started at 9 p.m. was in itself quite striking and would never have washed with any previous choir I'd known, where nine o'clock was scraping close to bedtime for many of the participants.

I really cocked up parking the car. And right in front of a man who I was about to learn was one of the linchpins of the choir, the '*buon* Nick' ('Nick, the good man') as he was known. First I parked in front of the choir building, then I noticed him looking at me strangely. '*Il coro?*' ('The choir?') I asked uncertainly. '*Si, si.* But you can't park there.' He gestured upwards – there was a huge unmissable '*sosta vietato*' (no parking) sign. He pointed me down a windy road where

227

I parked in front of a garage door before he had to again come to my aid and almost literally manoeuvre me into a safe spot.

He was very nice but I suddenly felt like I couldn't speak a word of Italian. Then along came Professore Baldassari, the man with whom I'd spoken, who turned out to be the conductor. 'Benvenuta,' he said as he hustled inside. There was a general flurry of people gathering – an avuncular man with a beard, a tiny lady who looked like the Old Lady Who Lived in a Shoe, a cluster of teenagers, two girls arm in arm in big silver bomber jackets, a joking dimple-faced man who pretended to strangle one of them as they went in laughing.

I felt very much a stranger. Not just in language or in culture but also in choral terms – I'd never seen a choir like this. Choirs I'd known – either been in or seen – were mostly women, invariably late middle-aged and up, inevitably conservative and ... well, with a sort of WI pre-*Calendar Girls* feel. Here, the age range was from seventeen to seventy, there were almost exactly equal numbers of men and women and everyone was bumping around playing practical jokes on each other and being terribly, well, *physical* about it.

Gradually everyone sat down in three or four neatish rows with the conductor at the front behind a Roland keyboard. He turned to me and then to them in what I can only assume was an introduction. It seemed to go on remarkably long given how little he knew about me, though I had told him about singing in choirs in different places before. Gradually the speech drew to a close with the unforgettable words, '... London ... Los Angeles ... Loro Piceno.'

There was a murmur and a general sense of 'welcome, welcome'. The conductor had suggested, at least I think he had, that I just sit in and listen to get the feel of things for now. So I sat on the margins feeling highly conspicuous as people took turns to spy over at me and then smile when I caught their eye.

They were singing Rossini's *Petite Messe Solennelle*. And they were singing it rather well. The conductor was a firecracker. Stamping out the time with his foot and stamping out the different parts with his hands and stamping out anything else that the other bits didn't cover with his voice. He talked a lot, and I couldn't understand a good deal of it. He was one of those people who couldn't speak slowly if he tried and I was pretty sure there was a lot of dialect, though it's always hard to be sure.

The sound of the choir was quite different from choirs I'd sung in before and the reason was youth. Nearly half of the singers being under twenty meant the overall sound had a freshness and clarity that was lovely. No creaks.

Every so often, there would be a mistake and Firecracker would stop and shout some more things out, usually telling the basses off for getting something wrong, and not mincing his words – well, at least not mincing his tone. Then once he stopped and leaped towards one of the sopranos, the little lady who lived in a shoe one, holding out a small wrapped sweet. When she went to take it, he whipped his hand away so she couldn't get it, and everyone laughed. I had the impression that this was some kind of recurring joke, but the significance was completely lost on me.

Realizing Firecracker was the type to single anyone out on a whim, I began to feel less comfortable in my seat. I had the sort of feeling you'd have if you'd gone to see a bawdy stand-up comic and only realized too late that your skirt was tucked into your knickers.

I sort of followed along with the music and even ventured a bit of quiet singing, though the only practice my voice had had with high notes in recent months was with the sort of involuntary one that comes out when your child is about to walk out in front of a car.

At the end of the practice, Firecracker came up and asked me how I'd found it and I said 'great'. Then he introduced me to another fellow member, the avuncular one with the beard who turned out to be the choir's president and who launched into a presidential-like speech about the choir. Thankfully he was much easier to understand, so I could react with genuine surprise when he told me the choir had been going for twenty-five years and that they had travelled to every continent together. In fact, all around the walls were photographs of the choir in different uniforms, in front of Big Ben, or in Red Square, or at the Munich Beer Festival. More surprising still, many of the original members were still present – he, Firecracker, and about ten others of the older ones – some of whom must have been barely teenagers back then.

Then Firecracker said something along the lines of 'Well, I think its time to put our new friend through her paces' and he beckoned me over to in front of the Roland keyboard. He called over a couple of other sopranos to act as embarrassment cover, which I thought was kind. Then he played some notes and asked me to sing them. Then he played some chords and asked me to sing the lowest or the highest or the middle notes. Then he played a series of notes and asked me to repeat the tune back to him. Then he played notes in a funny rhythm and asked me to sing the rhythm back to him.

Then he said 'Caterina. *Benvenuta alla Corale Buonagiunta* ('Welcome to the Bonagiunta Choir').

It was the *comune* who'd given me the first direction to the choir and it was the *comune* who came up trumps again to ensure that Jason would get his itchy feet round a football. We'd have to live here at least another twenty years before we worked out everything the *comune* did but some things were self-evident: one was that they spent a huge amount of money on local sports facilities. Loro Piceno has a population of a little over 3,000 but their floodlit, all-weather Astro-Turfed football pitch would be the envy of a town the size of Ipswich. I'm not sure if this was to do with the priority given to football in Italy or the priority given to the needs of young people (well, young male people at least) – but whatever the motivation, Jason wanted his piece of the action.

We already knew from the ever-helpful lady at the *comune* that the team practised several times a week. So one evening, at about seven, Jason took his luck and his boots and headed off to the stadium. There were various *ragazzi* hanging around, some already kitted up, others joking around. They were nearly all in their late teens or early twenties and Jason felt a bit like Dad as, pre-armed with a few bits of key vocabulary, he asked one of them where the coach was. They gestured towards a man over the other side of the field who bore a striking resemblance to Jesus Christ.

When Jason went over to introduce himself, he was surprised to find that Jesus already knew who he was. '*Ciao,*' he said warmly, '*e benvenuto.*' Was he really Jesus and knew everyone in the world? He noticed Jason was looking at him rather puzzled.

'*La tua casa*' ('Your house'), he said, '*ho messo tutte le piastrelle*' ('I tiled your house').

Another one?! We thought Elmedine's dad had tiled our house! No. Apparently he only does the outdoor tiling. Jesus had done all the indoor stuff – a big job, big enough to pay for his new car, he 'joked'.

Jason said that he'd like to come along to football training, just to do some exercise and keep his skills up. '*Ma certo. Iniziamo proprio ora?*' ('Of course. Do you want to start now?')

A bit embarrassed having seen what he was up against in the kit department, Jason headed back to the car to pick up his motley assortment of mismatched QPR socks, Liverpool shorts and raggedy football boots.   Everyone else was in pristine Loro Piceno kits, clearly ironed by their mothers, and carried everything around in state-of-the-art kit bags with equally pristine boots tucked away in the bottom. They had two sets of shoes each – trainers for training and football boots for footballing. This was all a bit of a shock to J, whose previous idea of an evening of football was a few fast physical games of five-a-side with plenty of bruises and swearing, then straight down the pub.

Training proper began. It transpired that Jesus wasn't the main coach – he was just God's number two, God being a guy called Ciocci who used to play for no less a team than Inter Milan, so in the eyes of the *ragazzi* was genuinely pretty close to the big guy. This was a man who had played alongside true footballing gods such as (Jason tells me) Jürgen Klinsmann. How on earth he ended up in Loro Piceno, the other God only knows.

The first bout of training involved playing … netball! One team had bibs, the other didn't and they had to throw the ball to each other while the other team tried to take the ball off them. It was all about keeping possession and nobody except Jason seemed to think it strange that they weren't playing with their feet. If one team managed to keep the ball in their hands for more than fifteen consecutive passes, the other was forced into punishment press-ups.

Then came another game which the coach (who tradition dictates is addressed as 'Mister' in deference to the fact that football was invented in England – a behaviour that seems uncharacteristically good-sportish of them) – referred to as 'psychological training'. For Jason it was more a case of a linguistic workout. There were four corners, each with a number. Players had to stand in the middle of this square as Mister yelled out 'run to 2', 'run to the opposite of number 3', 'run to the corner one point anti-clockwise of number 1' and so on. It produced a jelly feeling in legs and brain alike.

Then there was fitness training. This meant running up and back down the hilly next-door field, pausing only occasionally to let a tractor or a herd of noisy sheep pass by. Once they'd have to run really fast, another time really slowly, another time backwards, another time skipping. All the others had changed into their trainers but Jason soldiered on in his tiptappy football boots.

Things got worse. There was another game where they had to do one-touch kicking of the ball to their team-mates. The game was played thus: they had to shout out the name of the person to whom they were about to pass the ball, then pass it in one shot. Jason is much better with names than I am but even he struggled with this one, not least because at least half of the other players seemed to be called 'Lupo' or 'Luca'. They had as much trouble with his, and he also had to be on his mettle to realize that any of 'Joe', 'Jim', 'James', 'John', 'Joseph' and even the occasional 'Jahsson' might be destined for him.

After a couple of hours of all this, Mister said that was it for today. What?! They hadn't even played any football. They had just done training. Jason was shocked, knackered, and a bit relieved.

Even at shower time J found himself outplayed. Every other player had a perfect shiny dressing gown and a brand new pair of flip-flops, often colour coordinated with the dressing gown. And each one entered the shower with such a vast range of unguents that a marketing man would weep. Jason, with his bare feet and tatty QPR towel tied round his waist, was clearly the outsider, until the great unifier of towel-slapping games levelled the field.

Afterwards, the sound of hairdriers made conversation impossible, then the smell of aftershaves and gels and deodorants meant even breathing was a challenge.

'Where are you off to?' J asked, hoping to learn of the inevitable drinking hole they must surely all be about to decamp to.

But all this abluting and perfuming was for no one, it transpired, but their mothers. Everyone was just going home. 'Mum's making pizza,' someone said with a grin.

And so it was that J returned home, with aching limbs, to incredulously drink a solitary beer and eat a plate of solo spaghetti.

Rosie had her escape from the house, too, in the form of Titti.

When she went to nursery in London for a short spell, we used to be given a little slip to tell us about her day. Nearly all of it would be taken up with descriptions, written irritatingly in the first person, of what she had done. She had been less than a year old so this usually wasn't a lot and, of course, she couldn't speak yet, which was what made the use of the first person irksome. It would say things like:

'Today I enjoyed looking at the mobile with sparkly fishes on.'
'Today I banged spoons and other things to make a nice noise.'
'Today I rocked in the corner, pondering life's purpose, alone and lonely, but for some Day-Glo animals.'

At the end of the little slip would be a quick summary of whether she'd eaten 'all' 'most' 'some' or 'none' of her unspecified lunch.

At Titti, we were also given a slip at the end of each day to tell us about her day. The slip was divided into the following sections:

What she had eaten for mid-morning snack
What she had eaten for lunch for *primo*
What she had eaten for lunch for *secondo*
What she had eaten for lunch for *contorno*
What she had eaten for lunch for *dolce*
What she had eaten for mid-afternoon snack
Whether she had done a poo

It was 100 percent about food! Admittedly, there was reason to boast. The food was fantastic – fresh, high quality, varied and packed with goodness. And whether thanks to peer pressure, superior cooking or corporal punishment, Rosie was persuaded to eat things there that she would never have contemplated at home; we received reports of her yomping down second and even third helpings of salad and lentils and liver.

But we couldn't help feeling it was a bit strange that we had no idea what she had done all day in the possibly rather short chunks between feeding sessions. Occasionally there would be a clue when Rosie would start singing a song about sunflowers or washerwomen in Italian – one that we definitely hadn't taught her. Or when playing 'heuristically' (a word we had learned from the London nursery, which Jason had initially confused with 'hasidically', but which he later had learned meant, well, basically playing by herself. It was a slightly sad day when your less-than-one-year-old's daily report told you 'Today I enjoyed playing by myself') she would start talking, or rather shouting, at one of her toy animals in Italian to *'sta zito'* ('shut up') or *'guardateme'* ('look at me') and we had alarming images of these toddlers being yelled at to obey.

The philosophy on parental involvement couldn't have been more different here. In London there was a very open-doors policy, with parents invited and encouraged to drop in at any time, without any need to 'warn' of their arrival. They could sit in the corner and listen to a reading session or watch songs being sung or whatever. And if there was some special event – a little show or a fancy dress day or something – parents (well, mums) would be roped in to help, making costumes, baking cakes or chaperoning children. When Rosie was there she had been too young and it had been for too short a period for us to really experience this, but I have since seen from friends in London that this 'involvement' can turn into a ferociously competitive and bitchy display of parental one-upmanship. I didn't envy that in the least – there is something quite dreadful about seeing competitive mums living out their various neuroses in the form of a 'best Easter bonnet' contest.

But our new Italian version was no paragon either. Rosie's nursery here consisted of the main building and then a sort of anteroom where children took their coats off, put on their anti-slip socks and said goodbye to their parents. Parents were firmly not allowed past this room into the nursery 'proper'. They were not encouraged to go and listen to book readings or song singing or help with costume making. In fact, they were forbidden. It apparently upset the other children.

So off she went every day to feast on Italian food and play with her little Italian friends and we experienced the first of a probable lifetime of wondering what our child got up to when she was not with us.

Spaghetti with lemon and parmesan cheese

Spaghetti olio, limone e parmigiano

Ingredients for 2 people
Spaghetti – 200g
Olive oil – 2 tablespoons
Lemon – the fresh juice of a small lemon or
half a big one
Maldon sea salt and freshly ground pepper
Parmesan – 40g freshly grated

People are always giving me recipes here. Even men, who generally never cook, will suggest a twist on a popular dish. Giovanni, who is another 'choir widow', and whose favourite hobbies are identifying wild fungi and collecting guns (he has twenty-six), told me I must try spaghetti simply with lemon juice, olive oil and parmesan.

The trick is to mix the oil and lemon into an emulsion first, he told me. On a day when we have literally no food in the house, this recipe comes to mind.

Cook the spaghetti in boiling salted water with some oil to stop it sticking together. Pour 2 tablespoons of good quality olive oil in a cup and then squeeze in the juice of 1 lemon. Add a good pinch of salt and several grinds of black pepper. Grate the parmesan.

Drain the cooked spaghetti, keeping a couple of tablespoons of the pasta water in case the final dish is a bit dry. Stir the oil and lemon violently with a fork. Pour the mix over the pasta, then add the parmesan. Mix thoroughly and serve.

Trout preserved in olive oil

Trota sott'olio

Ingredients
Trout – 4 fish, 8 fillets
Sugar – fistful
Salt – fistful
Cold water – a cupful
Parsley – bunch
Garlic – 1 clove
Olive oil

With a mischievous grin my other 'choir widow' buddy, Angelo, asked if I wanted to go fishing with him. Given that I've been a vegetarian for thirty years it was a provocative request. The trouble is, I was mouthing off to him that I'd have no qualms eating meat if I'd caught and killed the animal myself. In this case I could be fully aware of its provenance and could be sure it had a good life.

Angelo caught me offguard, excuse-less, so I had to say yes.

In the end I couldn't bring myself to eat the fish, so Angelo showed me how to preserve it so I could bring it home for Cathy and Rosie to scoff.

With a very sharp knife, scrape the scales and underlying muck off each fish – run the knife from the head to the tail several times till you have some mucky looking goo of fish scales to show for it. Then fillet the fish, first gutting them, then cutting off the head and tail, and finally removing the flesh from each flank.

Lay the fillets out in a fairly deep-sided ceramic dish. Sprinkle over the sugar and the salt (the image of Angelo's giant hands with dark cracks in the skin holding a fistful of salt is an enduring one). Then add the cup of water. The water doesn't need to completely cover the fish. Cover with cling film and put in the fridge. Turn the fish over once a day for 4 days (it helps here if you have put the fish in the same way, that is to say skin up or skin down, so you can tell which ones you've turned over).

After 4 days, drain the water off and remove the skin, which should come off very easily at this stage. Chop the fish into 2cm square cubes, add the chopped-up parsley and a peeled clove of garlic and spoon into a sterilized glass jar (that is to say a jam or Kilner jar whacked in the oven – 10 minutes at 160ºC /gas mark 3 should do the trick). Leave room at the top of the jar for at least a couple of centimetres of olive oil with as little air as possible above. Put the lid on the jar nice and tight and this will store for months (or a few days, once it's opened).

14 The fruits of our labours

We had orders, we had oil, we had tins and boxes and we had annoying little cardboard strips to wedge in to make everything fit snugly. Now all that remained was to turn this little lot into 445 perfectly formed little packages and get the right tree's oil to land on the right people's doorsteps.

Whenever I do any new job, I am amazed to discover the effort and thought that goes into the smallest thing. When I first started working in TV, I couldn't believe that it took three months to make an hour-long documentary. I couldn't believe that the person narrating wasn't somehow just magically doing it live and spontaneously. I couldn't believe that you might film a hundred times as much material as might go in the final programme and that it might take six weeks in an edit suite to decide which bits you wanted in or out. I couldn't believe the tiny decisions that had to be made, right down to the type and size of font you wanted to have the end credits written in and whether you wanted the title to linger on screen for three or four seconds. The world which I thought I'd understood (as a viewer) was suddenly a different world entirely.

And so it has been with Nudo. I can still barely compute the amount of effort and decision-making that has to go into making even the smallest and humblest of companies function. There are the things that you do think of – you need to choose a name for example, but then you need to decide how you want the name written and where to find someone who can make you a sign or print you a stamp with that name on, written in the same way as you have decided you want it to be. And then you have to find out how to get headed paper with that name on and find someone who prints headed paper and work out what file type to save your new name as and on and on. And that's all just for your name – then there are accounts to work out how to do, laws to get your head around, a million suppliers to research and test drive, press and marketing to try to conquer, envelopes to order, printers to repair, computers to install updates on. For everyone, as with us, it must feel that you are the first people in the world to be finding out about all this.

And this feeling was at its height with our first 'spring packages', as we call them. These are the first packages that adopters receive and each contains all the olive oil that their tree has produced in that year's harvest. (It is actually impossible to press the olives from one tree at a time, so we harvest a group of say thirty trees of the same variety in the same area and then divide up the oil between those thirty adopters.) This year, the average amount of oil per tree was about two litres, so each adopter was to receive four half-litre tins of lovely fresh extra virgin olive oil.

It felt that every stage of sending out these spring packages had a little saga all its own. The tins, which arrived fairly on time in a small lorry, were the first bits of hardware to show up in the flesh. You don't think that 2,000 sounds a lot until you see them stacked on a pallet as tall as a man.

The man driving the truck said he couldn't get the truck down the drive (wimp) and asked where our 'equipment' was. We told him we didn't have any equipment because most drivers managed to tackle the drive. He snarled a bit. I suggested we tried to lift the pallet off by hand – they were only empty tins after all.

'Che cazzo dici?' said the driver, which roughly meant 'What the hell are you talking about?' but a little more aggressive.

It turned out he had a point. Even empty tins, when multiplied by a couple of thousand, are really heavy. It was impossible.

So I told the driver and Jason to wait a minute as I ran back down to the house to collect as many black bin bags and boxes as I could find.

Seeing me coming back laden with what looked like rubbish, the driver said, *'Che cazzo fai?'*, which roughly meant 'What the hell are you doing?' only a bit ruder.

Jason and I unloaded the first few layers of tins into the bags and boxes and I started to carry them down. J made towards the pallet in a way that clearly suggested the driver should grab hold of the other end. He was grumpy as hell by now but realized that this job was only going to be signed off if he assented, so he did, muttering *'Cazzo'* (which literally means 'dick') under his breath.

He and Jason, who were very different heights, staggered down our wiggly bumpy drive carrying the still very heavy pallet. They were like mismatched pall-bearers moodily carrying a gouty granddad. I ran along behind trying to gather the windfalls which were gathering momentum down the steep hill.

As we reached the office at the back of the house, about half of the pallet remained intact and the driver scarpered, realizing his duties had been completed. Jason and I spent another hour stacking all the cast-offs back into some sort of order. It was the kind of thing that makes you really appreciate, in case you hadn't before, the invention of the forklift truck.

So the tins were safely gathered in. Though they looked a bit bare all naked and white and topless and rather industrial. But that was in hand. Jason and my sister Madeleine had between them designed a beautiful sticker which we hoped to God was going to precisely wrap round the bland whiteness of the tin and cover it in gorgeous Nudo repeating olives. We'd decided to go for half with a white background and half with a black one so that each adopter's package would be composed, rather chicly, of a Mod mix of monochromes (well, and some green bits). J, in his impressive efforts to keep us green in the other sense, had found a printer in Wales who only used environmentally friendly dyes and who had said it'd be no problem to get the stickers to us in Italy. They had been due to arrive from Wales any day and we couldn't wait to see them.

The oil had been taken care of. We already had our precious golden booty stashed away in the cellar in about twenty or so shiny barrels all labelled and pretty. Fabiola was in charge of the boxes and, true to her word, delivered them on the precise day she had promised. Jason was as twitchy as could be about seeing them and, perfectionist that he is, managed to find fault in that they had used a slightly wrong font on the 'Adopt an olive tree' wording. I was the opposite – I couldn't believe how posh and grown-up we were to have our very own boxes with our beautiful Nudo tree with our logo underneath. To me it was absolute proof that we were a proper company and I think my enthusiasm even managed to bring J round a bit. We spent a day preassembling the boxes (sticking together the bottom part) and working out how to fold the inner cuff so that it fitted precisely.

That inner cuff became a bit of a symbol for me. You see I have this thing, through osmosis from my mother, that waste is a very bad thing. And these little pieces of cardboard, which existed only to make sure that the tins of oil were a bit more padded and a bit less likely to move around, and that would be, for sure, binned on the moment of arrival, became like little waste demons floating above my head. I grew to loathe every little corrugated inch of them as I folded them round in their fussy snug-fitting way.

Despite my metaphorical rash, 445 boxes were soon assembled

and teetering in piles like gigantic bacteria gardens all over our living room.

We had written our spring package letters and refined them again and again over weeks of nervousness about what tone to strike with our adopters. We wanted to be a bit jokey but at the same time convey the (true) idea that we took the business of olive oil seriously. We wanted to give people some genuine information without being preachy. We wanted to be edgy but humble.

This was the letter we sent:

Spring 2006

Rejoice – your *Adopt an olive tree* spring package has arrived. No more of that lacklustre stuff from the supermarket. It's time to let real olive oil take over your kitchen.

In your package you'll find four tins of oil – everything your hard-working tree has sweated and strained over this year, an average of two litres of oil. Not bad going when you consider it's been a rotten year weather-wise in Italy. A late frost spelled trouble for olive blossom, and since blossom more or less equals olives, which more or less equal oil, yields didn't reach their maximum.

But the thing about olive trees is they actually don't mind a bit of a hard knock life - if they did they'd have gone the way of the Roman Empire. It's a bit like with people: we all like a challenge and an effortless, overprivileged existence doesn't make for the tastiest fruit despite what the Eton prospectus might tell you. What we're trying to say is that the trees have concentrated on quality not quantity so the oil this year is particularly good.

246

Now, time to stop reading our ramblings and get down to the important business of tasting your oil. We don't want to scare anyone off, so if you're worried about being called pretentious, don't read the next bit – just neck your oil back like a drunk. If you fancy yourself as more of a connoisseur, sip a bit of olive oil 'neat' from a teaspoon, hold it in your mouth and think about the flavour. The first tastes to hit you are the fresh ones – summer meadows, cut grass, those sorts of things. Then breathe in a bit of air, trying not to let the oil spill out of your mouth (not a good look, even for a connoisseur), and think again. Can you identify other things? Artichokes maybe? A hint of pear? The smell of your dinner burning? Finally as you swallow the oil you'll feel a peppery kick in the back of your throat. Pretty fine we hope you'll agree.

Now we're getting to work on the soaps for your autumn package. And get ready for your lemon oil which will be arriving then too – it is sublime.

Buon appetito!
Nudo

PS In case you'd like to give someone else the gift of adoption, we've included a discount voucher to oil the wheels of generosity.

Of course, there were things we realized we'd forgotten only after we'd printed off 445 of these little babies. Such as the fact that our oil, being unfiltered, is cloudy. We worried that our customers, being used to clear oil, would think this meant there was something wrong. So we had to print off another little note explaining the cloudiness and advising about storage – and go back through each envelope restuffing every one with this extra nugget of information.

As to getting our packages to their destinations, I had spent hours on the phone to different courier companies getting quotes and trying to get a sense of them. It was hard when you were talking to sales people (who if nothing else should have been able to sell to you) and it was something you'd never done before so you were not even sure what questions to ask. In the end it came down to hunch. And in the end for us, this meant two people in the final running. They were chalk and cheese – one lady, Hedra, who was incredibly pernickety and wanted to know every detail (like even down to whether we would supply the addresses to her in an Excel document in a downwards or a crosswise configuration), and the other, Sharon, who was much more 'know what I mean, love' and who just generally seemed quite up for it in a cocky, confident way. In the end we plumped for Sharon. She would be responsible for delivering all our packages to people's homes, once we'd first delivered them to Sharon's godforsaken warehouse in the pits of London.

As to getting them to Pitsmouth in Godforsakenshire, we were calling in a major favour from our pals Bob and Ian. They lived a couple of villages along in the next middle of nowhere place and, by that weird six degrees of separation thing that happens, turned out to be best friends with a girl who was, in a friendly way, my chief rival at school. Bob and Ian were busy doing up their massive house, converting it into apartments to rent out, and spent a lot of time going back to the UK to load up with things like doors and windows which were, apparently, much cheaper there. The result was that they were often driving to the UK in a van that, while completely and probably illegally overloaded one way, was empty on its outbound journey.

One day they mentioned that if we ever wanted anything taken, they'd be happy to oblige. Another day we said, 'How about a tonne of olive oil?' and, as good as their word, they said, 'No problem.'

So things were pretty much in place, we had address labels and letters printed and boxes made up. It was time to get down to business and first off that meant filling the tins with oil. With each adopter due to receive four half-litre tins that meant 445 x 4 tins in all. Or just under 1,800.

We donned our pristine aprons, loaded up with trays and a radio and headed down into the cool of the cellar. Then Jason turned the tap of the first barrel and a huge gloop of thick cloudy yuk came out. He turned the tap off again.

'Oh my God,' he said.

'What?' I said.

'It's all gone lumpy,' he said.

'Oh my God,' I said.

'Exactly,' he said.

We went back upstairs and got the biggest containers we could find. We turned the tap back on, thinking that we just had to let it run for a while until the clearer oil starting coming through. Corrado had told us that unfiltered oil settles out after sitting for a bit, so the hope was that the yucky thick stuff was just at the bottom so would all come out first.

But there didn't half seem a lot of it. It ran and ran, filling our containers and more until we had half our kitchen saucepans deployed on the job.

Finally the oil started running through normally and I set to work, sitting on my little three-legged milkmaid's stool, filling and weighing each tin to make sure it had the right amount of oil.

Meanwhile Jason was trying to deal with our ... residue. The thing was, we knew that it was all just olive oil and we couldn't bear to waste it all – so Jason thumbed through his mental boy scout manual and within half an hour had rigged up an aerial (well, it hung from the ceiling) filtration system. It involved a large amount of very fine muslin which my mum had given us (offcuts from the products of her business making jelly bags and steamed pudding covers and whatnot) suspended at the corners, so that our unattractive gloop could be dolloped in. Underneath was our hugest casserole dish to catch the good bits of oil that we hoped would start to emerge. Later we learned from Corrado that it is totally normal for oil to become thick like this when it is stored at too low a temperature – it is basically the oil starting to freeze.

The radio kept us going. We mostly listened to RAI 3 which is sort of halfway between Radio 3 and Radio 4 in UK terms. It has earnest programmes, it has a lot of music of all kinds and it has a bit of cheek. As we sat filling tin after tin after tin we listened to programmes about everything from Beat poetry to Italian women's football to the philosophy of being a radical. A lot of it went over our heads but usually just as it was getting too much they'd put on a bit of chirpy music and we'd be back on track.

Again we learned respect for the number 2,000. As Jason carried the filled tins upstairs to the big wooden table we'd brought in from outside, rows became layers and layers became ... Unsustainable. Even our solid wooden garden table began to bow in the middle. So we started stacking on the floor. It just seemed to go on and on. At about five we had to stop to go and pick up Rosie from nursery. We spent a few hours playing with her before bed then resumed work in the cellar from about nine. We discovered that RAI 3 goes a bit off-piste in the evening. It becomes an outlet for avant-garde jazz, experimental shouting music and improvised fusion. The madness of its mood suited ours, as tins and lids floated in front of our eyes.

On the third day of this, I said to Jason, 'Should we be worried that the stickers for the tins haven't arrived yet?' meaning 'You promised the stickers would be here by now.'

Eventually he was persuaded to go and phone our eco-friendly hippy in the Welsh hills.

He came back looking ashen.

'Oh my God what?' I said.

'He hasn't even sent them yet.'

'But he knew we needed them this week at the latest. Why hasn't he sent them?'

'Some problem with the machine or something. Stupid Welsh hippy.'

'So what did you say?'

'I said send them now, as soon as you can, as fast as you can. With a good courier company it should only take two days, so we'll still be fine.'

By this point it was Thursday. Ian was going to be driving the van back to London the following Saturday, so we had eight days to fill the tins, put the stickers on, pack up and label each box then put those into big boxes. If he sent the stickers today there was a good chance that we would get them on Monday – which would still give us four and a half days to do everything, which would be OK.

By the end of Friday, all the tins were filled, the boxes were as prepped as they could be, the letters were folded and enveloped – in short, everything was now waiting for the Welsh hippy's stickers.

Monday came. Monday lunchtime came. 'Couriers usually come in the afternoon,' we told ourselves. Monday afternoon came. Then by any definition the end of the working day came. Jason phoned the hippy. I heard his raised voice from three rooms away, but could only make out words like 'tracking number' said loudly as if to a very stupid person.

'He sent it by the slow service,' Jason told me, incredulous.

'You are kidding me,' I said.

'He said the two-day service was going to cost a fortune and thought it would be better to go with the slower one – it's meant to take three to four days and it costs half as much.'

'I knew we should never have trusted a stupid fucking hippy,' I said.

'He's given me a tracking number so we should be able to find out where it is.'

The tracking news wasn't good. The stupid hippy liar hadn't even sent it on the Thursday as he'd told Jason; he'd sent it on the Friday evening, so it had only actually left the shores of the UK earlier today, Monday. There was *'una possibilità'* ('a chance') it could still get to us on Tuesday evening, the courier company said unconvincingly.

All this time I had been doing calculations. If the stickers had arrived today and we'd worked a twelve-hour day, we would have had to average about a label every two minutes – or each of us doing one label every four minutes. That seemed doable. By Tuesday, it'd be down to a label every three minutes and by Wednesday down to a slightly more alarming minute, including all the time to pack up and label the boxes. I didn't even want to do the calculation for Thursday.

Of course, the package didn't arrive on Tuesday. And it didn't arrive on Wednesday either, despite our pleading to the courier company that we would go and pick it up from bloody Rome if we had to. But that wasn't possible; it was on a lorry they couldn't say where so there was no chance of our collecting it ourselves. But they promised promised promised that it would be with us as early as possible the next morning, Thursday.

By this point, we just had to believe that they'd arrive and we had to get help. The only people we could think of were little Carlo, who God bless him, is up for anything, and Elmedine, who we persuaded to deviate from her normal career path for two days. I spent the rest of Wednesday doing slightly psychopathic baking, partly to use up nervous energy and partly because I thought if there was one thing that would get us through it would be cake.

Carlo showed up at eight the next morning. We'd told Elmedine we'd come and get her the moment the courier showed up and that she should be on standby.

The really infuriating thing by this point was that there was literally nothing we could do but wait – and it had been like that for three whole days now. Those tins sat there mocking us, those boxes all had eyes and the clock just tick tick ticked its message of our impotence.

At ten the phone rang. It was the courier company. '*È arrivato ancora?*' ('Has he arrived yet?')

'NO!' I yelled.

'Oh, well, he should be there any minute'.

Thanks a lot. Jason went to get Elmedine – we thought we might as well. So then we were four, sitting around, making chit-chat, trying not to eat all the cake yet.

At 10.45 there was a honk from up the driveway. The unduly cheery courier driver didn't want to negotiate our driveway. 'I've been here before,' he said. We didn't recognize him and weren't quite sure whether he was being metaphorical.

He handed over the package. None of us could quite believe that this tiny, slightly battered parcel of about fifty cubic centimetres could really have been the cause of all this anxiety. We waved off the courier and sprinted back down the hill to the house.

Ripping into the packet, there was hardly time to check the labels (God, what if the stupid hippy had made a stupid hippy typo?) before cracking on. Luckily the labels looked good – the colours were pretty and the design was really striking – and no typos. Next came the tests of seeing a. whether they fitted the tins and b. whether it was going to be a nightmare to get them on. Jason was the first to brave the job and … It worked! It was a fiddle, but if you made sure you lined the sticker up perfectly then unrolled the back part slowly as you wound the sticker round the tin, it sort of fell into place.

Well, the first one did. The second one went a bit wrong and ended up all wonky at the far end. Jason tried to peel it back off, but one part got ripped on its reverse journey. He tried yanking it really hard to shock it into coming off and that seemed to work better but took some courage. We didn't have stickers to waste though, so the best thing was to take a tiny bit longer lining up at the beginning and hopefully get it right first time. The knack was to nestle the front edge of the sticker between the two ridges at the top and bottom of the tin, then firmly, tightly unfurl the rest of it so that it stayed exactly parallel to the top of the tin. That way, there would be no bubbles or wrinkles and the repeating olive pattern at the far end would match up exactly. It was like wallpapering a huge mansion, with miniature tools, awkward paper, a team of apprentices and in an enormous hurry.

Carlo and Elmedine looked terrified. They had never really done work for us before that they could fail at. We each demonstrated one to them and then watched like nervous parents as they tried to have a go themselves. Elmedine switched into teenage girl perfectionism mode and slowly but surely managed her first sticker, pretty much on target. Carlo was the surprise – normally a quite relaxed person, he suddenly seemed a coiled wire of tension and his whole body language changed into this twisted, huddled mass. He started but it was wrong, he pulled it back without it tearing, just; he tried it again, we thought it kinder not to look, we were sure he'd get the hang of it – and instead got on with our own. There was plenty here for everyone after all.

After a while we settled into the sort of rhythm that one does when working at an essentially quite boring repetitive task with a group of people with whom one feels at ease. There would be fairly regular curses from all of us, and Carlo in particular, as stickers would go off on deviations, but after a while it became enjoyable, the race against the clock. We would take it in turns to choose CDs to accompany our labours, which meant a rich mix from Nelly Furtado one minute to Shostakovich the next. And there were lots of tasty cake breaks.

We carried on like this throughout the day, the piles of discarded sticker backs forming a moat around the table. By the time it neared five and Rosie collecting time, it was clear that a lot more than a normal working day was needed and both Elmedine and Carlo offered to stay.

Rosie thought it the strangest sight, all these adults looking so deep in concentration with what looked to her like a regular crafts table – but she had lots of people and lots of paper to play with so was quite content.

By eight we sent our helpers home. Carlo had an hour's drive and neither of them had had dinner and it was time for us to see to Rosie. We did Rosie's bath time and had a hurried meal of our own before putting her to bed and getting back to our table for more sticking.

By midnight we were starting to hallucinate stickers and thought maybe it would be good to start doing some boxing. We were more than halfway with the tin stickering, but what we didn't yet know was how long the boxing up would take. It was a bit of a fiddle as it involved writing the tree code on each tin, putting four tins in a box, inserting a letter, then closing it up while remembering which tree it was so that we could attach the correct address label. It wasn't really the sort of brainless job one desired in the middle of the night and it took two hours just to do the first forty. I didn't dare return to my calculations about timings per box for fear they wouldn't add up.

By three in the morning we were really on diminishing returns and turned in for a few hours' sleep.

The advantage of that feeling of hideous tiredness caused by work is at least you feel you have a proper job. And even though you'd pay anything for a bit more sleep there's something exciting about the idea of being on a mission, especially in Italy where you know there is delicious coffee to help bolster you through.

By the time Elmedine and Carlo showed up at eight, we were already well under way. I now realized that there was at least a full-time job of boxing to be done alongside the stickering. It involved ticking off which customers (tree adopters) had been boxed up by checking the document on the laptop, cross-referencing everyone's tree number and so on – so it wasn't really a job to be delegated. It pretty soon became clear that there was yet another full-time job for someone to be done assisting me doing the boxing job. It was a slight relief for all of us to be able to take Carlo off wonky stickering duty and put him onto a more fitting macho job of hefting heavy boxes around, sealing and labelling them, bringing fresh box supplies through from the other room and so on.

At about noon, Elmedine asked a strange question. *'Dove sono le altre etichette?'* ('Where are the rest of the stickers?'), she said.

The battered box in which the labels had arrived was indeed nearly empty but there were about 500 naked tins still to be dressed. We all stopped what we were doing and went on a furious sticker hunt, ferreting through bins in case we'd accidentally thrown a load away, sweeping through the sticker back offcuts in case they'd dropped in there. But no, search as we might, there were no more stickers. Out of 2,000 stickers, there were 500 short.

My fury at the hippy knew no bounds. It was very lucky for him at this point that he was in Wales or he would have been a dead hippy.

Carlo and Elmedine had never seen me or Jason angry before. Carlo in a tiny voice said, 'Is it my fault because I wasted so many?' At which point we had to laugh. I gave him a hug and told him that no, it was absolutely not his fault, it was the fault of a stupid, ugly idiot in Wales. I tried to explain what a hippy was in Italian to confused effect.

'Right, let's work out what to do,' Jason said. We had a little over twenty-four hours. There was no chance of getting more from Wales. We needed somehow to make something that first time took thirty e-mails, twenty phone calls and three months smoking dope to happen, happen in about an hour and a half. We need to find a place to get more stickers done here – and straight away.

'Grafos?' we said together.

Grafos was the little local printing place that we had passed a hundred times without going in. We'd seen their name about as they seemed to do all the printing a rural community required – posters for the artichoke festival, decals for farm vehicles, labels for *vino cotto* bottles. We weren't sure they would be quite a perfect fit for us, but nonetheless in our quest to make things more local, going to have a chat with them had been on our 'to do' list for a while. There's no time like lunchtime on a Friday in Italy with a disaster on your hands to make friends.

Jason found the right design files but there seemed to be twenty different versions in jpegs and pdfs and all sorts – so in the end I hustled him out of the door carrying the whole laptop. It was close to 12.30 now and if they closed at the normal time for lunch we could be done for. It was then only a little over twenty-four hours until the van was due to leave and we were a quarter of our orders short.

As Jason went out the door, I had the strangest mix of feelings. Rage at the hippy was definitely still there and half of me wanted to phone him up just to vent some of it, sorrow for Elmedine and Carlo who had been working so hard and who now looked so worried, sorry for myself that our nice little music-filled, cake-fuelled workers' idyll had been broken up, and utter confidence that Jason was somehow by some miracle going to make everything OK.

He rushed into Grafos with a nervous energy bordering on panic that probably isn't the norm in a little village printing shop. He waved one of the stickers in front of the lady on reception, who strangely was wearing sunglasses and sucking urgently on a cigarette, which seemed unwise (not to mention unnecessary from a narcotic point of view) given the array of chemicals surrounding her. 'Can you print these?' he asked, urgently. '500 of them?'

She took the sticker, felt it between her fingers, looked at the front and the back, sniffed it, then waved it at one of her colleagues round the corner.

She couldn't see why not. But probably best to come back next week as they were really busy just now. They'd definitely be able to do them in a week or two though.

'Erm,' said Jason, which in Italian is a sucked noise between your teeth. 'We need them today. We have had a disaster. Our printer didn't supply enough stickers for our tins and the printer's in Wales and we have to send our tins tomorrow to England because that's when our transport is leaving and we're a new company and this is the first time we've done it and we can't get it wrong. Which means we have to get the stickers done today.'

'*Mi dispiace*,' said the sunglass, smoking lady. 'I'm sorry ... but there's just no way.'

Jason rummaged around for ideas. 'How about,' he chanced, 'doing just a few of them – say a hundred?'

A perky looking fellow who'd obviously been eavesdropping said something very quickly to the sunglass lady. He had a kind face and Jason prayed to his new-found lord.

The sunglass lady looked slightly disapproving and said, 'OK, we will try and do some today. Come back at 8 p.m. just before we close.'

'Thank you thank you thank you,' said Jason, addressing his comments as much to the kind perky man who he knew had saved the day.

Back at base, at least we weren't short of things to do – and all the rest of the day we cleared the backlog of dressed tins into boxes and labels. So by eight, when Jason headed back to Grafos, all we had left to pack up were the 500 naked tins.

Five minutes later, the phone rang and I winced in anticipation. 'THEY'VE DONE THEM ALL!!!!' said Jason.

He was evidently still at Grafos and I was glad that he wasn't hiding his delight. Elmedine and Carlo and I did a special sticker dance round the room and all was suddenly OK again.

In fact, so great was our confidence now that we packed our helpers off home again and had dinner with Rosie. By ten, we got down to fixing on the new stickers, feeling confident that even though it was to be a rush to the finishing post, we were going to make it.

But when Jason tried the first sticker it didn't quite fit. Not quite fitting is a bad thing as it means the edge either creeps up over the rim of the tin or, worse, that it doesn't quite cover all the metal at the other end. All the stickers seemed to be just a tiny bit too big. If you were lucky and happened to find the middle way, you could get an acceptable fit, but it was mere chance really. At 10.30 on the eve of our van departure, though, I was prepared to go with it. 'We'll send the bad ones to the double-barrelled surnames,' I said, only half joking.

'I can't bear it,' said Jason. And he went into the office to get what I knew was going to be the guillotine. 'If I cut down each one and you stick, we'll be able to get them just right and I think we can still do them in time.'

'Oh my God, are you serious?' I said. Cutting them would mean a painstaking shaving off of maybe three millimetres on each side of the sticker at slightly tapering angles.

'Look, let's try one,' said J. 'I'll show you.' And damn it, he was right. It did make a difference and they did then fit and they did then look so much better. I knew that protest would be useless so I gave into the inevitable.

'One condition,' I said. 'We're having a Montenegro (a sickly sweet liqueur we'd recently discovered) first.'

And so we did and then we spent the whole night, well, until four, deliriously slicing and sticking the last 500 stickers on to the tins and leaving them in neat piles ready to be packed up the next day. When we closed our eyes, they had repeating green olives etched all over them.

It was the final hurdle that Saturday. No help this time, plus Rosie to try and distract. It hurt that day. By the time Bob and Ian arrived at six in the evening we were loading the last oil boxes into the last big packing box and were so exhausted that we couldn't even quite celebrate. I smoked a cigarette to try to bring on a festive mood but it tasted revolting, while Rosie asking, 'What doing Mummy?' also extinguished some of the pleasure.

After we'd loaded all the boxes into their transit van – they fitted but only just – we'd promised to take Bob and Ian out for a pizza to say thank you. And so it was that we sleepily headed down to L'Approdo. I soon found that any attempts at bright and bristling conversation were completely useless and half an hour later Jason had to kick me under the table as I was falling asleep in my pizza. We paid the bill, drove back up the hill and finally waved goodbye to Bob and Ian and our tonne of oil.

Ricciarelli biscuits

Ingredients for about 16 biscuits
Egg whites – 2
Plain flour – 15g
Baking powder – $^1/_3$ teaspoon
Icing sugar – 125g
Ground almonds – 175g
Almond extract – 3 drops

Preheat the oven to 220ºC /gas mark 7. Beat the egg whites until they are stiff. In another bowl, sieve the flour and baking powder together then fold into the egg whites. Fold in the icing sugar, the ground almonds and the almond extract to make a sticky paste.

Dust a clean dry surface with a bit of extra icing sugar. Dollop a teaspoon of paste onto the surface and roll it in the sugar to make an oblong shape. It helps if you put some extra icing sugar in your hand to stop the mixture sticking to you. Repeat this for every biscuit.

Put the biscuits on a very well greased baking tray (or the marvellous Bake-O-Glide which nothing sticks to) and bake for 10–12 minutes or until they are just going golden and are slightly cracked. They still want to be soft inside so take care not to overcook them. Take them out and when they've cooled a bit, sprinkle some more icing sugar over the top.

Mandarin breakfast cake

Ingredients
Olive oil – for greasing
00 flour – 250g
Caster sugar – 200g
Baking powder – 10g
Ground almonds – 100g
Salt – pinch
Zest – 2 oranges, 1 lemon and 1 lime
Milk – 150ml
Freshly squeezed orange juice – 50ml
Mandarin olive oil – 100ml
Almond essence
Eggs – 3
Icing sugar – for dusting

Prepare a bundt (ring) tin with greaseproof paper on the bottom and a small amount of olive oil up the sides, making sure also to coat the central spout.

Sift the flour, sugar, baking powder, ground almonds and a pinch of salt together in a large bowl. Add the zest of all the citrus fruits.

Make a well in the centre and into it pour the milk, orange juice (squeezed straight from the oranges), mandarin olive oil, a few drops of almond essence and the eggs. Mix well – using a hand or electric beater – for a few minutes until you have a smooth batter.

Pour the batter into the bundt tin and put into a preheated oven at 180°C /gas mark 4. It'll take about 45 minutes with a fan-assisted oven, a little more in a normal oven. You can tell it's cooked when you start to smell delicious orangey aromas in the kitchen and when a skewer comes out clean. Turn out onto a wire rack to cool then sprinkle with icing sugar.

The cake can be eaten warm as a pudding served with fresh summer fruit and cream – but is also delicious the next morning as a breakfast cake. The cake keeps really well, retaining its moistness and zest.

Hazelnut meringue layer cake

with strawberries and cream

Ingredients

Egg whites – 6 large
Caster sugar – 225g
Toasted shelled hazelnuts – 225g
White wine vinegar – $1/4$ tsp
Mascarpone – 350g
Double cream – 50g
Icing sugar – 25g
Vanilla pod – 1
Strawberries – 250g

Preheat the oven to 150°C /gas mark 2. Separate the egg whites and whisk them until they form stiff peaks, then gradually add the sugar, spoonful by spoonful, continuing to whisk. Chop the hazelnuts finely – you can grind them in a machine, but it's nice if there are some bigger bits to give some crunch. Add the vinegar and fold the hazelnuts into the egg whites.

Spread the mixture out into 2 or 3 large circles (depending if you want a tall thinner cake or a shorter wider one) on a very well-oiled baking sheet or Bake-O-Glide anti-stick sheets. Make sure the circles are spread out quite smoothly with a spatula or the final cake will be wonky.

Cook for about an hour then turn off the oven and allow the meringues to cool inside.

Make the filling by mixing the mascarpone with some double cream – just enough to make the mascarpone mixture more workable. Add the icing sugar and the seeds from the vanilla pod (or you can use good vanilla essence). Chop the strawberries, setting aside the most perfect specimens for the top of the cake.

To assemble the cake, put the first meringue sheet on a large plate, face down to give you a nice flat surface. Pile on half the mascarpone mixture, then half the strawberries. Repeat this process. If you've made three sheets, repeat this process twice, using a third of the mascarpone mixture and a third of the strawberries for each layer. For the top layer, put the strawberries point up like sentinels. Present your cake to the sound of whoops and cheers.

Oven-baked perch with potatoes, olives and mandarin olive oil

Persico al forno con patate e olive in olio al mandarino

Ingredients for 2
Potatoes – 400g
Perch fillet – 300g
Olive oil – a glug
Mandarin olive oil – a glug
(you could use lemon olive oil)
Salt and pepper to taste
Black pitted olives – 40g
Rosemary – a sprig

We gave little Carlo a tin of mandarin olive oil and asked him to experiment. A couple of weeks later we got an email from him saying something along the lines of 'I'm not an inventive cook like you, but I baked a perch with some potatoes, black olives, rosemary and mandarin oil, and it was very nice.' It was a bit of an understatement; Cathy and Rosie went potty for it.

Slice the spuds into 1cm thick slices, parboil and drain. Preheat the oven to 200ºC /gas mark 6. On a clean plate pour half of the oils over the fillet and rub them in with a good dose of salt and pepper. Place the fillet in a ceramic dish and arrange the potatoes and olives around the edge. Put the rosemary on top of the fillet and cover everything with the rest of the olive oils. Cover with a piece of kitchen foil and put in the oven for 25–30 minutes. Remove the foil halfway through cooking. Serve immediately.

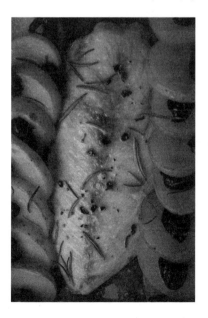

15 Mangiamo

We did a lot of eating over the next week. Partly to make it up to our stomachs for a week of bad eating and partly because eating is one of life's major pastimes when you live in the middle of the Italian countryside.

It took a while to get used to the eating times. They were just so strict. If you found yourself in search of a proper lunch in the countryside at 2.30 you might as well forget it. We were more or less used to it but when friends came to visit, we saw them fall into the same traps again and again. They'd arrive on the plane at one, drive around a bit admiring the scenery. By about two their stomachs started giving lunch hints and by 2.30 they really meant it. They'd try in vain to find a restaurant open but instead come across only little bars, empty except for a table of wiry old men playing cards, whose food options amounted to one or two slightly curling sandwiches in the display cabinet. They'd then arrive at us about an hour later, hungry as horses, and we'd spend the first hour of any visitor's trip putting plate after plate in front of them, until they reached that feeling, first of relief that they were not going to starve to death and then a short while later, panic that they would never move again.

The thing about restaurants in Le Marche, at least outside of the bigger towns and sometimes even there, is that they are usually quite hidden away. You have to know where to go or know who to ask – and know how. It took us a long time to realize this. Well, actually I should clarify – there are evening restaurants which tend to be in the middle of villages and which are easy to find, but the lunchtime restaurants are different. They are generally very cheap, very basic in terms of décor and lighting and very good in terms of the most honest, most typical Marchigiani food. They exist to service the workers of the world – the builders and plumbers and road-cleaners and tree fellers and policemen – so the food is substantial and utterly traditional. There is nothing on the menu which any of these fellows wouldn't have been served since they were off their mother's milk. I am invariably the only woman in these places, bar the odd travelling saleswoman trying to look nonchalant in the heaving sea of grubby testosterone.

It is here that the 'I don't understand where they put it all' Italian meal comes into its own. Most Italians don't eat breakfast – well, they say they do but what they actually mean is a cup of coffee and a sort of croissant thing loaded with Nutella. But these guys have generally been up since early and by lunchtime they are ravenous. This explains the antipasto – usually a simple and, crucially, *immediate* plate of local speciality meats and cheeses. Round our way this usually means a bit of prosciutto, some *ciauscolo* (an extremely soft pork salami, halfway to being pâté in terms of consistency, and very delicious) and an assortment of pecorino cheese in different stages of life – usually a young *ragazzo* cheese soft and smooth, going right up to the grizzled elder of an almost unsliceable crumbly version which is as strong as can be stomached. So the point of the antipasto is to quell the panic of a stomach which hasn't been fed for often fourteen or fifteen hours.

Crisis averted, it's time to move on to the *primo* (what the English often refer to as 'the pasta course'), whose purpose – like the Yorkshire pudding or the baguette – is to put some serious carbohydrate fullness into the belly. The *primo* could be pasta, could be risotto, could be *orzo* (barley), could be a thick pulse soup in winter – but whatever it is it will definitely be filling. By the time the pasta course is finished there is rarely 'hunger' in any true sense but there is still a desire for other types of food – for protein and fibre in particular. So then comes the *secondo* – the 'meat course'. In Le Marche this is often as simple as a few lamb chops grilled over open flames or perhaps a piece of chicken with olives and tomatoes – simply prepared and full of the flavour given to the meat by nature rather than added to it by man. Obviously, to follow the meat and complete the nutritional requirements, it is desirable and necessary to have something vegetable-ish. Again, in Le Marche, often nothing more complicated than some braised chicory or some *patate al forno*, preened with rosemary and toned with olive oil.

All of this is washed down with water – always water, without having to ask and remind the waiter – and some local cheap but good wine. The philosophy of the wine is the same as the food – it comes from probably less than a few miles away, you can taste the grapes in it and if you're paying more than 2 euros for a litre carafe, you must have flashed your Rolex on the way in.

The stomach has been filled and rounded. But there is still room for a touch of sugar, so a small dessert or more usually a piece of fruit – a local pear or apple or orange – is presented with a sharp knife, the tool that at least doubles the pleasure of eating fruit. In fact, even at home now, I will offer a 'fruit service', which means I wield the sharp knife onto whichever fruit Jason or Rosie request. The pleasure of a pre-peeled, de-pithed orange presented in slices, rather than the presentation of a complete sphere, is so great that I even get some back by diffusion.

The only thing that remains is the essential espresso. Not, never, ever, a cappuccino, but a small strong coffee which will cut through all this food and wine with enough of a jolt to propel all these workers back into their cars en route to work.

Of all the things we English do wrong in Italy, probably the one that the Italians find most incomprehensible and laughable is the post-meal cappuccino. For a start, cappuccino is full of milk and therefore very filling – so it is almost an insult after all this food to suggest you still need more calorific content. Secondly, milk is for babies really, so can only be forgiven for being drunk by adults in the morning (before 11 a.m.), when we are all still a little foetal. It is not uncommon, ordering a cappuccino after noon, to be asked whether you are OK.

So that's lunch – the lazy, greedy, drunken indulgence it's seen as by Northern Europeans or the reason for existence it is seen as by Italians? Whatever, it serves many purposes: it gets workers out of the hot part of the day, taking as it does at least two hours, usually from 12.30 to 2.30 (you can see why you don't stand a chance if you appear at 2.30 of getting more than 'a quick plate of pasta'), and it is nutritious and rounded enough to propel you through the many hours of work still left in the day. Most Italians don't eat dinner until late in the evening, especially in the summer, so this lunch is servicing probably another seven or eight hours of work. And it is sociable. Even though these workmen restaurants are filled with men, they talk! They laugh. They communicate. They lark about with the waitress and with each other. Work is less painful afterwards, filled with food, wine and the stimulus of contact with one's fellow man.

Northern Europeans don't know what they are missing.

Italian TV

Food was one thing but even after nearly a year, we still couldn't get used to Italian TV. We secretly wondered if there was a glitch in the transmission system to Loro Piceno which meant they were accidentally still broadcasting programmes from the 1970s. But the presence of the same vile contemporary hit shows like *Big Brother* quashed that unlikely theory.

Every programme had an ageing perma-tanned man and a young lady in a bikini. Every programme. The only exception was the endlessly repeated *Texas Ranger*, a weird American show straight out of the '70s with a brawny moustachioed star solving improbable crimes. Every other programme had a bikini girl. I wondered if it was a law that Berlusconi slipped through. Even during the World Cup, the post-match analysis show would have a bikini girl perched upon a high stool (presumably to show off her nice long legs), sitting there and sometimes *not even saying a single word*. Should one have appreciated the honesty of this? We all like a bit of eye candy, and at least here there was absolutely no attempt to dress it up as anything else. In fact, there was hardly any attempt to dress it at all. Or should we have been depressed about the state of gender relations and sexual stereotypes in this mother-adoring nation? Unreconstructed doesn't even half do it.

One evening we noticed there was a programme on called 'Cambia moglie' or 'Exchange wife' and knew it could only mean one thing. *Wifeswap* Italian style. This sort of programme is actually rather fascinating to watch in another cultural context. Dealing as it does with the minutiae of daily life, it gives you interesting clues as to the petty preoccupations of one's adopted countrymen.

That night there was to be a double bill, something I'd have found hard to stomach in English but which in Italian was compelling. The first episode revolved entirely around food, with the main bugbears between the two swapped wives seeming to come down to whether they slightly over-or slightly undercooked their pasta. Uninteresting in itself, but interesting to see just how upset they could get about it. In fact, this made me think about other times when our new Italian friends had found amazing mileage in talking about the teensiest detail of something they had just planned to/wanted to/refused to eat.

Take pizza. I mean pizza is a bit of bread with stuff on top, isn't it? My mum can never eat pizza when she comes here because she says it's really just the same as the bit of bread and cheese she has every lunchtime at home, but hot. And she has a point. I mean the pizza bread part can be nice and light and crunchy, and it's good if the things on top taste fresh and flavoursome. And that's about where I'd stop in terms of pizza small talk. Such lack of interest would be taken as at best ignorance and at worst insult in the context of discussion with Italians.

After a choir concert once, we went for pizza and the post-pizza analysis had gone on for a full ninety minutes. There were those who preferred the crust to be slightly less thin, so that there was a bit less crunch and a bit more chew. Some didn't like the bubbles rising up in the crust because the crest of the bubble meant that the toppings tumbled off, so there was a bare patch. Some were insistent that *pizza bianca* – without the tomato sauce – was invariably better because you tasted the other ingredients more. Others were insistent that if you had aubergine the only way to go was *rossa*. Then there was the discussion of the digestion of the pizza, a subject apparently as rich as discussion of the dish itself. Some believed that enough fizzy beer made the pizza palatable. Others detailed how they would always be up all night after evening pizza with terrible bloating.

Italians remind me of Americans in the level of their intimacy with every tick and whir of their inner selves. It makes me feel there is something to be said for British stoicism, where for the most part people aren't really aware – much less care – if tomatoes give them a slightly peaky feeling in the forehead or if eating after ten causes flatulence. Italians love to tell you about all this – and transfer it, exaggeratedly, to their children, who 'have terrible pain' if they eat sausages or 'unbearable fever' if they encounter an egg.

The second episode of the *Wifeswap* double bill was a wicked pairing. In one couple the husband had a wandering eye. In the other the woman was a terrific flirt. The combination did everything the producers could have dreamed of and more. Previously I wouldn't have thought it possible that *Cambia moglie* could make me feel physically sick. But the sight of these two self-fanciers feeding strawberries to each other in a restaurant and ending up snogging on the sofa – all obviously highly aware of the ever-present camera – was as unstomachable as *pizza bianca* at bedtime.

We are told that TV has done some good in uniting Italy. There is one simple reason. Dante aside, only since the advent of TV has Italy really had a shared language. Until then, everyone spoke in their local dialects. And local really means local – the dialect in Loro Piceno is distinctly different from that of Civitanova Marche, half an hour away. So you can imagine if you take a Sicilian and ship him up to Genoa, neither stands a chance. So now, although most people still speak dialect at home, the great TV unifier has meant that Italians also have a language in common. Albeit with some of the creativity ripped out – particularly with swear words. Dialect is full of rich and toothsome swear words. But watch an American film with Italian subtitles and you would think that the only

Italian swear words involve the words 'cazzo' (literally, dick) and 'va fanculo' (fuck off).

We went to carnival in a pretty nearby town called Amandola and felt very foreign. All the floats carried allegorical or political messages – all written in dialect and completely incomprehensible to us. In fact some were even incomprehensible to the Italian friends we were with because they're from miles away (like twenty). There were jokes which relied on an in-depth knowledge of the unique sufferings of particular saints and others which were satires on current political debate. It was one of those occasions that made one feel rather hopeless about the chances of ever feeling at home.

But not only we were confused. Italy is a peculiar mixture. On the one hand, from the outside, wherever you go, everything just seems so *Italian*. But the reality is that Italy has only existed as a nation for a babyish amount of time – since 1871 or so. It's younger than America and think how snobby we are about *its* lack of history. The contradiction comes from the fact that Italy has this very short history, coupled with the long history that is evident in every medieval hilltop village. It is young and old, has seen it all, and yet seen nothing. And particularly now, when so many aspects of Italian culture are changing so quickly. In little more than a couple of generations, the average family size has gone from households of twenty or thirty being lorded over by the grand patriarch to families with often only one child, living in little nuclear units. For all the apparent influence of the Pope, Italy somehow has the lowest fertility rate in the whole of Europe.

Italy is confused. More and more women go out to work (a large chunk of the explanation for the declining birth rate) but men domestically haven't accepted the change. That's why it's only possible for women to cope with one child – because as well as working, they still do all the work in the home, the cooking, the washing-up, the cleaning, the childcare – with the man clinging desperately to a role based on a dead past and the Bible. There is consumer modernity – the *ragazzi* all wave around the latest mobile gadgets – but every food festival will still boast of the ancient flavours that will be on offer, giving a sense of warmth and comfort about the past as reassuring as mamma's lasagne.

Italy needs immigrants but is terrified of immigration. It is terrified that the Italian way of life – in practice having to change because of the crude facts of global economics – will be wiped out by a few hundred thousand Eastern Europeans quietly praying to Allah. But without immigration – or an unprecedented change in the country's fertility habits – the Italian population will be half its current size within a few generations. It already has a worse problem with pensions and an ageing population than most of the rest of Western Europe. But denial sometimes is a helpful ruse.

Perhaps all this uncertainty explains why symbols like the olive tree endure. The olive tree has been there, done that, seen the Roman Empire come and go, waved off Mussolini, and will see through plenty more corrupt comings and goings. It's just there, hanging out, producing its blameless fruit and casting its sheep-like shadow. Making the landscape and the world a better place.

Antipasti: Meat, cheese and bruschetta

Ingredients for 4 people
Prosciutto crudo – 200g thinly sliced
Ciauscolo – 200g sliced
Honeydew melon – 1
Pecorino cheese – one young, one seasoned
Honey
Country bread – 8 slices
Garlic – 1 clove
Ginger – small lump
Olive oil – to drizzle

Arrange the meats on a platter with slices of melon.

Slice the cheese and arrange on a platter. Lightly drizzle with runny honey.

Toast the bread on each side on a grill till golden. While still hot rub half the bread with the peeled garlic clove and the other with the peeled ginger. Sprinkle with salt and pepper and drizzle a z shape of olive oil over each slice.

Spaghetti with anchovies, olives and capers

Spaghetti con alici, capperi e olive

Ingredients for 4 people
Salted anchovy fillets – 90g
Garlic – 2 cloves
Olive oil – 4 tablespoons
Tomatoes – 400g
Black pitted olives – ¹/₂ cup
Capers – 3 tablespoons
Oregano – a couple of sprigs
Spaghetti – 350g
Parsley – 4 tablespoons chopped

Cut the heads and tails off the anchovies. Press along the backbone with your thumb and turn over and remove the bones, which should come away easily. Soak in cold water for 10 minutes.

Peel the garlic and fry the whole cloves in the olive oil. Add the chopped and peeled tomatoes, the olives, capers and oregano and simmer for 10 minutes.

Cook the pasta in salted water. When it's nearly ready add the anchovies and parsley to the sauce and take out the garlic.

Toss the cooked pasta with the sauce and serve.

Secondo piatto:
Breaded veal cutlets Cotolette di vitello impanate

Ingredients for 4 people
Veal slices – 500g
Eggs – 2
Salt to taste
Breadcrumbs – 80g
Flour – for dusting
Butter – 40g
Meat stock – 200ml
White wine vinegar – 1 tablespoon

Lightly pound the meat with a meat mallet. Get everything ready for covering the meat; beat the eggs with a pinch of salt, spread the breadcrumbs out on one plate, spread the flour on another plate. Now dust each slice of meat in the flour, then the egg and finally the breadcrumbs.

Heat the butter and fry the meat until it is golden brown on each side.

Pour in the warm stock, cover and cook over a low heat until the stock has completely evaporated. Quickly whack up the heat and put in the vinegar until that has also evaporated. Serve with your choice of veg.

Contorno: Potatoes roasted with garlic and rosemary

Patate al forno

Ingredients for 4 people
New potatoes – 750g
Garlic – 3 cloves
Olive oil – 5 tablespoons
Rosemary – couple of sprigs
Maldon sea salt and freshly ground pepper

Par-boil the whole potatoes in salted water. Preheat the oven to 180°C /gas mark 4.

Drain the spuds and cut them up into rough chunks. Add them to all the other ingredients in a baking tray and make sure they are well coated in everything.

Roast in the oven for 30 minutes or until golden.

16 Waking up from the Italian dream

We first noticed it in a busy and filthy metro carriage between Termini and Repubblica in Rome. It wasn't rush hour packed. It was a normal busy weekday packed – full but not nose-in-someone's-armpit full. Rosie had managed to squirm her way into a seat and Jason and I were standing up, feeling like Romans who knew the movements of an underground train well enough that we didn't need to hold on. We were in Rome for a couple of days to get a dose of city life and to get a coffee without having to drive.

Then I noticed it.

'Have you noticed it?' I asked Jason.

'What?' he replied, which meant he hadn't.

'Feeling … at home, being surrounded by people,' I said.

'Yes!' he said.

'I think it's do with electricity,' I went on. 'When you're around lots of people, there is some sort of charge that is given off that we pick up and that recharges us – just like electrical power, or some kind of battery power. Yes, a rechargeable battery that needs electricity from people. That's what makes us feel at home.'

I realize there's a danger here of sounding like some mad hippy, but I think it's clear from our earlier experience (not to mention a general life principle) that hippies are high on my hit list. So you have to believe me when I say it's not at all a hippyish notion. I see it more like this – when you are in a room with lots of people, the room is warmer than if you were in a room by yourself. No one doubts or thinks there is anything mysterious about this – it is just a simple transfer of power in the form of bodily heat from people to their surrounding air – and thence to surrounding people. It is almost too obvious to point out. All I am suggesting is that there is some other kind of power which is also transferred from one person to another when they are in close proximity. We've all had that experience at a big concert, or a rally or a gathering to hear the Pope – whatever your tickle – of the excitement of being in a big crowd, of experiencing something together with lots and lots of other people. Well, that's probably the same sort of thing.

The thing that made this moment so clear though was its banality – we were on an underground train. We weren't with anyone else we knew and we weren't even talking to anyone else around us. We were just in an enclosed space with other human beings. And we were being energetically recharged in a way that made us feel happy, and even more than feel happy, made us feel energized, made us feel that things were possible, that we could conquer whatever we wanted to conquer, achieve our life's dream, answer all our uncertainties and so on.

And this is a thing that only cities give, this energy. Of course, when we miss 'home', London, we think about our friends there and how nice it would be to hang out with them and with our families. We think about how nice it would be to have such a choice of cultural stimulation – to be able to see art, to go to movies, to see a play, to wander through some fair, to listen to almost anyone giving a talk about almost anything. And also we think about how nice it is, among a huge sea of people, to have familiar places where you go to roost or to relax – a pub where someone knows you probably want a pint of Guinness, a park where you always bump into someone you know and even if you don't the natural sociability of toddlers will mean that soon you will, a takeaway where you always take ages to decide and then order the same thing as always.

Those are all the sorts of things we are very conscious of missing. But in that moment on the underground, it was clear that there was a much bigger thing that we were really missing – and it was this sheer physical fact of being around people, around strangers, energized by the presence of humanity. It was this that was the real miss, the significant life-affecting miss, as this is the thing that makes us feel that we are alive.

It was really at this point we realized we might have a major problem living in the countryside.

Notwithstanding these disconcerting revelations we're still living in the countryside. And realizing that, there are lots of things about living in the countryside that make us feel like idiots. Idiots, that is, that we are only learning them now. One thing, so obvious to any sane person it's almost embarrassing to write it, is that if you live and work in the countryside you are entirely driven by the seasons. This extends to everything, from what you do each day to your mood in doing those things. Could anything be more obvious?! Yet we didn't really think of it. We naïvely thought urbanite things like 'Oh won't it be nice to have clearly differentiated seasons.' In LA the whole year is one long sunny fug; the sun gets a bit hotter in the summer and a bit cooler in the winter but blink and you'd miss the changing of the seasons. Then in London you're protected just by the fact of a city so densely packed. The tube might be boiling hot one day and a pleasing respite from a bitter winter wind another – but you're still on the tube every day, doing your tube thing. The seasons have little more than a superficial warming or cooling effect on your dash here or there.

But now we lived in a place where in the winter, we could be literally unable to leave our house if the snow was too thick. And in the summer we might be unable to leave through sheer heat-induced inertia. A day of rain in the city just meant that you might have to remember your umbrella. (Though as an aside, I have never been an umbrella owner. I hate the things. People drive their umbrellas worse than their cars and they are at least as antisocial to pedestrians.) But a day of rain in the Italian countryside really meant something – either 'hooray the trees are getting a drink', or 'bugger we can't prune today' or 'poor farmers – their hay crop has just been trounced'.

This dawned on me because I realized that as winter came, we entered a dark wintry closed-in time within ourselves. And when summer arrived we entered a time of expansiveness, lightness and warmth. And it wasn't just us. That surly neighbour lady who had her head turned down against the cold for four months now strolled about in a flowery skirt eating *gelato* on the street and looking and I'm sure feeling at least a decade younger. The grumpy goitre post office lady now had a cheeky smile photo-shopped onto her cynical frowning face. The ever-smiling *carabiniere* now positively skipped out of his car to arrest the latest petty criminal. Spines straightened, necks rotated, mouths opened, eyes brightened. None of us are more sophisticated than the sunflowers in the next door field, living for this warmth, this heat, this sociability – then slowly breaking and fading again for our winter reclusion.

But then we came into the heat. It was warm enough to go to the seaside most weekends, Rosie finding ever more pleasure in the tiny waves. We walked along the promenade and in the weird pine tree place eating our *gelati* like everyone else and passing for locals as long as we only opened our mouths for the next lick. Isn't it funny that pistachio is pronounced 'pistackyo' in Italian? How did that get corrupted? It felt wrong whenever we said it right and we felt downright pretentious if we had to say it in front of visiting English friends. But we had to say it a lot because 'pistackyo' and chocolate is the best possible combination of flavours, and as it happens colours – as long as the 'pistackyo' is pale green and the chocolate dark as night.

It was just such a huge pleasure not to be cold. It was such a pleasure not to have to put on layer after layer of ugly underlayers. It was such a pleasure to have some sun on our faces and no shoes on our feet.

By June the temperature of the water in the sea was sometimes higher than the temperature on land – something to remind yourself of when it still seemed to make you go 'ooh ooh ah ah' as you waded in inch by wettened inch. Rosie never admits she's cold, even when her lips have gone blue and she has goose bumps from neck to ankle. 'Me no cold,' she says, 'me happy,' as if the two things are mutually exclusive. Which we're beginning to think maybe they are.

Other things than the warmth had been diverting us. For me, one of the greatest of these had been the choir. I was still not quite sure of my place in it, and there were many other mysteries about the relationships between people in it, but there was an ease of being among the members that only comes from a group that has spent so long together. Luckily this ease was potent enough to wrap in relative newcomers like me.

The choir made several foreign trips every year and my first was to Monaco. (I thought we were headed to a small tax-avoiding principality until passing the North Italian border resulted in the revelation that 'Monaco' is Italian for 'Munich'.) Being imprisoned on a coach for hours and hours talking Italian was as close as I'd come to intensive language study and what was nice was that everyone moved about so you ended up having all kinds of deliciously varied chats. One with 'Cric e Croc', two cheeky nicknamed *ragazzi* thick as thieves, asking how much hair English women shave off (their intrigue sparked by frank pubic sightings on the beach, on bodies of evidently non-Italians), another with the jowly bank manager (the one who inevitably also looks after the choir's coffers) trying to help me understand the pensions crisis being focused on in that day's *Corriere della Sera*, and another with Edyta, the only other foreigner in the choir, Polish, confessing her undying love for Billy Idol and wondering if I'd like to have a listen to her Walkman?

These choir trips (and there are many – forty-eight concerts in 2006) often involved exchanges with other choirs. We'd go to their place, do a concert or two and they'd put us up and feed us. Then they returned to be similarly hosted in San Ginesio.

We spent three lovely days with the Monaco gang, brought together by our unusual shared pursuits. These ranged from singing a quite challenging, very angular, modern Mass written by a German composer who also conducted – it was the first public airing of this work and even he said it was amazing to hear it aloud for the first time. For us it was even more so, as we'd been practising it in parts for weeks but had never put it together because without an orchestra it was just too dissonant. From that, we went to being whisked around Oktoberfest by our choral host Elisabetta, dressed in one of those Heidi outfits, and sampling all her favourite rides, fish snacks and beer.

A few weeks later, the German choir came back to San Ginesio. The occasion this time was somewhat marred by 80 percent of their choir getting food poisoning from the first dinner, a lively social event organized (and, embarrassingly, cooked) by our choir. The next morning, the Germans were meant to be singing a church mass in Loreto at the celebrated cathedral. They had to leave very early in the morning, most clutching their stomachs. Within half an hour of departure the coach toilet had apparently overflowed. But there was worse to come, as the bugs weren't finished yet. In fact, at almost any point on the winding road from San Ginesio to Loreto, a passing driver could have glanced out of his window to see tens of erstwhile immaculately mannered German ladies squatting down behind trees and hedges in any field near to where the coach could pull over. The Germans didn't make it to the mass. Luckily for them the new Pope was a local Bavarian so will hopefully sort out some sort of exoneration.

As well as the usual array of masses and requiems and whatnot – usually in Latin – we sang many songs in other languages. This meant mastering the Italian pronunciation of French, Spanish, Norwegian and so on – since if I sang in those languages using English pronunciation it didn't sound right and, of course, it was important for a choir to sing with one voice. The hardest of these hybrid languages for me to master was Italian-English. If I sang English-English it sounded really odd as it was so far from what everyone else was singing. Instead I had to learn to sing English with an Italian accent. So 'Can't help falling in love', for example, became 'Cont elp forling in loff.'

When we sang English songs, someone in the choir who predated me (I suspect this job might be coming my way soon), who had a reasonable grasp of English, had taken on the job of transliterating the English so that everyone in the choir knew how to pronounce the words. To give the gist, here are some of the lines I have had to sing. Try it (*you have to do it out loud*); you'll be amazed what you find. It's like the lyric equivalent of those 'magic eye' puzzles which had everyone squinting one year at Christmas time.

Song 1
 Hallo darknes mai ol fren
 Aivcamtu tolkuif iu eghen
Song 2
 Eemajin derz no evan
 Eetsizi ifutrai
 Noell bilowuz
 Hopovos olischai
Song 3
 Waiz men sai
 Honlifuls rosheen
 Bot ai cont elp forling in loff weethu
Song 4
 Aiv bin so lokee
 Aiemze ghel wuif golden haia
 Ai wonnassing eet owt to evribodi

The choir was not a church choir. So we didn't have to sing at mass every Sunday or anything like that. But when there were big religious festivals, there was usually something brewing. In these situations, Nicoletta usually served as my cultural translator. She moved to Le Marche at a similar time to us, from Milan, and as such is almost as much a foreigner as we are. She is left wing, very well educated (in psychology) and very well travelled (she's lived in Libya among other places), all of which things make her pretty exotic in the eyes of local Marchigianians, and she wrestles with the cultural homogeneity here as much as we do. Because she is a bit of an outsider, there are questions I can ask her which I would be embarrassed to ask others for fear of appearing like a lawless infidel.

Recently, we sang at some San Ginesio do, celebrating I'm not sure what – even Nicoletta couldn't help with this one, it was something very local. There were bishops everywhere, in the pews, in the aisles, taking the service. There were priestly robes of all hues. There was a group of about twenty all in royal blue gowns. (I say all, but there was one whose gown was definitely a few shades lighter than royal, as if his mum had washed it in too hot a wash.) Then there was a group who all had these massive necklace things on with different size pendants – the size of the pendant seemingly inversely proportional to the size of the man. So one tiny little baby bishop had one so huge that it looked like it was actually physically pulling his neck down into a supplicant position. Then there were these three in really scary Ku Klux Klan-looking outfits with full face hoods with tiny eye slits. Two were white and one was a sort of sackcloth colour which made him look for all the world like he was about to slaughter a pig rather than be a lamb of God himself. In fact, I was so distracted by this thought, that when it came to singing the words God will forgive *'alcun male'* ('any badness') I accidentally sang that God will forgive *'alcun maiale'* ('any pig') instead.

Can priests give themselves communion? Or is it like hairdressers or dentists who need another one to do the business for them?

It is strange for me, a heathen, to spend a lot of time in churches. For Italians – or certainly at least those round our way – church is like a second home. There is an ease of behaviour that feels completely alien to me. I've often seen teenagers walking into church, talking on their mobiles, reaching for the dab of water and cross-ing themselves and doing the sort of bobbed kneel all while still chatting happily about arrangements for later that evening. It's all just part of the normal daily ritual, and in a way although God is the Big Guy – it's also as if he's a bit down to earth. Like with your grandparents, you don't quite always have to be on super best behaviour. I was amazed that, in a country where people will dress up for the slightest thing, the people whose turn it is to do a read-ing during mass don't dress up for the occasion – jeans and a T-shirt seem to be fine. It's the sort of confidence and comfortableness that only comes with familiarity.

I shouldn't give the impression that it's for everyone and of course there are plenty of people who don't go to church. And plenty more who loathe it. Nicoletta's husband Angelo recently told us that he'd worked out that every kilometre the Pope travels costs something like 500,000 euros – so when he does one of his big world tours, the cost is in multiple millions. The irony isn't wasted on Angelo and his point was the simple one: spend that money on the poor instead of a stupid popemobile and bodyguards and you wouldn't have to go around telling the poor to pray to God about their plight.

While I have the choir by way of extra-curricular entertainment, J has his football buddies – and particularly his pal Giancarlo (Jesus) to keep him occupied. They have even started going out for drinks together when there isn't the excuse of football, something which I guess can only be called friendship.

It started almost like a first-date sort of date. Giancarlo had said to Jason after football one evening, 'Would you like to go for a beer after practice next time?' and Jason had said yes. Before the next practice, Jason had checked with me about going out, been given his late pass, put on slightly more going-out sort of clothes than he'd usually wear to football, and suffered a certain amount of the butterflies one has about the first move of intimacy with someone new. We'd speculated about what the evening might involve (even thinking it might end up riotously stumbling into somewhere awful like the famous 'Sexy Disco' in Piediripa) and off he'd gone. Football practice went off normally enough, with no mention of the impending evening ahead.

At the end Giancarlo waved at Jason and said, *'Alla prossima'* ('See you next time').

Jason had said, trying to appear casual, *'Una birra?'* ('A beer?')

But no, GC was just too tired. 'Next time?' he said. It was obvious that to him the previous engagement had been made with an Italian casualness, 'next time' meaning 'some time soon' rather than the English 'after the next practice, at 9.30 sharp' that Jason had read it as.

J returned home, posh clothes still uncreased, slightly despondent.

Next practice, he didn't make any assumptions but this time GC was clearly in business. He'd roped in another pal, Gio, who looks about fourteen and giggles like a teenage girl, and the two of them after practice spent even longer than usual tousling their hair, and slavering a cacophony of unguents over themselves. Emerging shiny and perfumed from head to toe, GC said to the gel-free zone that was Jason, 'Ready?' and off they all went.

Gio spent large chunks of the evening composing text messages to his new girlfriend – looking up periodically for advice from his older friends about how he should phrase a particularly romantic sentiment or, more often, how to spell something. Meanwhile J had done a bit of preparatory language research to be sure that he would have some things to talk about. The Italian football league was in the midst of its latest referee-bribing scandal so that was an obvious – and fascinating – starting point.

The scandal had come to light when telephone conversations between Moggi (the General Manager of Juventus) and the head of the Referees Federation were made public. To understand the importance of what followed, it's worth knowing the status of Juventus as a football team – they're like the Italian Manchester United – the team of default support, with something like 40 percent of Italians claiming allegiance to the black and white flag. Well, Moggi was basically phoning through his referees shopping list for the season. 'We'd like Ref Mr White for the game against Inter and Ref Mr Black for the game against Fiorentina,' because, obviously, those referees would be sympathetic to Juventus and would be duly rewarded for their partiality. The tape recordings were made public (leaked somehow by the careless police) before any legal case was being pursued. Anyway, further investigations found that not only were Juventus up to naughty tricks, but so were AC Milan, Lazio and Fiorentina. At least those were the ones who were found out.

There was outcry, gnashing of teeth and so on and it was decided that all the teams should be relegated a division and have points deducted. Then, in true Italian style, there was contra-outcry, contra-gnashing of teeth and an overturning of most decisions, with the result that in the end only Juventus were relegated (and even then with fewer points deducted).

The interpretation of who are the real goodies and baddies obviously varies depending on who you're talking to. GC is an AC Milan supporter. AC Milan are owned by Berlusconi, which I'm sure has nothing at all to do with the fact that they were let off more lightly than any of the other teams. GC shrugs off any insinuation, saying basically, 'everyone's crooked'; 'we're just one of the ones that got caught'; 'let's move on'.

But the really striking thing, J said later, was how much the conversation demonstrated that Italians are completely inured to the idea of corruption. All the time here, one has had conversations – with anyone from a football coach to the fishmonger – that further illustrate the Italian view that *everyone else* is always breaking the rules. The belief of this fact is as big an impediment to tackling the problem of corruption as the corruption itself; for if everyone believes that corruption is everywhere, then every secondary person in the chain acts in a way to protect themselves or exploit the situation or react in some other way. As such, it really does extend to affect everyone.

To me, the strangest thing about Jason's new social life is the fact that he often comes back really late – two-in-the-morning sort of late – but sober. 'Going out for a drink' here, even in macho football-playing circles, means not much more than that – going to have a drink, maybe two, probably getting some food, but mainly sitting and chatting. It takes a while to get used to because obviously in the UK going out for a drink means going out to get totally plastered, the success of the evening often being judged in terms of the level of unconsciousness reached. Now we find it strange to go back to London and hear people saying things like 'God yeah it was a wicked evening, I was completely out of it.' It now seems strange that anyone would want to be 'out of' a wicked evening rather than in it. But of course we don't say anything for fear of sounding like grandma.

Seafood fritto misto

Fritto misto di mare

Ingredients for 4 people
Mixed seafood – 1kg of sardines, anchovies,
whiting, baby sole, small crabs, scampi, baby
octopus, cuttlefish
(or what your fishmonger recommends)
Plain flour – 2 cups
Vegetable oil – 500ml
Sage leaves – several
Lemon – 1 large
Salt and white pepper

We always seemed to arrive at the beach at lunchtime. We headed to the nearest fish restaurant and Cathy and Rosie ordered big steaming heaps of spaghetti alle vongole followed by crispy fritto misto – a mountain of battered scampi, baby squid, anchovies, small crabs, fresh sardines and tiny juvenile flatfish like sole.

Trouble is I don't eat fish and I usually settle for a pretty bland pasta pomodoro. More recently, though, things have turned around with a new restaurant which opened in Porto San Giorgio. They made me a gem of a pasta pomodoro. The secret according to the friendly waiter is the ricotta cheese in the sauce.

The seafood should be quite small, so it's probably not worth gutting. Anyway they say that the intestines give a slightly sharp taste, and the fried heads are pleasantly crunchy. Sometimes Cathy takes out small bones as Rosie tucks in.

Wash, clean and pat dry the seafood. If you do have big squid and cuttlefish cut away the mouth parts and the bone of the cuttlefish. Cut into rings if necessary.

Spread the flour out on a shallow dish. Dip the fish in the flour and shake off any excess. Heat the oil in a large pan with the sage. Once hot enough (test with a piece of old bread, which should brown in about 30 seconds) remove the sage leaves and fry the seafood, starting with the larger pieces. Once golden brown remove and drain on kitchen paper. Serve on a warm plate with lemon wedges and season with salt and pepper.

Spaghetti with clams
Spaghetti alle vongole

Ingredients for 4 people
Clams – 1kg (or a 200g jar)
Dry white wine – 1 glass
Olive oil – 4 tablespoons
Chilli – 1
Garlic – 3 cloves
Salt – but not much
Spaghetti – 400g
Parsley – 1 bunch (¼ cup chopped up)

Put the clams in a bowl of cold, salted water for half an hour. Then rinse them under some running water and throw away any that are open (i.e. dead). Heat the wine in a pan and add the clams. Cover and cook at a high heat for 5 minutes until they have opened. Take the pan off the heat and scoop out the clams. Sieve the nice liquid that is left in the pan and set aside.

Heat the olive oil in a large pan, add the chopped chilli and garlic and cook for a couple of minutes. Then add the liquid from the clams and simmer uncovered. Salt to taste.

Meanwhile prepare the spaghetti as directed on the pack. When the sauce has thickened up, add the clams and the parsley and simmer for a couple of minutes.

Drain the pasta and add it to the sauce. Mix and serve with a garnish of parsley.

Spiralini with ricotta and tomatoes

Spiralini ricotta pomodori

Ingredients for 4 people
Olive oil – 1 tablespoon
Onion – 1 large
Garlic – 2 cloves
Tomatoes – 800g
Spiralini – 400g (or fusilli or riccioli)
Parsley – 1 bunch ($^1/_4$ of a cup chopped up)
Tomato paste – 1 tablespoon
Salt and pepper
Ricotta – 150g
Parmesan

Heat the oil in a frying pan and cook the finely chopped onion and garlic for a couple of minutes. Chop the tomatoes into 2cm-ish square chunks, cutting out the stalky bit as you go. Add to the frying pan. Bring a big pan of salted water to boil and cook the pasta according to the instructions on the pack.

As the tomatoes simmer add the chopped parsley and the tomato paste. Salt and pepper it to taste and add a tablespoon of water from the pasta. When the pasta is nearly ready add the ricotta to the sauce and stir in. Drain the pasta and put it back in the saucepan. Pour the tomato sauce on top. Serve immediately with a generous sprinkling of freshly grated parmesan.

297

Vincisgrassi

For the pasta:
00 flour – 500g
Eggs – 3

For the filling:
Butter – 50g
Olive oil – 2 tablespoons
Onion – 1
Celery – 1 stalk
Carrot – 1
Minced chicken breast – 200g
Chicken giblets – 200g
Dry Marsala – 5 tablespoons
Passata – 1 litre
Rabbit bone
Salt
Parmesan cheese – 50g

For the béchamel sauce:
Butter – $^1/_4$ cup
Plain flour – $^1/_4$ cup
Milk – $^1/_2$ litre
Salt and pepper

I asked my football buddy Giancarlo if he knew any local recipes. I wasn't sure how seriously he would take me. Very seriously indeed, it turned out. Before I knew it I was invited round to his gaff to cook the locally famous vincisgrassi. A lasagne made from chicken innards, named after an Austrian general, Prince Windischgraetz, who saved the region from Napoleon. In the end Giancarlo's mum, Gigia, took me by the hand and showed me her version of vincisgrassi.

Preheat the oven to 180°C /gas mark 4. Make the pasta dough (following the pasta instructions for ravioli on page 12). Leave to rest.

Melt half the butter in a pan with the olive oil, add the finely chopped onions then the chopped celery and carrot. Cook for several minutes over a low heat. Add the minced chicken and crank up the heat a bit. Once that is browned add the trimmed and chopped up giblets and cook for a few more minutes. Then add the Marsala, bring the heat down again and cook until half of it has evaporated. Then add the passata and the rabbit bone, cover and cook for another hour. Check for salt. Once it's cooked, take out the bones.

Roll out the pasta into long thin strips, about 10cm. Bring a big pan of salted water to boil. Cut the pasta into 10cm by 20cm sheets and partially cook in the water. Scoop them out, run under cold water and lay on a tea towel.

Make the béchamel sauce: melt the butter, stir in the flour, add the milk gradually and simmer till thick. Season with salt and pepper. Grease a lasagne dish with a bit of butter. Place a layer of the pasta at the bottom. Cover with a layer of béchamel, a sprinkling of parmesan, then meat, then pasta again. Repeat this till you have about 10 layers, with béchamel at the top. Cook in the oven for half an hour and serve.

Osso buco

Braised veal shank

Ingredients for 4 people
Butter – 80g
Onion – ½
Veal shank – four 3cm thick slices of shank cut across the bone
Plain flour – for dusting
Salt and pepper
Red wine – ½ a glass
Meat stock – 175ml
Carrot – 1
Celery – 1 stalk
Lemon – rind of 1
Parsley – small bunch

Cathy's friend from choir, Nicoletta, is from Milan. She promised to cook us a Milanese speciality to show us how different it is from Marchigiani food. She chose osso buco, which uses braised veal shanks. The name comes from the Italian for 'hole in the bone' and the bone marrow itself is one of the real treats of the dish. It is invariably served with saffron risotto (page 300), one of the pillars of Milanese cooking.

Melt the butter in a deep-sided frying pan and cook the diced onion over a low heat for 5 minutes. Lightly roll the shank in flour and add to the frying pan with the heat turned up until browned all over. Season with salt and pepper and add the red wine. Let the wine evaporate.

Add the stock, diced carrot and diced celery, turn down the heat and cover. Carry on cooking for up to an hour or more. If it starts to go too dry add more meat stock. If it's too runny add butter and flour to thicken it. When it's about ready mix in the grated lemon rind and finely chopped parsley, and cook for at least a couple of minutes more. When ready, place a slice of the meat on top of the risotto and drizzle some of the remaining juice from the frying pan over the top.

Saffron risotto

Risotto con pistilli di zafferano

Ingredients for 4 people
Chicken stock – 1.5 litres
Butter – 80g
Onion – 1
Risotto rice – 350g
(Carnaroli or Vialone Nano, if you can get them, are better than Arborio)
Dry white wine – 1 glass
Saffron threads – ¹/₂ a teaspoon
Parmesan cheese – 80g

Bring the stock to the boil. Melt two-thirds of the butter in a saucepan and add the finely chopped onion, stirring occasionally on a low heat for 5 minutes. Stir in the risotto rice so it's evenly coated in butter and starts to turn translucent. Pour in the wine and cook until it has evaporated. Then start to add the stock, one ladle at a time, so the rice slowly absorbs the liquid. Add more stock as the saucepan goes dry. This will take about 20 to 25 minutes. The rice should be tender with a pleasant bit of bite in the middle. Before you add the last ladle of stock, stir in the saffron threads and a pinch of salt. After all the stock has been absorbed, take the pan off the heat and stir in the remaining butter and the grated parmesan. Serve.

17 Nudo gets all dressed up

When we lived in London, we used to go into Selfridges food hall and look at all the amazing produce and the perfect flowers and the immaculate fish displays and the huge choice of olives and of course at all the beautiful olive oils on the shelves. We'd pick up a bottle of olive oil and imagine that one day, maybe in ten years' time, maybe as few as five, we might walk in there and be able to hold up our very own oil. We'd imagine how proud we would be and how when that happened we'd really feel like we were definitely a proper grown-up company.

Well, one day we got cocky and wrote to Selfridges. We had a lead. Someone we knew was related to someone who had adopted a tree as a Christmas present for her husband. The lead part was the fact that the husband/gift recipient was the Head of Food at Selfridges.

We spent a whole day composing the e-mail. We had heard that Selfridges were looking to revamp their Christmas hampers this year, so most of the e-mail was suggesting different ways of getting our tree adoption scheme to work in hamper format – a tin of oil with the promise of the next harvest to follow, a whole range of Nudo products (some of which didn't actually exist yet, but we knew adrenalin would be a great spur), Nudo as part of a 'Bella Italia' hamper with other sumptuous Italian delicacies. There was no part of the hamper world we left untouched. We attached photographs of products, pieces of press and of course sent examples of anything and everything we could. We read the e-mail and reread it twenty times each, making sure the tone was confident but not cocky, excited about doing business without seeming desperate, flattering without being obsequious. My finger quivered with the sheer cheek of it all when I finally pushed the send button.

Of course there was no reply that day and there was no reply the next. But a very reasonably short amount of time later, the reply came back:

We love the idea, just need to figure out how we make it happen.

We did actually get up and dance around the office. We could not believe it. We had been in business nine months and we were going to be doing business with Selfridges. Selfridges! I mean, this wasn't some low-rent deli in the suburbs; this was the place where consumers go to die. It felt like we had produced our first Nudo baby.

This was the first step in feeling like our company was moving up to the next gear. We suddenly felt that anything was there for the taking if we only bothered to think what it was and then went out and asked for it. Neither of us are natural sales people but we both liked the feeling of success enough to kick ourselves into action.

One thing we knew we had to address was our presentation. We had, thanks to Madeleine, beautifully designed products. But they were being let down by the detail – the tins themselves with their slightly pug nose tops weren't the most beautiful thing in the world and we weren't going to rely on any bloody Welsh hippies again. And, in fact, the whole idea that we were going to hand-stick each label onto each tin just suddenly seemed quaint, and not in a good way. We also knew, from some sample tins we'd kept at home, that the stickers could start to unpeel a bit at the corners in a not very Selfridges looking way.

J was the first to broach the subject of getting printed tins. No stickers at all – just tins stamped and printed with our lovely Nudo olives all over their metallic outsides. Surely that was too posh to be possible?

Well, first enquiries seemed to confirm this. Minimum orders were in the hundreds and even tens of hundreds of thousands. Quite apart from the financial outlay, we had nowhere to store quantities like that.

But once J has an idea in his head, it is hard to shake.

And a little while late, well, I can hardly bring myself to say it but we were in the midst of another tin saga. After the first time and the horrors of finding tin makers and tins that were a nice shape and lids that fitted, we were somehow, a few short months later, going through a whole new nightmare with those little metal buggers.

The problem stemmed from the fact that in the printed tin world we were minnows. After much bowing and scraping, Jason man-aged to persuade the fellow at the tin printing place to reduce their minimum order to 14,000 for the small 250 millilitre tins and 7,000 for the larger 500 millilitre ones. To us, these numbers were almost incalculably massive and the cost (nearly £20,000) would leave the Nudo bank account hovering dangerous close to the zero level. But to the tin factory, used to doing orders for companies like, er, say Heinz, we were little more than an offcut.

Every stage of the process was a compromise for us. The first shocker was that they said it would be impossible to produce a sample. It just didn't work that way, they said; to set the machines up to do one tin was the same as setting the machines up to do 10,000, so no, a sample was impossible. The best they could do was send us a paper version (by e-mail) of the tin that they were about to print – which at least meant we could check they hadn't made any typos but gave us no security about what colours they'd turn out.

Then there was the compromise on the money. To cut the story of a long and ineffective battle short, we had paid them the whole payment up front – in fact, back in April. So we had written a cheque for thousands of pounds for thousands of tins that we wouldn't even be able to see in advance. There was a lot of trust on our part.

Then there was the problem of timing. Until now, we hadn't really had due respect for Italian summer holidays. When they say they close for August they really mean it. No one will even answer the telephone. And what that in turn means is that everyone is trying to get everything done in June and July so they, too, can holiday in peace. What *that* in turn means is that if the minnows are also trying to minnow their way through before summer, they ain't gonna stand a chance with all the sharks in the way.

Of course, one can be sanguine if one knows all this in advance, you can just rethink and reschedule and work around. But it doesn't happen that way. When you phone up to ask whether things are going to happen on time, they don't say, 'Hey minnow, forget it.' They say, '*Certo*' ('Sure').

And so it was that we had been promised our order of 21,000 printed tins on the week beginning 12th June, 'or the week of 19th June at the very latest'. They knew – or at least we'd told them – that our schedule for sending out our autumn packages meant it was important that that deadline was met. This promise had been made back when we started talking to them about the tins in April. Jason would phone his contact, Signor Ferranti, at least once a day to check on the tins and would be treated with the sort of contempt a mafia boss might have for a fly, but he would manage to reaffirm that 'the schedule is the schedule'.

So when J phoned up the week before the one commencing 12th June to just check that everything was going to plan and Ferranti more or less said, 'What plan?' the blood drained from both of our faces. Things had been put back, he nonchalantly explained, and ours would be done 'a few weeks' later than planned.

Though he didn't know it, we could actually cope if the delivery was up to three weeks late as, after our experience with the Welsh hippy, we'd built in a contingency buffer. We tried to pin him down to a more exact idea of timing, but he always promised to get back and never did.

Then Jason went on holiday, scuba diving with friends. I phoned up Signor Ferranti the next day hoping that hearing a tirade from a harridan on the phone might melt a hard heart. Au contraire. Ferranti told me that there was now 'almost no chance' that the tins would be delivered before the summer holiday. But that he would make sure they were among the first to get done afterwards.

I took a deep breath. My reaction was stuck halfway between fury and despair, so a sentence that began 'You made us a commitment, we have paid you and this is completely dishonourable and unprofessional' ended with 'please please please please please'. The mixture of anger at the situation and frustration at my lack of fluency in expressing my upset led inevitably to tears and big, gulping not-very-businesslike sobs.

That seemed to do the trick. Signor Ferranti grudgingly said he would go to the warehouse and see what he could do. Later that week, he phoned back to say that the tins would be printed the next day.

Finally, at the end of July, six weeks after they had been promised and four months after we'd paid, we were told that the tins were on their way from Liguria on an articulated truck. We were both relieved and nervous. They were finally coming, but would the sizes be wrong or the colours too garish? We also had to quickly get ready to store eight pallets of tins. There wasn't room at our house for them so Jason had pestered his fellow footballers about whether they knew of a bit of storage space.

His persistence paid dividends when he went to see Andrea, who runs the new pizzeria in town. Jason had heard that his brother-in-law had a shoe-making business that had gone down the drain (reflecting the general crisis of shoe-making in Le Marche) and as a consequence there was a garage, round the corner from our house, which was available. J's credentials as feisty British bulldog with FC Loro Piceno seemed to mean that we would be allowed tenure gratis, as long as we gave it a clean and made sure to eat plenty of Andrea's pizza.

Ignoring the overpowering and dizzying smell of volatile industrial glue the garage was perfect, and as soon as we heard that the tins were in transit we set about covering it, from floor to ceiling, with plastic sheeting.

By the time the truck arrived it was late and we were dirty and tired. Rosie was also losing her patience with the initially fun great tentacles of white masking tape with which she'd now managed to straitjacket herself. The garage was looking good and we were nervously expectant about our blind date with our tins.

With the sun setting over the Sibillinis the lorry pulled up outside the garage. A short, sweaty man jumped out of the cab, apparently surprised to see a young foreign couple and small child as the welcoming party for his delivery. But our smiles were big and excitement evident as he proceeded to open the back of the truck.

Inside the vast, gloomy trailer stood eight enormous pallets of shiny new tins. Each pallet stood nearly six feet high and was carefully wrapped in that pallet-wrapping cling film. They looked beautiful. The green was good. There were no obvious typos, but all we could really tell through the plastic was that they didn't say 'Nupo' or something.

Then we noticed that the driver, exhausted from more driving than he should probably have legally done, was waving at us madly. He seemed to be acting out a sort of mock lift, straining as if picking up an invisible dumbbell. As we looked around for a tailgate or any kind of lifting gear in the truck, we realized that the long and short of his performance meant, 'Where, in God's name, is the forklift truck?'

I like to think our expressions batted back the question with another, namely, 'Where, in God's name, is your tailgate?'

Then the driver started elaborating, a tone of desperation in his voice. *'Non ce la facciamo, non riusciamo scaricarle'* ('We can't do it, we can't unload them').

'Ce la facciamo,' Jason said. 'We can do it.'

The driver looked at us with a terribly sad look in his eyes. We would have preferred the grumpy swearing version any day.

J jumped up into the back of the trailer, grabbed the corner of the nearest pallet and put all his considerable strength into an almighty pull. His arms nearly came out of their sockets. The driver's look of sadness turned to a look of pain, and I noticed that Jason couldn't even bring himself to look me in the eye. It was only later that he confessed to me that this was one of the moments in his life when he felt he had failed as a man, as if by some Y gene he was meant to have miraculously predicted the forklift shortage.

But Jason isn't one to give up. He checked with me what the Italian word for 'unload' was and, grabbing the keys to the Mini from my hand, said he was going into town to get help. With a Tarzan-like 'Me return soon' to the driver he jumped into the car and sped off, leaving an unlikely trio of me, Rosie and despondent lorry driver sitting on the curbside.

I hadn't a clue what J thought he was going to do, and I was pretty sure he didn't either. But on his side was the fact that he knew pretty much every young male in Loro Piceno who was fit and agile. Because if you are young, fit and male, you play football – it's like conscription, but more compulsory.

About twenty minutes later, J returned with a Mini full of testosterone-oozing gristle. Jason had struck Loro Piceno gold. He breathlessly summed up what had happened. Sitting outside the main bar in town, sipping an espresso, was Manu, a young left-footed midfielder with deep-set eyes and a permanent five o'clock shadow. Strong, too. J had screeched to a halt and shouted out of the window something along the lines of 'I need a favour. It takes 10 minutes. I have a lorry with many tins. I need to unload it.'

Manu had looked slightly baffled as Jason added, 'Very heavy. More people!'

Manu had nodded then as if he understood what J was talking about. Maybe this kind of thing happens all the time in Italy. He knocked back the dregs of his coffee and casually walked off, reappearing seconds later with Andrea and Silenzio. Andrea is the star striker (the only player in the team who gets paid, thanks to a generous local sponsor) who looks like a beefy version of Prince and Silenzio (only ever known by his surname) is a tall, wiry defender whose dad runs the *consorzio*. Anyway, they jumped into the Mini and as they arrived Jason was still smiling at them so hard it almost looked painful.

Andrea took one look at the giant pallets and whipped out his mobile phone. It was obvious to him that even these four couldn't do it. It was like a scene from *Zulu*: literally within minutes two *ragazzi* arrived in an *apé* (those motorized three-wheelers that buzz round town, making a noise like a bee, an *apé*), then another. We were now nine strong and on a roll.

It still took a Herculean effort. At one point, I remember standing in the truck looking up and seeing a tsunami of tins wavering four feet or so higher than the top of my head. I was certain we were going to lose the whole pallet into the road but somehow only a couple of hundred tins fell out before the wave righted itself. A pair of the other pallets had split open as we levered them off the back of the truck, but there was an amazingly low casualty rate. As we looked at the pallets lined up in the garage, we could have cried. Even the lorry driver looked suitably impressed. Or maybe it was just relief that he could now finally get out of there and get some sleep.

It was about ten o'clock when the empty lorry trundled off into the distance. We were lost for words to say to those lovely footballers who had just completely saved our bacon. And it hadn't been a ten-minute job at all; it had taken about an hour and a half, though none of them had uttered a word of complaint. How could we thank them? I caught Jason's eye and I knew we were thinking there was only one possible way: with food.

Spaghetti for hungry footballers

Spaghetti dei giocatori

Ingredients for 4 people
Onions – 2
Garlic – 3 cloves
Butter – 100g
Artichoke hearts – 300g (frozen or canned)
Dried spaghetti – 500g
Egg yolks – 3
Parmesan – 60g
Pecorino – 40g
Basil – handful of fresh leaves

What do you feed nine hungry Italian footballers with five minutes notice and an empty fridge? The answer – a rich spaghetti with artichokes (frozen), aged pecorino, parmesan and a big handful of fresh basil leaves to cut through the cheesy richness. And lots of big bottles of ice-cold Moretti beer.

Finely chop the onions and garlic and fry in half the butter. As they start to go clear add the frozen artichoke hearts.

Cook the spaghetti in a pan of salted and oiled water.

Off the heat vigorously swirl in the remaining butter and the egg yolks to the artichokes. Then add the cooked spaghetti. Mix in the grated cheeses. Finally add the basil leaves.

Our dish often ends up really orange because the eggs we use, from our neighbour, come from chickens fed with corn. But even without that, this dish is always rich and luxurious.

Cherry and pine nut focaccia

Ingredients
Dried yeast – $^1/_2$ a teaspoon
Warm water – 160ml
Flour – 250g
Salt – big pinch
Sugar – 60g
Olive oil – 25ml
Cherries – 350g (about 300g stoned)
Pine nuts – 25g

We have five cherry trees dotted around the grove. Once the cherries have turned fat and red, it's a race against the birds to pick them. I went down to a tree that hangs precariously over the gulch, which meant a perilous climb, but gave me about two or three kilos of smooth firm cherries in about twenty minutes.

Rosie helped sort out the 'baddy ones', shoving handfuls into her mouth along the way, cherry juice dripping down her chin. Then she helped me make a cherry and pine nut sweet focaccia.

Put the yeast and the warm water in a bowl and leave for half an hour in a warm place. Add the flour to the bowl, through a sieve, and add the salt and half the sugar. Then slowly add the olive oil as you mix the dough in the bowl. When it's in a big lump put it on a well-floured surface and knead for 5 minutes. Put the soft lump back into the bowl, cover and leave to rise for 1 hour.

While you're waiting, stone the cherries. With our home-grown cherries I noticed nearly every one had a small, white, wriggling grub in the middle. It's one of the problems of being organic, I said to myself, and scooped them out. If I don't tell anyone, they will never know.

Preheat the oven to 180°C/gas mark 4. When the dough is ready, brush a thick oven tray with olive oil and roll or flatten it onto the tray with your hands. Cover the surface with the cherries. Sprinkle the pine nuts over the top, pressing everything into the dough as you go along. Splash a bit more olive oil over the top. Cook for 40 minutes and halfway through take it out and sprinkle the sugar over the top. Once it's done eat immediately.

Fig jam

Ingredients for a jar
Juicy ripe figs – 500g
Sugar – 350g
Lemon – 1 small

Nothing gives me a bigger buzz than going down to the grove, picking something fresh and cooking with it pronto. The fig trees were full of fruit, and although I always thought jam making was for grannies, Rosie and I had a bash at it. A couple of hours of great fun later we had enough fig jam to last us a year.

Roughly chop up the figs and cook in a pan until they start to boil. Add the sugar and juice from the lemon and continue to boil until it hits 220⁰C or starts to go gooey. Let it cool till a skin forms and then put in a sterilized jar (10 minutes in boiling water will do the trick).

18 The outside world pays a visit

People have started coming out to visit their adopted trees. It is the strangest thing. When we put on the website 'You can even come and give your tree a hug' it was half as a joke. Then we got the first e-mail enquiring about visiting, then a call, then more and more. By the end of the year we'll have had about fifty adoptive parents coming out to just say hello and hang out with their temporary adoptees.

When people first got in touch, we were intrigued to find out what sort of people make a reasonably big trip just to visit an olive tree. So far, we have been unable to draw any firm conclusions.

We had one chap who drove all the way here with his son in his Aston Martin (to take advantage, I suspect, of the fact that the Italian highway police would be more likely to nod and say 'Che bella' than ticket them as they flew fly past at 100mph+). He spent maybe an hour with his tree, asking well-informed horticultural questions, then turned and drove all the way back to the Midlands, barely even stopping for a cup of tea.

Then one large family arrived, with three children ranging in age from early twenties down to four years, plus a chirpy mother-in-law. It was only after we'd sat around for a couple of hours with Rosie and their little one playing in the paddling pool that the older daughter admitted that today was the day she was to receive her degree results and would I mind terribly if she borrowed our computer for a couple of minutes to go and see what she got?! So we were party to the family celebrations as she learned moments later that she'd been awarded a 2.1.

There are some people who have clearly read and digested every word of the literature we send them with the adoption packages – some even to the very flattering and slightly cringe-inducing effort of quoting back our half-baked jokes to us.

One lady came because she had writer's block that she was trying to unplug.

Another chap came with his family tartan ribbon to tie around his tree.

Another family came but, when we told them their tree was a bit of a walk away, said they didn't really need to see the actual tree and could we just pretend it was one of these nice ones at the top?

One of the most unlikely groups was a trio of elderly gentlemen from Morecambe. One of them had the strangest accent, a mix of his Sicilian past and his Northern English present. The second was a wizened sea fisherman who had a few fingers short of a handful. Both of them were soundly working class. The third was a posh and portly man who spoke over the others, laughed loudly and often, and who we thought must be paying for their trip. They were travelling around in a small van, which the two workers slept in, having banished their friend to the tent because apparently he snored loudly enough to wake a sloth. The fisherman was trying to learn how to drink wine while the other two – one by dint of being posh, one by dint of being Italian – were appalled that he could have gone so long without this essential life skill. But the fact was he didn't really like the stuff too much, unless it was diluted about one part to three with lemonade. He claimed to be gradually reducing the lemonade percentage as the holiday went on.

Another couple came armed with picnic hampers and a lunch big enough for ten. They spent a good six or seven hours under their tree (I say 'under', but our trees aren't really big enough to be under and the noon sun makes its presence felt on noses and shoulders) – just admiring the view and chewing on tasty treats.

Now that's being on holiday.

Most of the visitors are from the UK but we've also had visitors from California (full of questions about organic farming), the Netherlands (full of jokes about the name Nudo), Ireland, Spain and even someone from Milan. We couldn't help feeling a bit shy with him, as he quizzed us about things to do with olive trees which we were sure he must have learned at school – you know, along with football, opera, fashion and Catholicism. When he went away seemingly satisfied we did feel we'd pulled off our first coal deal to Newcastle.

One time, some visitors arrived just as a herd of sheep was being driven up through the grove by a shepherd wearing Armani sunglasses. That's the kind of publicity you can't pay for.

Almost without exception, visitors proclaim themselves envious of our life. They say things like 'I bet it's a load of work but wow you're so lucky' and 'I just wish I could do something like this. You lucky things.'

This obviously gets us thinking. It gets us looking around the grove in a different way. We allow ourselves to feel a tiny bit proud of what we've achieved in the battle against nature; it really does sometimes look like paradise down in the grove these days. And we even let ourselves feel a bit pleased that we have a company that just about makes money and that hopefully does more good than harm in the world. And it makes us think about our lives and how we are gradually making friends and learning the strange ways of the countryside and doing business with Italians and … almost starting to fit in.

But it also gets us thinking in other ways. It makes us wonder if we are secretly envious of our visitors' lives in the way they are envious of ours. It makes us think about what we are missing. About the lives we had, the friends we could drop in on, an ease of communication, a city which could continue to surprise and stimulate, the thrill of being surrounded by others.

And all this gets us asking ourselves, 'Have we done the right thing?' We think about that trip to Rome where we had the strange sensation of feeling at home on the underground. We imagine another cold, cold foggy winter with a shudder of dread. At the same time, we try to suppress these negative thoughts because the implications of acting on them are too huge and frightening.

Maybe this is what having a 'life change' is all about. It's about putting yourself face to face with big questions about your life. It's about asking yourself what you really want and trying to measure the importance of one thing against another. As such, it is probably inevitable that there should be contradictions and uncertainties. It is probably inevitable that you should sometimes tie yourself in knots trying to work out the 'right' answer. It is probably inevitable that all this confronting life sometimes all gets too much.

So thank God there is always another tree that needs liberating from brambles.

Adopt your own olive tree.

To get an authentic taste of Le Marche and the story behind Nudo you really need to try some of their delicious produce.

Only when you drizzle some divine Nudo lemon oil over your salad or let some sapa-soaked polenta melt in your mouth will you really understand what all the fuss is about.

Better still, you can adopt one of the Nudo olive trees. It's the perfect excuse to come out and see the Nudo olive groves. Give your tree a hug and while you're at it, give Jason and Cathy a hug too.

Since you've already bought the book, how about a 10% discount for adopting an olive tree? Just use the secret code iboughtabook on the website and promise not to tell anyone.

See you at **www.nudo-italia.com**.